The Brontës'
WEB OF CHILDHOOD

Undated Portrait of the Duke of Zamorna
Drawn by Charlotte Brontë

The Brontës'
WEB OF CHILDHOOD

By Fannie Elizabeth Ratchford

We wove a web in childhood
A web of sunny air

NEW YORK
RUSSELL & RUSSELL · INC
1964

823.809
b869zr

To HELEN SAFFORD BONNELL,

Generous trustee of Brontë treasures

ACKNOWLEDGMENTS

To those whose help in my long-continued Brontë study is gratefully acknowledged in *Legends of Angria* I would here add Mary Jourdan Atkinson and William Clyde DeVane. Mrs. Atkinson's contributions in both nature and extent might well justify her name on the present title-page. Mr. DeVane generously read the manuscript and offered suggestions which, adopted, have clarified and strengthened the story this volume tries to tell.

INTRODUCTION

⌈No FAMILY in English literature has provoked so many books and monographs as have the four Brontës, Charlotte, Branwell, Emily, and Anne; and no individuals, except Shakespeare and Byron, have received so much attention as the two older girls. Mrs. Gaskell's *Life of Charlotte Brontë,* published within two years of Charlotte's death, holds its place after eighty-three years as one of the most popular biographies in the language. Later research has added little of essential value or interest to its story of the outward lives of the remarkable family of Haworth Parsonage. Yet the thoroughness of Mrs. Gaskell's work, rather than deterring others, has tempted innumerable enthusiasts into the Brontë field.⌋

When the simple facts of Charlotte's thirty-nine years lost their novelty through much repetition, writers took to inventing mysteries and indulging in fantastic speculations leading to endless controversy. "Lives" gave place to "Secrets," "Keys," "Defenses," and "Vindications" in long procession. Interest, spreading first to her nearest of kin, came eventually to include all who touched her life, even to her remote ancestors and slight acquaintances, producing a long list of such titles as *Charlotte Brontë and Her Circle, The Brontës in Ireland,* and *The Maternal Relatives of the Brontës.* Nor has interest stopped with persons; it has concerned itself voluminously with the region in which the Brontës lived, until the personalities of the three sisters are inseparably identified with the Yorkshire moors; and books about the Brontë country are as numerous as books about the family that made that country famous. A complete bibliography of Brontëana would fill a sizable volume.⌋

It would seem, then, that the subject has been exhausted in all its aspects; yet every year brings forth an undiminished quota of volumes colored by the literary or intellectual fad of the moment. Thus we are now emerging from an orgy of Freudian studies and psychoanalyses of Brontë complexes and repressions into a staggering succession of Brontë plays and novels. It has become the fashion to exalt Emily and debase Charlotte, in utter ignorance that their genius—the ability to realize the imaginative with the vivid intensity of the actual—was identical, and that Emily's one point of superiority was her full surrender to the creative spirit which Charlotte fought with all the strength of her tyrannical conscience.

Though the existence of voluminous Brontë *juvenilia* has long been known to a small group, no biographer has made understanding use of it. Mrs. Gaskell describes a curious package confided to her when she was compiling her *Life,* "containing an immense amount of manuscript in an inconceivably small space; tales, dramas, poems, romances, written principally by Charlotte, in a hand almost impossible to decipher without the aid of a magnifying glass." And she quotes the twenty-two titles listed by Charlotte in a "Catalogue of My Books," dated August 3, 1830, five months after her fourteenth birthday. The biographer marvels at the quantity and thinks the quality of singular merit for a girl of thirteen or fourteen, but her silence regarding her heroine's tremendously greater production between 1830 and 1839 indicates that she did not see it or attached no significance to it. Indeed she misses entirely the point of the few early fragments that she quotes.

In 1894 Mr. Clement K. Shorter visited Mr. Arthur Bell Nicholls, the husband of Charlotte Brontë, at his home in Banagher, Ireland, and purchased from him for Mr. Thomas J. Wise the greater part of the Brontë manuscripts and letters in his possession, including the package mentioned by Mrs. Gaskell. The letters Mr. Shorter incorporated in *Charlotte Brontë and Her Circle* (1896), and *The Brontës Life and Letters,* 1908; the manuscripts as a whole he passed over as worthless, pausing only to remark of "An Adventure in Ireland," the one exception he printed: "Perhaps the only juvenile fragment which is worth anything is also the only one in which she escapes from the Wellington enthusiasm."

By the Wellington enthusiasm he meant Charlotte's habit of weaving her romances around the Duke of Wellington; but he was mistaken in thinking the fairy tale which escaped his general condemnation the only one of its kind, just as he was mistaken in his judgment of the others. Neither did he know that by Charlotte's fifteenth year the Duke of Wellington had given place to his elder son, whom she fashioned as an unrestrained Byronic hero retaining few Wellesley features. Mr. Shorter might with more accuracy have spoken of Charlotte's Byron enthusiasm.

It would seem that neither Mrs. Gaskell nor Mr. Shorter was equal to the forbidding and apparently interminable task of reading in chronological order the hundreds of pages of microscopic hand printing which guarded the secret of Charlotte's childhood and early womanhood. Thus they missed a record far more revealing of the mind and genius of their subject than the letters which they made the basis of their biographies, and a romance more interesting than the speculations that have gathered around the Brontë name. Perhaps they found themselves unable to reconcile the contradictory revelations of letters and manuscripts and chose the more understandable one—the letters. It is quite certain that neither grasped the value of the treasure in hand. No later biographer saw the precious mass intact with the Brontë touch still warm upon it; no one else has even seen the whole of it, for Mr. Wise, after selecting a few pieces for his own library, committed the rest to the fortunes of the auction room, even breaking some into parts which he bound and sold separately. The little booklets and separate sheets were eagerly seized upon by collectors for their romantic association and odd appearance, rather than for their content, and soon became widely scattered through England and America. Many, fortunately, came into possession of Mr. Henry H. Bonnell, a singularly sincere and intelligent Brontë devotee, of Philadelphia, who bequeathed them to the Brontë Library and Museum at Haworth, where they are available to students.

It is now almost twenty years since my interest in these diminutive Brontë manuscripts was excited through one of the curious little booklets in the Wrenn Library at the University of Texas. It is a small octavo of thirty-five pages measuring 7½ x 4½ inches covered with minute hand printing. Its unusual appearance, together with the signature, "C Brontë, June 29th, 1837," offered a temptation too great for my curiosity to resist.

The transcribing proved an alluring but disappointing task. The story was little more than a series of vignettes held together by no stronger tie than the shadow of a common character and an unrealized tendency towards a unifying plot. The typed transcript of more than one hundred pages presented a puzzle in every line. Who were the characters and what the incidents mentioned with the casual familiarity of everyday friends and neighborhood gossip? Such names as Wellesley, Castlereagh, and Townshend indicated that its actors were real personages, yet not one could be identified with the statesman whose name he bore. The setting proposed the greatest puzzle of all. The landscape and social manners were plainly English; the political situation suggested Ireland; the presence of Arthur Wellesley at the head of an army indicated the Continent; while as if to complete the confusion, one character says of another, "There goes the most skilful compound of malignance and dissimulation in Africa."

My puzzled brain echoed fervently a remark on the paper before me, "The whole is a mystery," but I was far from heeding its accompanying admonition, "Pry no further." I could not dismiss the sketch from my mind as merely an unfinished exercise, for it possessed an intensity of feeling and a subtle realism that were more than accidental or momentary. It could never have come into existence alone. I guessed that it must be a section of a longer whole, and began a search for its antecedents and sequels. The usual reference books yielded nothing, but protracted effort brought to light a few pieces of the *juvenilia* in obscure periodicals unenlightened by editorial matter. Such crumbs of information as I picked up tended to confirm my guess that the Wrenn manuscript was one of a closely connected series. My first considerable help came from a still smaller and more finely written booklet in the library of Mrs. Miriam Lutcher Stark, now at the University of Texas, which, though written three years before the one in question, presented the same characters and the same setting. At this point, in 1923, Mr. C. W. Hatfield prepared the text and supplied the notes, for more than sixty posthumous poems included in Shorter's *Complete Poems of Charlotte Brontë*. Many of these were taken from prose tales, where they occur as songs or effusions of one of Charlotte's fictitious poets; but Mr. Hatfield's notes were brief, suggestive rather than definitive, and I had to look further for the full story. Again, in 1925, he prepared the text, this time without editorial matter, of thirteen prose selections from unpublished manuscripts illustrating Charlotte's style of writing from her thirteenth to her twenty-second year. The critical value of this little volume, published under the title *The Twelve Adventurers and Other Stories,* was little understood, and did not receive the attention it deserved. A letter to Mr. Hatfield after I had read it brought kind response. He not only lent me transcripts which he had collected, but he introduced me to Mr. Bonnell, who until his death made his originals freely available to me, a kindness continued by Mrs. Bonnell.

My search, prolonged to the present time, through public and private libraries of America and England, has yielded astonishingly rich returns. I have studied in originals or in copies more than a hundred manuscripts by Charlotte and her brother Branwell, equaling in mass the published works of the Brontë family. Nearly all of them are in the minute hand printing described by Mrs. Gaskell; the earlier ones have the appearance of printed books varying in size from miniatures of 1½ x 1¼ inches to small octavos, with elaborate title-pages, prefaces, and colophons containing signatures and dates; their covers are of blue, brown, or gray wrapping paper.

Since I began this work, probably one-third of the stories I saw first in original manuscript have been printed, most of them in the Brontë Society Publications from transcripts made by Mr. Hatfield. In 1933 I published, in collaboration with William Clyde DeVane of Yale, a group of hitherto unprinted stories and poems under the title *Legends of Angria,* with an introduction outlining the origin, contents, and critical importance of the entire series. In 1936, the Shakespeare Head Press, under the editorship of Thomas J. Wise and Alex Symington, reprinted most of the material which had previously appeared, with the additions of a few pieces by Branwell Brontë.

The present volume is the first essay towards a comprehensive evaluation of the Brontë *juvenilia.*

And what is the conclusion? Have the tedious little booklets any literary value in themselves that escaped Mrs. Gaskell and Mr. Shorter? Or do they yield enough of biographical and critical interest to justify the prodigious labor of collecting and transcribing them? The answer is inherent in their nature. They are a closely connected series of stories, poems, novels, histories, and dramas having a common setting and common characters, written through the sixteen years between 1829 and 1845, a period comprehending approximately one-third of Charlotte's life and one-half of Branwell's, each making its definite contribution to a highly complex creation. They are the epic cycle of an imaginary world in which the four young Brontës lived, moved, and had their being, into which they projected themselves and all that they knew of life from narrow experience and wide reading. They are the frank, unembarrassed, unselfconscious diary of a Charlotte the world has never known, who built for herself a refuge in the "silent, unseen land of thought" where her romantic spirit found escape from the discipline and restraints of ordinary life, a refuge shared by no one but her brother and sisters. Even more, they are the laboratory in which developed all the elements that in their several combinations make up *The Professor, Jane Eyre, Shirley,* and *Villette.* They are the clearest and fullest extant record for the study of a group of highly gifted children through their formative years. Finally, they are the conclusive answer to most of the longstudied, much discussed Brontë problems.

They explode the myth of Branwell's mental endowments, showing that his early precocity held not a spark of genius and that his development ceased after his fifteenth or sixteenth year. They reduce to an absurdity the contention that he wrote or inspired any part of *Wuthering Heights,* yet, paradoxically, they reveal that his influence upon one, at least, of his sisters was greater than his champions have claimed. They upset the orthodox belief as to the originals of Charlotte's best-known characters by showing that all evolved from childish conceptions, however they were finally modified by actual models for realistic effect. They deny conclusively that Charlotte's Belgian experience had any part in awakening her genius, for they show that her genius had no sudden awakening, but developed gradually and normally in response to all her formative experiences, and was full-grown and self-conscious in all its fire and passion before she set foot on the Continent.

In contrast to the oft-repeated, tragic picture of the four little Brontës, frail, neglected, and prematurely old, crouching in terror before the ever-threatening monsters of disease and early death, the *juvenilia* show us singularly happy beings, possessed of an Aladdin's lamp through whose magic power they transcended time and distance, walked with kings, and swayed the destiny of a mighty empire. In the light of analogy shed from their pages, Emily, long miscalled "the sphinx of literature," shows herself through her poems the frankest and most self-revealing of women, fearless and unembarrassed, entirely aware of her own genius.

These little books hold in their tiny script the most remarkable romance in literature and the most accurate record of the evolution of genius extant in any language.

FANNIE E. RATCHFORD

Jerrycroft, Irvington-on-Hudson
August, 1940

CONTENTS

CONTENTS

ILLUSTRATIONS

The Brontës'
WEB OF CHILDHOOD

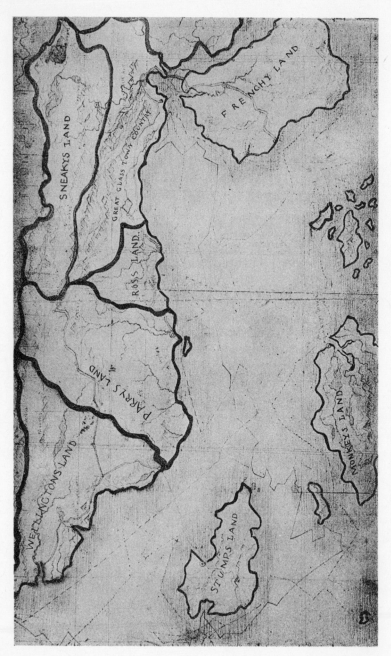

Map of the Glass Town Confederacy, Drawn by Branwell Brontë
at Fourteen

Chapter I

THE PARSONAGE SECRET

O NCE UPON A TIME four gifted children built themselves a dream world, magnificently wrought and marvelously beautiful. Taken by death, they left their creation intact, glorious in imagination, exquisite in fancy, but invisible save through a long unrecognized talisman. The father of the children was a curate, their home a parsonage at the top of a Yorkshire hill. From the back of their house stretched purple moors, while in front their small garden joined a churchyard leading into a church dedicated to the glory of God in honor of St. Michael the Archangel. In that church lay buried their mother and two older sisters. A stone's toss beyond the church stood the Black Bull Inn and beyond that a village of wild, rude millhands. Such was the careless challenge dropped by fate at the feet of four gifted children.

Today with Mrs. Brontë, Maria, and Elizabeth lie the Reverend Patrick Brontë, Branwell, Emily, and Charlotte. Anne, who followed Emily into death, is buried at Scarborough. The Parsonage itself, now a literary shrine, is open to all. A central hall sets an atmosphere of austere comfort, and simple dignity. To the right—if imagination harks back to former days—is the Reverend Patrick Brontë's study, and to the left the main living room, each with a fireplace. Behind the study is the familiar flagged kitchen, and across from it, a storeroom. There are no curtains—the Reverend Patrick Brontë feared fire—but rugs he permitted. The furniture is haircloth and mahogany. There are bookcases in the study, containing a few Greek and Latin classics, histories, and antiquarian treatises, while occasional shelves in the bedrooms hold family favorites worn shabby by much reading, such as *The Arabian Nights* and titles by Bewick, Johnson, Scott, Byron, and Southey. Seen also about the house are volumes borrowed from the Keighley public library and the rich collection gathered by generations of the Ponden House Heatons.

Soft gray tones prevail throughout the house, and exquisite cleanliness and delicate regularity give it an air of fastidious daintiness. Narrow stairs lead to two large front bedrooms, each with its adjacent smaller room, while over the lower hall is a cupboardlike space with a window looking across grave slabs to the square church tower. This is the so-called children's study, where Charlotte saw visions and Emily sketched herself, writing desk in her lap and her dog at her feet. Here, if anywhere under the Parsonage roof, the spirit of the dream world lingers.

Dominating the scene is the Reverend Patrick Brontë, sturdy and handsome, of Irish peasant stock, raised above his class by ambition and superior mental endowment. He is a Bachelor of Arts from Cambridge University and a clergyman in the Established Church. Four printed volumes from his pen in the study bookcase betray literary ambition. Since Anne was a few months old, he has been perpetual curate of Haworth with a living of two hundred pounds and this house rent free. He is a proud man, absorbed in his sermons. Presiding over the Parsonage is Miss Elizabeth Branwell, Mrs. Brontë's sister, from Penzance. A gentlewoman by birth, she is admirably equipped to teach the little girls manners, morals, and needlework, and to maintain household order. A matter-of-fact person, however, she is equipped neither by nature nor experience to deal with, or even to recognize, problems which call for understanding discipline, particularly the problem of overindulgence in the evasive mechanism of daydreaming.

Both the Reverend Mr. Brontë and Miss Branwell like privacy, and the four children enjoy large freedom from the questioning eyes of grown-ups.

Occupying an important place in the household is the servant, Tabby—faithful, unlettered Tabby. Knowing the old fairy paths along the "beck" she is the best qualified of the grown-up three to share in the magic secret which she feeds with her stories, and, by the same token, the least qualified to win the children from its dangerous charm. Nevertheless, not even she is initiated into their circle.

Nor was anyone else. No childhood friend was the young Brontës' confidant, for the shy, sensitive children did not mingle with the rude youngsters of the village. The Reverend Patrick Brontë took a pastor's interest in the parochial school at Haworth, but as an instructive medium he considered it beneath the station of a clergyman's family. Thus the four Brontës had their lessons in their father's study and in their aunt's bedroom, and indulged themselves, uncensored, in wide reading from the Parsonage shelves and neighboring libraries.

Charlotte's and Emily's single breath of the outside world ended in stark tragedy when they, eight and six years of age, together with Maria and Elizabeth, ten and nine, were sent to a half-charity boarding school maintained at Cowan Bridge for daughters of clergymen. The oldest two of this brood of six, born in as many years of a not too robust mother, broke under the school's routine. In less than twelve months they were dead, and Charlotte and Emily back at home with Branwell and Anne.

Mr. Brontë did not at any time consider submitting his son's education to hands other than his own. Hence the boy, of the remaining four children, became most acutely the victim of class and geographic isolation, and, eventually, the most complete slave of the druglike Brontë dream.

What happened in the immediate six years after Charlotte inherited Maria's mantle of leadership is the first half of the true Brontë chronicle. The impelling dream dominated the second half also, but the girls, unlike Branwell, were able at last to shape it to a constructive purpose.

Where then, did the four young Brontës conceal the key to the secret world so long closed to their biographers? Oddly enough it has always lain in open view, awaiting recognition.

Chapter II

A PARADE OF WOODEN SOLDIERS

O N THE NIGHT of June 5, 1826, a year after Maria and Elizabeth died, the Reverend Patrick Brontë, returning from Leeds, placed beside the bed of nine-year-old Branwell a box of wooden soldiers requested by the lad to supplement older sets now battered and broken. A set of ninepins, a toy village, and a dancing doll he gave to Miss Branwell for the girls. Early the next morning Branwell was at his sisters' door, calling them to see his new soldiers. Out of bed jumped Charlotte and Emily, Charlotte in the lead. Snatching up one of the soldiers, the tallest and handsomest of the lot, Charlotte exclaimed, "This is the Duke of Wellington! This shall be the Duke!" [1]

Emily then picked out for herself a serious looking fellow, derisively dubbed "Gravey" by the others. Anne followed, choosing "Waiting Boy." These soldiers Branwell good-naturedly agreed the girls might claim as their own, though they were still to be his in reality. Last of all, he selected his favorite from the remaining nine and called him "Buonaparte."

In these wooden soldiers the children had at hand *dramatis personae* for an ever-lengthening series of games. Around the toys raged battles and campaigns in which Wellington and his staff fought

---

[1] Charlotte Brontë: "The History of the Year." March 12, 1829. 550 words. (Bonnell Collection, Brontë Museum and Library, Haworth, Eng.)
———— "Two Romantic Tales: The Twelve Adventures." April 15, 1829. 4,500 words. (In the Library of Sir Alfred Law, Honresfeld, Littleborough, Eng., recently dispersed.)
Branwell Brontë: "The History of the Young Men, from Their First Settlement to the Present Time." By John Bud. December 15, 1830–May 7, 1831. Folding map and plate. 18 pp., 15,000 words. 7¾" x 6½". (Ashley Library, British Museum.)
All notes refer to original manuscripts, unless it is otherwise indicated.

Napoleon and his marshals according to formulas that were commonplaces of conversation in every English household. Branwell, encouraged by his father in his taste for military science and the study of tactics, directed their movements. Wearying in time of battles, the children turned the Young Men, as they called the new soldiers, to other occupations and arts suggested by their reading, changing them into make-believe publishers, authors, and antiquarians and crediting them with exploits surpassing the achievements of ancient and modern masters. In their various roles the toys were designated, according to physical or supposed moral characteristics, as Cracky, Cheeky, Monkey, Goody, Naughty, Rogue, and so forth. Again, in view of their ligneous nature, they were called General Leaf, Captain Tree, Sergeant Bud, Corporal Branch, Stumps, and so forth, and each was invested with a personality which was to be perpetuated long after the toys "had departed and left not a wreck behind." As this first play progressed, its several conceptions tended to run together, and soldiers, literary men, artists, prophets, and rogues fused in a complex and representative society.

Branwell, because of his proprietary interest in the soldiers and his knowledge of military technique, was master of this show—the Young Men's Play.

After a year his domination of the stage was broken by the invention of a new game, Our Fellows,[2] in which each child had as his own a large island inhabited by people six miles high, a convention taken from Aesop's Fables. Hay man was Charlotte's chief man; Boaster, Branwell's; Hunter, Anne's; and Clown, Emily's. All the chief men were ten miles high, except Emily's, which was only four.

Our Fellows held sway until a cold, gusty night in November,[3] when the children sat around a blazing kitchen fire, having just concluded a quarrel with Tabby concerning the propriety of lighting a candle. Tabby came off victorious, and Branwell grumbled gloomily, "I don't know what to do." Once again, Charlotte proposed the choos-

[2] Charlotte Brontë: Fragment: "The Origin of the O'Deay's is as Follows." 57 words. (Bonnell Collection.)

[3] Charlotte Brontë: "Tales of the Islanders." In four volumes. June 31, 1829–July 30, 1830. (The location of the manuscript is unknown to the present writer; printed in *Nash's Magazine*, December, 1911.)

ing of islands. Branwell spoke first, appropriating the Isle of Man. Charlotte took the Isle of Wight; Emily, the Isle of Arran; and Anne, the Isle of Guernsey. Thus was launched the Play of the Islanders, the third "great play" in the Brontë cycle.

The next step, following a now accepted convention, was the choosing of heroes to inhabit these islands. Branwell chose John Bull; Astley Cooper, a distinguished surgeon of the day; and Leigh Hunt, writer and editor. Emily chose Sir Walter Scott; Mr. Lockhart, Scott's son-in-law and biographer; and Johnnie Lockhart. Anne chose Michael Sadler, social reformer; Lord Bentinck, governor-general of Bengal; and Sir Henry Halford, another distinguished physician. Charlotte chose the Duke of Wellington and his two sons, Arthur and Charles, together with Christopher North and Co., pseudonymous editors of *Blackwood's Magazine,* and Mr. Abernethy, writer on anatomy and physiology.

Just at this point the children were interrupted by the "dismal sound of the clock striking seven," the regular summons to bed, but the next day they resumed the task of peopling their respective countries. As the weeks passed each added to his group of personages until their combined lists included most of the great names of the British Empire.

In the following June Charlotte gave the play, now beginning to lag, fresh impetus by shifting the machinery from a group of real islands to a fictitious Island of Dreams, where she erected a school which was to contain one thousand children. This island, according to her description, was "fifty miles in circumference, and certainly appeared more like the work of enchantment and beautiful fiction than sober reality." From the center towered a magnificent palace of pure white marble so finely wrought and so beautiful that it seemed the work of mighty genii and not of feeble men. Within the palace was a magnificent room called the Hall of the Fountain. Behind one of its statues a door, hidden by a curtain of white silk, discovered a small apartment at the far end of which was a very large iron door. This door, in its turn, opened on a long dark passage terminating in a flight of steps leading to a subterranean dungeon, "a wide vault dimly lighted by a lamp which cast a death-like, melancholy luster over a part of the dungeon, leaving the vault in the gloomy darkness of night. In the middle was a slab of black marble supported by four pillars. At the end stood a throne of iron. In several parts of the vault were instruments of torture."

There were also darkly vaulted cells appropriated to the private and particular use of naughty children, so far down in the earth that the loudest shrieks could go unheard by inhabitants of the upper world. In them, as well as in the dungeons, cruelest torturing might have gone on without fear of detection if it had not been that Charlotte kept the key of the dungeon and Emily the key of the cells and of the huge iron entrance, which would "brave any assault except with the lawful instrument."

Only young nobles were admitted to this magnificent school. The chief governor was the Duke of Wellington, and his sons, the Marquis of Douro and Lord Charles Wellesley, were guards keeping the children in order and taking them out to walk. They were "particularly fitted" for their task, Charlotte asserts, inasmuch as they led their charges into the wildest and most dangerous parts of the country, leaping rocks, precipices, and chasms, little caring whether the children went before or stopped behind. Often as not they came home with about a dozen wanting, who might be found a few days after in hedges or ditches, with legs or heads broken, "thus affording a fine field for Sir A. Hume, Sir A. Cooper, and Sir H. Halford to display their different methods of setting and trepanning."

There were other guards for thrashing the school children when they needed it, and Branwell kept a large black club with which he thumped them upon occasion, "and that most unmercifully."

From mere invisible *dei ex machina* of the play the little Brontës were now actors on the boards, with the titles Little King and Queens, and as such they constituted a court of last resort, to whom even the great Wellington and his sons must bow. When the school children rose in bloody rebellion and besieged their governors in the palace, Little King and Queens hastened in balloons to their relief, restoring order, bringing the dead to life, and healing the wounded by means of fairy remedies.

The rebellion put down, the school went on very well. "All rules were observed with scrupulous exactness; the governors attended admirably to their duties." The make-believe children, to all outward appearances at least, were becoming something like civilized beings; gambling was less frequent among them; their quarrels with one another were less savage; and some little attention was paid by them to order and cleanliness. The governors constantly resided in the grand palace of the institution, so that "nothing was left entirely to the care of servants and underlings."

This last sentence suggests that Charlotte had heard dependence on servants and underlings blamed for the bad conditions at Cowan Bridge, which were probably responsible for the death of her sisters, Maria and Elizabeth.

The Play of the Islanders ran for almost another year when the Brontës, becoming tired of it, as of their former inventions, sent the young nobles to their homes and left the Island of Dreams to irresponsible fairies.

Chapter III

TWELVE HEROES IN AFRICA

FROM THE PLAY of the Islanders the little Brontës turned again to the wooden soldiers and the Young Men's Play in a new guise suggested by the Reverend J. Goldsmith's *A Grammar of General Geography*.[1] Inspired by its section on Africa, they now sent their twelve wooden heroes on a voyage ending in shipwreck on the Guinea coast near the mouth of the Niger River.[2] Incidents for this great adventure were suggested now by Charlotte, now by Branwell, and Emily and Anne joined in playing them out. Action began with the sailing of the good ship *Invincible*, seventy-four guns, bound for Ashantee, a country looming large on the new map of Africa. The crew consisted of thirteen men, the twelve new heroes and Crashey, the captain, a battered survivor of an earlier set of soldiers, a "patriarch full of years and full of wisdom."

Charlotte would have hastened the *Invincible* to its destination with nothing more untoward than storms and scuffles and fist-fights among the crew, but Branwell, having read the story of the early struggle between the English and Dutch for colonies and trade, must have the ship touch at Ascension Island, then in possession of their rivals. There its crew fought a desperate battle. The Dutch, ignorant of the small number of English, "imagined them a legion of ghosts and demons let loose upon the garrison like an overwhelming torrent." So fiercely and so strategically did the Twelves fight, under Branwell's direction,

---

[1] Copy used by the Brontë children containing notes and drawings is in the Bonnell Collection.

[2] "The Twelve Adventurers" and "The History of Young Men." See note 1, p. 6.

that by nightfall they had nothing to do but seize their prisoners, "collecting every one, soldier, man, or child, both in the Town and Fort," to the number of one hundred and eighty, and cramming them all, *à la* the Black Hole of Calcutta, into a small room in the castle.

When morning came the survivors of this desperate struggle deliberated upon what should be done with the prisoners, and "at last came to the conclusion of blowing them up with the castle in which they were confined. This may to some seem monstrous and cruel in the extreme," observes Branwell, "but let us recollect that these people had wounded CRASHEY, and after this who would think of sparing them?" When "this act of justice and vengeance had been performed," the remaining heroes gathered up the bodies of Crashey, Ross, Bravey, Gravey, Monkey, Cracky, and Tracky, "which they soon *made alive* by the usual means, though after the most diligent search the remains of Stumps could nowhere be found."

The custom of "making alive" the fallen soldiers was the girls' antidote against Branwell's bloody slaughterings.

The unwounded survivors of the fight with the Dutch were Guelf, Wellesley, Parry, and Sneaky. Parry, Ross, and Sneaky or Sneachi were Emily's, Anne's, and Branwell's original favorites rechristened. The real William Edward Parry and John Ross were Arctic explorers then high in public interest. Only Charlotte's Wellington retained his original name.

Their dead having been "resuscitated or made alive again," the company of "renovated companions, 12 in number, but all true heroes," left the island, and fifteen days later, "on the 5th of June, A.D. 1770," anchored the *Invincible* in a deserted, stormy, and reed-choked bay, on the shore of Ashantee.

At this point the children, inspired by the reading of *The Arabian Nights,* hit upon a new and fascinating self-dramatization. They became the Chief Genius Talli, the Chief Genius Branni, the Chief Genius Emmi, and the Chief Genius Annii, and under their powerful protection the little band of shipwrecked adventurers proceeded to explore the country. To their great astonishment they found it cultivated. Grain of a peculiar sort grew in great abundance, and there were large plantations of palm trees and likewise an immense number

The Wooden Soldiers in Action, Drawn in Colored Crayon
by Branwell Brontë

of almond trees. There were also many olives and large enclosures of rice. Traveling two miles inland, they met a band of twenty native blacks, and had a "very fierce encounter." The whites triumphed gloriously, killing ten Negroes, wounding five, and taking their chief a prisoner. The remaining four of the enemy withdrew from the fray!

The next morning the blacks, represented by the set of ninepins pressed into the game, ransomed their chief and signed a treaty of peace. Immediately thereafter the heroes set about building a city, aided by the genii. "The situation was in the middle of a large plain, bounded on the north by high mountains, on the south by the sea, on the east by gloomy forests, and on the west by evil deserts. . . . Far off to the east the long black line of gloomy forests skirted the horizon. To the north the Gibble Kumri or Mountains of the Moon seemed a misty girdle to the plain of Dahomey; to the south the ocean guarded the coasts of Africa . . . to the west lay the desert." The little Brontës were making good use of their *Grammar of Geography*.

The building of the city "went on prosperously," the Hall of Justice, the fortifications, and the Tower of All Nations were completed, and the Grand Inn of the Genii was begun. One night when the twelve founders were assembled in the Hall of Justice, Arthur Wellesley, "at that time a common trumpeter," proposed that they immediately send word to England of the newly discovered world and its riches, hoping an army should come to their aid against the threatening blacks.

I am not so rash [he said] as to suppose that we of ourselves could cross the ocean in the damaged and leaky vessel we possess, or that we could build another in time to avert the danger which I fear is coming. But in what a short time have we built the city we are now in! How long has it taken to rear the Grand Hall where we now are? Have not those marble pillars and that solemn dome been built by supernatural power? If you view the city from this Gothic window and see the beams of the morn gilding the battlements of the mighty towers and the pillars of the splendid palaces which have been reared in a few months, can you doubt that magic has been used in their construction? Now, if the genii have built us our city, will they not likewise help us to call our countrymen to defend what they have built against the assaults of the enemy?

The Young Men's Play in its African phase gradually became the all-absorbing interest of the children's circumscribed existence. Into its crucible they tossed indiscriminately happenings of their everyday life, observations of their village neighbors, and borrowings from their omnivorous reading, transmuting all into glowing romance. Exhausting their sources of inspiration, they dramatized the growth of the play itself, patterning every detail into "The History of the Young Men." Branwell's request for a new set of soldiers and their purchase in Leeds thus became the thunderous summons of Chief Genius Branni, speaking out of earthquake and fire:

When the sun appears above the forests of the east, be ye all on the border of the evil desert, for if ye fail, I will crush you to atoms.

And the trip to Haworth in a closed box in a jolting cart, was a journey into the desert to meet the summoner:

The sky which till then had been blue and clear, was suddenly covered with black and tempestous clouds which hurried to and fro as if in some great and awful convulsion.

Himself in his night clothes when he discovered the toys by his bed, Branwell pictured through the eyes of the Young Men as an immense and terrible monster, "enveloped in a dim, misty and indefinable robe," his head encircled with a red and fiery halo, touching the clouds, and his nostrils flashing flame and smoke. The Parsonage, to the tiny mortals in the monster's hand, was a palace of diamonds, the pillars of which were ruby and emerald illuminated with lamps too bright to look upon; and the girls' bedroom, a hall of sapphire with thrones of gold, on which sat the Princes of the Genii. The choosing of favorite soldiers became the Genii's promise of protection and future glory: "I tell you all that ye shall one day be kings."

This prophetic communication being delivered, "all the fairies and genii joined in one grand chorus which rose rolling to the mighty dome and stately pillars of the genii palace, and reached among the vaults and dungeons beneath; then gradually dying away, it at last ceased entirely."

The decision to admit the old and battered Crashey to the company of the Twelves as their high priest and mediator was dramatized as a spectacular phenomenon:

While [the Twelve were] sitting together in the Common Hall . . . the wine cups standing upon the round table filled to the brim, the air suddenly darkened, the hall shook, and streams of fire continually flashed through the room, followed by long and loud peals of thunder. While all were standing pale and affrighted at the unusual phenomenon, a dreadful monster . . . entered the room with Crashey in his hand. He put him down and said in a loud voice: "I am the Chief Genius Branii. With me there are three others. She, Wellesley, who protects you, is named Tallii; she who protects Parry is named Emmii; she who protects Ross is called Annii. Those lesser ones whom ye saw are Genii and Fairies, our slaves and minions. . . . We are the guardians of you all. Revere this man Crashey. He is entrusted with secrets which you can never know. I prophesy unto you that ye shall one day become a great and mighty nation and rule all the world. Be not afraid; go on as ye have done. Adiu [sic]. Ye shall see us again." After thus speaking, the monster spread his dragon wings and flew away.

Whatever the temporary lightness of fancy Charlotte might introduce, Branwell, calling himself Bany-Lightning, always brought the Young Men's Play back to a game of destruction and war. His taste for the gruesome found rich provender in African battles, culminating in a last desperate conflict between the Twelve Heroes and ten cannibal chiefs from Acroofcroomb—the ninepins—"who had all vowed to eat the flesh and drink the blood of the 12s." The vow was partially fulfilled when Cheeky, Gravey, and Cracky, killed or wounded, were borne a short distance from the capital, where "horid to relate," their enemies "roasted and made a feast of them."

This atrocity excited their comrades to such superhuman effort that they forced the blacks to give way in a confused and dishonorable retreat, leaving behind 1,500 dead on the field of battle, among them five of the chiefs, the other five being prisoners. Crashey now implored the genii to fulfill their promise and "descend with the spirit of life." Instantly the dead and wounded Twelves, including "the half-eaten victims of the Acroofcroombers started from the ground, living, vigorous, and free from wounds."

The spirit of all being greatly refreshed by this miracle, the reunited band of heroes rushed after the fleeing blacks and fell upon them with such fury "that not a vestige of the Ashantee army remained."

In course of time the preëminence accorded Charlotte's Wellington brought forth grumblings from the other children. Thereupon the ex-

tensive territory conquered by the Twelves was partitioned into kingdoms ruled by the four heroes "best qualified to hold them" and named
accordingly Wellingtonsland, Parrysland, Rossesland, and Sneakysland
or Sneachisland, each with its capital called, in imitation of the original
magic city, "Wellington's Glass Town," "Parry's Glass Town," "Ross's
Glass Town," and "Sneaky's Glass Town." Together these kingdoms
formed a confederacy centering in the city of the genii, "The Great
Glass Town," a name taken from a book on African travel, signi-
fying in the children's minds the glasslike harbor in whose smooth
waters the magic buildings were reflected as in a mirror. Islands discovered off the coast were assigned to two other heroes, Monkey and
Stumps, and were added to the confederacy as Monkeysland and
Stumpsland. For the sake of Branwell's Wellington-Napoleon battles
a third island was peopled with French and called Frenchland, its
capital Paris.

Chapter IV

SOLDIERS TURNED AUTHORS

WHILE CERTAIN of the wooden soldiers made history, others recorded it in prose and verse. The great Sergeant Bud, representing Branwell himself, produced voluminous accounts of the discovery, conquest, and organization of the Glass Town Confederacy, and equally voluminous antiquarian treatises on the origin, manners, and customs of the Twelves, while Captain Tree, Charlotte's mouthpiece, turned the same material to lighter use in tales and novels.

Literal minded, Branwell must needs give material form to these imaginary volumes, for both he and Charlotte were already experienced authors. He himself had two volumes to his credit: "The Battell of [Wehglon?]," [1] a small pamphlet of a few leaves almost wholly covered with water-color pictures of soldiers charging a fort or lying stiffly on the ground where they have fallen, and "History of the Rebellion in My Army," [2] recording an incident in Our Fellows: Goodman, who, despite his name, is a rascal, aided by Boaster, raises a rebellion among the wooden soldiers and presses the rightful commander so hard he has to send an ambassador to "Charlotte's country" for help.

Charlotte's first extant book, written when she was twelve, a year before she wrote her first letter (September 23, 1829), has no apparent connection with the family games. It is a diminutive volume of six leaves measuring 2½ x 2¼ inches made up, like Branwell's first volume,

[1] Branwell Brontë: "The Battle of [Wehglon?]." March 12, 1827. Water-color illustrations. 8 pp. 2½" x 2¼". (Brontë Museum and Library.)

[2] ——— "History of the Rebellion in My Army." 1828 (Longhand and large printing). 6 pp. 4½" x 4¼". (Brontë Museum and Library.)

of few words and many illustrations. It begins "There was once a little girl and her name was Ane." [3] Anne with her mother and father goes on a journey which includes a boat trip. The mother is seasick and Anne cares for her and gives her medicine. The illustrations show the house and garden where Anne lived, the boat on which she sailed, and the castle she saw near London. Following this story, though not necessarily connected with it, is a map, tinted with crayons, divided into four sections labeled "Taley," "Brany," "Vittoria," and "Wating."

Blackwood's Magazine, beloved of the Parsonage family, served as a model for the earliest written literature of the Young Men's Play. With surprising manual skill, Branwell, in January, 1829, fashioned a tiny periodical [4] of four leaves measuring about 2¼ x 1¼ inches, proportionate in size, as he calculated, to his wooden soldiers. Its diminutive sheets, printed in the smallest characters Branwell could then contrive, were enclosed in a cover made from a leaf which advertised books by and about John Wesley. The finished volume was labeled simply, "Magazine 1829."

His leading article, "Kairail Fish," describing a marvelous creature eighty to one hundred feet long with a horn twenty to thirty feet long and hooked at the end, which, when cut off by sailors, grows back in the space of half an hour, he illustrated with pencil drawings which depict the strange fish and the boats used by sailors in capturing it.

Following this scientific article comes a section labeled "Poetry":

> Oh my America
> Yeild to our Monarch's sway
> And no more contend
> May they their interest see
> . With England to agree
> And from oppression free
> All that amend.

A note signed C. T. (Captain Tree) informs the reader that this adaptation of the English national anthem "was sung at our oratorio and was much approved."

[3] Charlotte Brontë: "There was once a little girl and her name was Ane." *circa 1824.* Six colored illustrations. 16 pp. (4 blank), 125 words. 2½" x 1½".
[4] Branwell Brontë: Magazine. January, 1829. Illustrations. 8 pp. 2¼" x 1¼". (Amy Lowell Collection, Harvard University Library.)

An editorial in the Young Men's tongue (invented by Branwell speaking rapidly with his nose held tight between forefinger and thumb) harks back to his earlier book, "History of the Rebellion in My Army":

Bany do ought not to Punit de Doung Mōanct for having rebelled against do
For they did deix Duty
                    Goopy

The remaining article, an account of the author's voyage to Mons Island from Glass Town, contains the earliest extant picture of the magic metropolis, a "city with its houses, palaces, cathedrals, and churches glittering in the sun before the sea." The inhabitants of Mons Island were personified puppets other than the wooden soldiers—presumably toys belonging to the girls. The men were dressed in three-cornered hats, blue coats, red waistcoats, white breeches, tawny stockings, and black shoes, and the women in red waists, blue skirts, white aprons, and white caps bordered with red ribands.

If Branwell brought out his periodical for the four months (February–May), following the initial volume, the issues must have been lost. The next that has survived, dated June, 1829, gives evidence of Charlotte's improving hand. She, hungry for a literary medium and quick to see the possibilities in her brother's newest innovation, reached out itching fingers for it. The leading article is hers: "The Enfant, Part 2 by Charlotte B——të," and beneath the table of contents her name is written in ordinary script. The publication is now "Branwells Blackwoods Magazine Chief Glass Town. Printed and sold by Sergt. Tree." [5] It has an elaborate title cover, a formal table of contents with imprint repeated below, an editorial, and a page of neatly printed advertisements. Its most significant feature from the critical view point is an announcement revealing that the little Brontës had lately read Macpherson's *Ossian*—probably the copy Charlotte gave Branwell, now in the Brontë Library, Haworth—a book which influenced Branwell superficially and Emily profoundly:

[5] June, 1829. 18 pp. 2″ x 1½″. (Amy Lowell Collection.)
July, 1829. 22 pp. 2″ x 1½″. (Amy Lowell Collection.)

To the Editor

Glasstown,
June 1, 1829

Sir,

I write this to acquaint you of a circumstance which has happened to me and which is of great importance to the world at large. On May 22 1829 the Cheif Genius Tally came to me with a small yellow book in her hand. She gave it to me saying that it was the POEMS of that Ossian of whom so much has been said, but whose works could never be got. Upon attentive perusal of the above said works, I found that they were most sublime and excellent. I am engaged in publishing an edition of them, Quarto—3 vols with notes. commentarys, &c. I am fully convinced that it is the work of OSSIAN who lived 1,000 years ago—and of no other. There is a most intense anxiety prevailing amongst literary men to know its contents. In a short time they shall be gratified, for it will be published on the first of July, 1829.

I remain
Yours &c, &c.
Sergt. Bud, Jun. T S C

To the Cheif Genius Bany.

By July friction between Charlotte and Branwell as to the tone of the magazine reached a crisis, and Charlotte persuaded her brother to launch a newspaper and leave the magazine entirely to her. The number for that month carries his agreement of surrender:

Concluding Address

To My Readers P.B.B——të.

We have hitherto conducted this magazine, we hope, to the satisfaction of most (No one can please all), but as we are conducting a newspaper which requires all the time and attention which we can spare from our other employments, we have found it expedient to relinquish the editorship of this magazine. But we recommend our readers to be [word omitted] to the new editor as they were to me. The new one is Chief Genius Charlotte. She will conduct it in the future, though I shall write now and then for it.   ΔΘΗ'

July 1829. P. B. Brontë

ΔΘΗ' are symbols of "the old Young Men's Tongue," a by-product of Branwell's Greek lessons with his father.

The children, having settled this editorial dispute to their common satisfaction, proceeded to make literary capital of it in two doggerels published in the December issue of the magazine. The first, headed

"Lines Spoken by a Lawyer [Captain Bud] on the Occasion of the Transfer of this Magazine," voices Branwell's foreboding that the dignity of the periodical is a thing of the past:

> All soberness is past and gone;
> The reign of gravity is done.
> Frivolity comes in its place;
> Light smiling sits on every face.
>
> . . . . .
>
> Foolish romances now employ
> Each silly, senseless girl and boy.
> O, for the strong hand of the law
> To stop it with its powerful claw!

"Lines by One Who Was Tired of Dullness upon the Same Occasion," asserts Charlotte's opinion that the change is for the better:

> Sweep the sounding harp strings,
> All ye winds that blow,
> Let it loudly swelling
> Make sweet music flow,
>
> . . . . .
>
> Sweetly, sweetly breathe, flute,
> Pour your gentle strains,
> Let thy music rise, lute,
> No more Dullness reigns.

These effusions are signed "U. T." (Us Two).

From the real *Blackwood's*, the editors of the play magazine took over the famous "Noctes Ambrosianae," setting up a Glass Town symposium of congenial spirits gathered in the famous local tavern where mine host, Bravey—the "fire-eater of the conquest"—having "thrown away his sword and become pot-valiant," waxes rich in the realization of the highest ambition of his soldier days, "to become one day master of a snug pot-house."

Here, before a blazing fire, with bottles and glasses conveniently at hand, the puppet Wellington is wont to meet his familiars and lead discussions on military science, politics, literature, and art; nor is petty gossip beneath his enjoyment. With him, rapidly pushing him to the background in the play, are usually found his sons, Arthur, Marquis of Douro, and Lord Charles.

They were tall, slender, remarkably handsome, and were so much alike that it would have been difficult to distinguish the one from the other, were it not for a shade of thought which occasionally passed over the features of the elder. His fine wavy hair was also a little darker than that of the other, whose merry smile, which now and then lighted up his handsome face, and the gaiety with which he would sometimes toss his light curly hair and the playful manner in which he spoke to his brother when he observed the shade of thought come across his fine features, all betokened a more gay disposition than that which belonged to the older.

Also usually found at these gatherings are Wellington's fellow kings of the Glass Town Confederacy: Parry, Ross, and Sneachy; together with such celebrities as Gravey, Sir Alexander Hume Bady, Young Soult, the poet, Captain Tree, and Sergeant Bud.

These "Conversations" or "Nights" in Bravey's Inn reveal that Glass Town abounded in newspapers, such as "The Young Men's Intelligencer," "The Grog Bottle," "The Courier du Francais," "The Quatre Deinne," and "The Glass Town Intelligencer"; that a literary detective discovered the initials "U. T." stand for the Marquis of Douro and Lord Charles; and that the Palace of Waterloo was haunted. They disclose also that Charlotte had in her possession a magic fluid which forced the taker to tell the plain, full truth, no matter how prejudicial to his interests. Three times she administered it with startling effect, once to a young boy who admitted thereupon that he had violated the usage of good society by going to see his own uncle hanged; again to a mysterious visitor who confessed himself many times a murderer; and still again to Bud (Branwell), who owned himself the author of "Causes of the Late War," "which he got his Grace (the Duke of Wellington) . . . to have published in his name that it might sell the better."

At one of these gatherings, according to the July issue of the magazine, Bud is prevailed upon to read a portion of the text of *Ossian*, with his notes:

Hem-m! hem! Part of the beginning of the First book of the poem of Fingal by Ossian: Cutthullin sat by Turas Walls by the trees of the rustling sound

His spear leant against the rock His shield lay on the grass by his side. Amid his thoughts of mighty Cairbar a hero slain by the Cheif in war. . . .
[Note:] Tura's Wall Tura the dwelling of Cuthulin it is by some thought to be a cave by others a castle. In those times their great cheifs lived in caves very often and to have a rock and grass and dust by a castle is not very likely. I think it is a cave.

Well, what think you of that?

Douro's answer to this challenge, typical of the manner in which Charlotte constantly caught up Branwell's pomposity, was:

Ossian is sublime. The commentary is in many parts very good, sound, and just, but that which relates to Tura is unjust in the extreme. It says that Tura is a cave whereas by your own account it must be a castle, for Ossian says that Cuthullin sat by Tura's WALL. No cave could have a wall. A castle could, nay must have walls, can you answer?

Before the discussion can become more heated, Branwell in his lighter character as Young Soult, the Rhymer, interposes with a song:

> One day I went out a-walking
> and I saw a sheet of fire
> hovering oere the mountain
> kindled was my ire.
>
> . . . .
>
> I saw it was a Genius now
> so that I ran away
> for fear that he should see me
> if this were my last day.

Bud's great work is reviewed in the same issue as "Commentary on Ossian 29 vols folio. 2 edition," concluding:

This is one of the most long winded books that have ever been printed we must now conclude for we are dreafully tired. July 1829. P B B

The tyranny of the Genii hinted at in Young Soult's song—an expression of the rebellion complex which was beginning to dominate Branwell—is a frequent and exciting subject of discussion at all public gatherings in Glass Town. At one time Parry reads to his fellow citizens from the "Young Men's Intelligencer," the proclamation: "Whereas Bany wants some cash he requests 500,000,000 £ and if this is not complied with he will let the Genii upon the world. Signed by order of Bany-Lightning."

Again, the magazine carried the impressive communication:

Sir,—It is well known that the Genii have declared that unless they [the Young Men] perform certain arduous duties every year, of a mysterious nature, all the worlds in the firmament will be burned up, and gathered together in one mighty globe, which will roll in solitary grandeur through the vast wilderness of space, inhabited only by the four high princes of the Genii, till time shall be succeeded by eternity.

On another occasion Young Soult rouses the tavern gathering by singing:

> If you live by the sunny Fountain
> if you live in the streets of a Town
> if you live on the top of a mountain
> or if you wear a crown,
>   The Genii meddle with you.

And the Marquis of Douro wins the hearts of all present through his courageous toast, "THE DOWNFALL OF THE GENII," drunk with "nine times nine and thunders of applause."

Forgetting the geographical location and the climate of the African city, Charlotte often projects into her "Nights" details of purely Yorkshire color, such as Lord Charles's grumblings against Haworth weather:

When all the old women traverse the streets in red woolen cloaks and clanking iron patteens, when apothecaries are seen rushing about with gargles and tinctures and washes for sprained arches, chilblains and frost-bitten noses, when you can hardly feel your hands and feet for the cold and are forced to stand shuddering over the fire on pain of being petrified by the frost, how pleasant this is, Arthur! . . . Consider of the frosty nights and windy, showery, uncertain days, when you can't stir about without an umbrella in your hand, and if you unfurl it, you are in danger of being lifted over the tops of the houses. Or perhaps you may be going over the bridge, and in that case nothing but death stares you in the face. Oh, summer and autumn for me. . . . The pleasantest season of the year!

With the August issue, Charlotte, now in full control, changed the title page of the periodical to read:

"Blackwoods Young Mens Magazine [6] Edited by the Genius C.B. Printed by Captain Tree And Sold by Captain Cary, Sergeant Blood, Corporal Lidell, &c &c &c.,"

and advertises to the effect that:

"A magnificent painting of the Chief Genii in Council is now to be seen at Captain Cloven's house terms of admittance 3d."

Other departments of the magazine, too, contribute their part to the Glass Town picture, celebrating in song and story such familiar landmarks as the Tower of All Nations (an adaptation of the Tower of Babel), apostrophized in a poem entitled "The Walk":

Oh, thou great, thou mighty tower!
    Rising up so solemnly
O'er all this splendid glorious city,
    This city of the sea.

Thou seem'st, as silently I gaze,
    Like a pillar of the sky.
So lofty is thy structure grey
    So massive and so high!

The dome of Heaven is o'er thee hung
    With its maze of silver stars;
The earth is round about thee spread
    With its eternal bars.

"Scene on the Great Bridge by the Genius C B," leading article in the November number, pictures one of the architectural treasures of the city, and at the same time illustrates the antagonism between the "bluff, hardy, original old Glass Towners" and the more showy, overbearing Englishmen who accompanied the Duke of Wellington on his return after "delivering Europe from Napoleon," an incident of Glass Town history recorded by Branwell in "The History of the Young Men." The narrative, in part, runs:

[6] August, 1829. 20 pp. 2″ x 1½″. (Amy Lowell Collection.)
October, 1829. 16 pp. 2″ x 1½″. (Amy Lowell Collection.)
November, 1829. 16 pp. 2″ x.1½″. (Amy Lowell Collection.)
December (1), 1829. 1⅞″ x 1⅜″. (Brontë Museum and Library.)
December (2), 1829. 18 pp. 2½″ x 1½″. (Ashley Library.)
The September issue has not come to light.

We had traveled thus for some time, when, emerging from the trees, we entered the highroad, and the great and splendid city, with its majestic towers and glorious palaces burst upon our view, and the running to and fro of its horses and of its chariots and the noise of its mighty multitude resounded in our ears like the rushing of many waters.

In a short time we came to the Great Bridge and truly the arches are so high that they are dreadful; and when I stood on it and looked down on the tremendous waters which were rolling and raging beneath with a noise like distant thunder, I could not help thinking of the intrepidity of those little mortals who had erected the great fabric on which I stood.

There is at each end of the Bridge a beautiful and elegant tower, in which the keepers of the toll reside, and no one is permitted to pass without paying the requisite sum. . . .

I had stood a little while on the bridge when a dashing English Captain came galloping up, mounted on a stately war-horse.

"What's to pay, old boy?" exclaimed he to the toll keeper, a fine, venerable-looking old man [one of the Twelves].

"6d, Sir," replied he, "and in the meantime I beg that you will be a little more respectful."

"6d? Who ever heard of such a thing? I'll report you to the Duke, you old rascal. I suppose you keep a good half in your own stupid pouch."

"I don't though, and I've a good mind to throw you over the bridge for such a lie."

"I'll not pay you a farthing."

At this point a genius appears and reduces the cocky captain to terms by threatening his life if he fails to pay.

Charlotte concludes the magazine for the year with two issues in December, stating merely: "We have been obliged to have 2 numbers this month." One carries her review of a great painting: "The Chief Genii in Council by Edward De Lisle." Of gigantic dimensions, it represents "the genii seated upon thrones of pure and massive gold, in the midst of an immense hall surrounded by pillars of fire and brilliant diamonds. A large and cloud-like canopy hangs over the heads of the genii, all studded with bright rubies, from which a red, clear light streams, irradiating all around it with its burning glow, and forming a mild contrast to the flood of glory which pours from the magnificent emerald dome."

"The Chief Genii in Council" represented, of course, the four little Brontës planning new adventures for the wooden soldiers.

As an accentuating background to this highly colored romantic life of imagination, comes Charlotte's faithful record of Parsonage routine,[7] written on March 12, 1829.

Once Papa lent my sister Maria a book. It was an old geography book; she wrote on its blank leaf, "Papa lent me this book." This book is a hundred and twenty years old; it is at this moment lying before me. While I write this I am in the kitchen of the Parsonage, Haworth; Tabby, the servant, is washing up the breakfast things, and Anne, my youngest sister (Maria was my eldest), is kneeling on a chair, looking at some cakes which Tabby has been baking for us. Emily is in the parlour, brushing the carpet. Papa and Branwell are gone to Keighley. Aunt is up-stairs in her room, and I am sitting by the table writing this in the kitchen. Keighley is a small town four miles from here. Papa and Branwell are gone for the newspaper, the "Leeds Intelligencer," a most excellent Tory newspaper, edited by Mr. Wood, and the proprietor, Mr. Henneman. We take two and see three newspapers a week. We take the "Leeds Intelligencer," Tory, and the "Leeds Mercury," Whig, edited by Mr. Baines, and his brother, son-inlaw, and his two sons, Edward and Talbot. We see the "John Bull"; it is a high Tory, very violent. Dr. Driver lends us it, as likewise "Blackwood's Magazine," the most able periodical there is. The editor is Mr. Christopher North, an old man seventy-four years of age; the 1st of April is his birth-day; his company are Timothy Tickler, Morgan O'Doherty, Macrabin Mordecai, Mullion, Warnell, and James Hogg, a man of most extraordinary genius, a Scottish shepherd.

Perhaps Charlotte at thirteen was already balancing the actual against the imaginative.

The magazine of 1829 had several companion volumes from the pens of its editors. In April—the month that saw the completion of her thirteenth year—Charlotte wrote under title of "The Twelve Adventurers" a unified and dramatic account of the founding of Glass Town, not to be recognized as part of a loosely organized and long-continued play of four small children until one reads Branwell's very literal companion volume of two years later. And near the end of the year, in December, she selected from the incongruous processions that march

[7] "The History of the Year." See note 1, p. 6.

and frolic and caper across the odd little pages of her tiny booklets ten favorites for a daguerreotype view, presented in a diminutive volume reminiscently entitled "Characters of the Great Men of the Present Time" by Captain Tree, for Captain Tree uses the word *characters* in its Popeian sense. The Duke of Wellington, of course, heads the list, his portrait savoring most deliciously of the thirteen-year-old author, who was drawing, not the real Duke of Wellington and his achievements, but a wooden soldier and his exploits in the Young Men's Play. "There was," she says, "a certain expression of sarcasm about his mouth which showed that he considered many of those with whom he associated much beneath him."

Earlier in this same year, Charlotte read Branwell's recently acquired copy of *Childe Harold,* and though but dimly understanding the hero's character, she immediately grafted his salient qualities upon Arthur Wellesley, Marquis of Douro, older son of the Duke of Wellington, thus creating a personality that dominated her imagination for the rest of her life.

His songs [she writes] consist of grand and vivid descriptions of storms and tempests—of the wild roaring of the ocean mingling with the tremendous voice of thunder when the flashing lightning gleams in unison with the bright lamp of some wicked spirit striding over the face of the troubled waters, or sending forth his cry from the bosom of a black and terrible cloud. . . . [The] strains are like the soft reverberations of an Eolian harp, which as the notes alternately dye and swell, raise the tone to a pitch of wild sublimity, or lead it to mournful and solemn thought; and when you rise from the perusal of his works you are prone to meditate without knowing the cause, only you can think of nothing else but the years of your childhood and the bright days now fled forever.

In the *character* of Captain Bud Charlotte initiates the teasing satires on her brother which run through the whole of her *juvenilia*. Captain Bud's physical appearance, as she presents it, comes from the wooden soldier of that name after years of battering adventures, but his literary style is Branwell's own, as Charlotte judged it, and his eccentricities of disposition are exaggerations of her brother's occasional exhibitions of egotistical temperament:

[8] Charlotte Brontë: "Characters of the Great Men of the Present Time." By Captain Tree. December 17, 1829. 16 pp., 2,500 words. 2″ x 1⅜″. (Law Collection.)

This great politician is now 45 years of age. He is tall, bony, and muscular. His countenance is harsh and repulsive. His eye is deep set glittering and piercing. All his movements are rather slow and lagging. His gait is awkward. One of his shoulders projects above the other, and in short, his whole appearance is not of the most pleasing kind. He is, however, the ablest political writer of the present time, and his works [show] a depth of thought and knowledge seldom equalled and never surpassed. They are, however, sometimes too long and dry, which they would be often, if it was not for their great ability. Flashes of eloquence are few and far between, but his arguments are sound and conclusive. Some of his apostrophes are high and almost sublime but others are ridiculous and bombastic. He never condescends to be droll but keeps on in an even down course of tiresome gravity—so much so that I have often fallen asleep over his best works, and have as often taken shame to myself for it.

His disposition is nervous, crabbed, and irritable, but nevertheless his integrity is upright and inflexible. It is said that he is a hypochondriac, and that at different times he supposes himself a flame of fire, a stone, an oyster, and a crayfish, and that he even sometimes believes himself to be a heatherbell apt to be blown away at every blast of the wind; but that upon such occasions his friends always take care to keep him out of sight. What credit may be put in these assertions I know not, but I believe them to be founded on fact.

In the same spirit she pokes fun at Branwell's poetic effusions in the *character* of Young Soult, the Rhymer:

This truly great poet is in his 23 year. He is about the middle size and apparently lives well. His features are regular and his eye is large and expressive. His hair is dark and he wears it frizzed in such a manner as to make one suppose he had lately come out of a furze bush. His apparel is generally torn, and he wears it hanging about him in a very untidy and careless manner. His shoes are often slipshod and his stockings full of holes. The expression of his countenance is wild and haggard, and he is eternally twisting his mouth to one side or another. In his disposition he is devilish but humane and good natured. He appears constantly labouring under a state of strong excitement occasioned by excessive drinking and gambling, to which he is unfortunately much addicted. His poems exhibit a fine imagination, but his versification is not good. The ideas and language are beautiful, but they are not arranged so as to run along smoothly, and for this reason I think he should succeed best in blank verse. Indeed, I understand that he is about to publish a poem in that meter which is expected to be his best. He is possessed of a true genius which he has cultivated by great effort. His beginnings were small, but I believe his end will be great and that his name will be found on the pages of history with those of the greatest of his native country.

Captain Bud's son, Sergeant Bud, a bad fellow according to Tree, is interesting by reason of the punishment meted out to him in Charlotte's imagination: "If I had it in my power I would first duck him in water; next I would give him seventy stripes with a cat-o-nine tails; then I would make him ride through the Glass Town on a camel with his face turned to the tail; and, lastly, I would hang him on a gallows 60 feet high. When he was dead, he should be cut down and given to the surgeons for dissection."

"Given to the surgeons for dissection!" These were the days of Dr. Robert Knox's explorations in anatomy in the University of Edinburgh —the days of the "resurrection men" scandal. On January 28, 1829, William Burke was hanged for committing murder that he might sell the corpses to Dr. Knox and his students. In the "Noctes Ambrosianae" of *Blackwood's Magazine* for March, 1829, John Wilson attacked Dr. Knox for his trade in human bodies, obtained in many cases from "grave snatchers" who disinterred newly buried corpses. All this and much more the Brontës read and projected into the Glass Town Play. The theme is played out at still greater length by Branwell in "Letters to an Englishman," [9] in which he has the writer tell how, having wandered into Dr. Hume's house, he was seized by Ned Laury, Young Man Naughty, and other "rare lads" and dragged to the doctor's dissecting room to be sacrificed to science. Just as he was being bound to the table, the Duke of Wellington, guided by Lord Charles, arrived to save him.

Charlotte's conception of a villain at this stage of her development is presented in the *character* of Alexander Rogue:

Rogue is about 47 years of age. He is very tall, rather spare. His countenance is handsome, except that there is something very startling in his fierce gray eyes and formidable forehead. His manner is rather polished and gentlemanly, but his mind is deceitful, bloody, and cruel. His walk (in which he much prides himself) is stately and soldier-like, and he fancies that it greatly resembles that of the Duke of Wellington. He dances well and plays

---

[9] Branwell Brontë: "Letters from an Englishman." September 2, 1830–August 2, 1832. 6 vols., 27,000 words. 2¾" x 2¼". (Brotherton Collection, University of Leeds.)

cards admirably, being skilled in all the slight-of-hand blackleg trick of the gaming tables. And to crown all he is excessively vain of this (what he terms) accomplishment.

More important, however, than all the others because directly prophetic of the future, is the *character* of Dr. Alexander Hume Badry, the wooden soldier Bady in process of becoming Sir Alexander Hume, Duke of Badry, physician to His Grace the Duke of Wellington and father-in-law of the Marquis of Douro—ultimately Mr. Home, Count de Bassompierre of *Villette*.

Branwell, even after giving up his magazine to Charlotte, was quite as busy as she through the memorable year of 1829. The justice of her satire against him as Young Soult is evident from a volume [10] published in September, which, though bad verse even for a boy of twelve, like his edition of *Ossian,* joins astonishing bibliographical technique to childish conceptions:

A collection of Poems by Young Soult, The Rhymer. Illustrated with Notes and Commentarys by Monsieur De La Chateaubriand, Author of Travels in Greece, the Holy Land, &c., The State of France, Review of the Empire, &c., &c. Sept. 30, A.D. 1829. Paris: Published by M. De La Pack, le eleve, M. De Brunnette, &c.; Chief Glass Town: Sergeant Tree, Corporal Bud, Captain Legrand, &c., &c.; Tweney's Glass Town: Captain Leg; Parry's Glass Town: Col. Wind; Rosses Glass Town: Seargt. Snow.

Several editions of the Works of Chateaubriand in translation are listed in the sale catalogue of the Ponden House Library.

Volume I of Young Soult's poems, the author announces, contains "6 poems, 35 verses, and 30 notes and commentaries"; "Volume II has 5 poems, 28 verses, and 11 notes." The first and longest poem of the collection is "The Ammon Tree Cutter," comprising three books in blank verse. Where the author got his notion of an Ammon Tree Cutter is not made clear, though, as Chateaubriand, he offers two notes explaining his title: "An ammon tree is a tall and stately tree which produces the fruit called ammons"; and "These ['ammon cutters'] are a most dangerous class of men, inhabitants of Paris and its environs. They go out into the night and cut down all the ammon trees and burn all the vineyards of those against whom they have a spite. . . . If they can catch

[10] Two volumes. 2¾″ x 4″. (Brontë Museum and Library.)

the owners they flay them alive and then tie them to a tree with their skin."

> O vile ammon tree cutter,
>   Thee do I hate
> And some day when I see thee,
>   I'll clash thy dismal pate,

sings Young Soult who, later, while he is out on one of his habitual moonlight walks, comes upon an "ammon tree cutter" at his bloody work.

> His face was haggard, and his sleeve tucked up;
> A knife which reeked with blood was in his hand.
> He trampled upon a victim skinned,
> Who writhed about in dying agonies.

The poem goes on to say that the murderer was brought to justice before Judge Murat, and here Chateaubriand notes that Judge Murat was "Napoleon's brother-in-law, a savage man who would not care for the death of his own son more than that of a rabbit. His name at full length is Jean Joachim Murat, Mayor of the city of Paris." Murat sentences the culprit "to death by the guillotine," which so infuriates him that

> . . . . .he flew
> Upon the Judge Murat and like a madman
> Tore him in pieces, saying, "Revenge!"
> The soldiers and police did now rush in,
> Like to the waves driven against the rock,
> To take him from the dead Joachim
> Who was torn piecemeal in a thousand bits,
> And lay in his last agony on the floor.
>
>   . . . .
>
> But at last the murderer was took.
> They flayed him then, and roasted him with salt,
> And laid him on a grid-iron to roast alive.
> And oh! the horrid yells that burst from him
> Was like the roaring of wind 'mid trees
> And rocks and mountains in a misty vale,
> Until at last they slowly died away
> Into a low hoarse murmur, then were gone,

> And naught was heard but dripping blood and fat
> Into the raging fire which blazed around.

Branwell, still writing as Chateaubriand, follows Young Soult's long poem with "Concluding Observations," informing the reader that the book is "certainly the best of the Rhymer's creations, and also the longest," and that "the reason why he wrote it was one of them ['an ammon tree cutter'] had been spoiling his father's trees." The critic continues:

In this poem [Young Soult] evidently makes fun of Murat, as any person will see who reads it. Some will not understand why he speaks of persons living after they are skinned alive, and, if to them, especially those living in England, it seems improbable and erroneous—but it is neither, for it is known how hard Frenchmen are to kill. Some can't be killed for a day, others for 2 days, and Pigtail cannot be killed for 3 days!!! Certainly these cases are not common, but a vast number will live 12 hours after they are skinned alive or their hearts cut out. But no Frenchman or Englishman or any other man can remain alive after their heads are cut off.

> Frenchmen can live while their heads are on;
> Frenchmen can live while their hearts are gone;
> Frenchmen can't live while their heads are off;
> Frenchmen can't endure a scoff.
>
> Tree. Vol. 2, 411.

This saying of Captain Tree is very true, for Frenchmen can never endure a scoff or thrust or bitter joke. They rather will fly out into an ungovernable fury or go and hang themselves in prison without more ado.

Chateaubriand.

Chateaubriand neglects to explain that Pigtail is a Frenchman "7 feet high . . . ugly as can be imagined and tremendously cross to those unhappy mortals who may happen to get into his clutches." In one phase of activity he kidnaps children and puts them to torture for profit, such as suspending them by hooks, for example, and capping their heads with burning pitch for the amusement of street crowds.

"The Ammon Tree Cutters" is indeed a fair sample of Young Soult's art and the two volumes of his poems contain nothing of greater literary merit. "Ode to Napoleon," "in exceedingly rambling and irregular meter," according to Branwell's note, is amusing. Composed while Young Soult was "drunk and under the influence of passion," it so displeased the Emperor with its reference to Wellington as

> . . . the one
> That thee has done
> Because all thy followers run,

that he exclaimed: "This is hatred under the mask of *Friendship*. If this fellow writes any more such trash, he shall be guillotined!"

The remaining poems of the collection celebrate the destructive power of Chief Genius Bany, as in the following stanzas:

> Onward thou rushest, destruction thy name,
> Onward thou rushest, companion of flame,
> Onward thou rushest, ally of war,
> Onward thou rushest, of Famine the star,

and,

> It is a genius hideous form,
> But in his hideousness he prides.
> See how he strides upon a cloud
> And blows his trumpet strong.
> Ah 'tis the dreadful note of war,
> 'Tis loud, impetuous—long.

"Ode to the Chief Genius Bany," warns that great being against undue pride in his power:

> O, thou mighty Genius,
> Thou ruler of the world,
> Take care, lest from thy power
> Thou shouldest soon be hurled.

It would seem that the wine of power Branwell drank in the Young Men's Play was going to his head.

Front Cover of an Early Book by Charlotte Brontë
(Actual Size 2″ x 1½″)

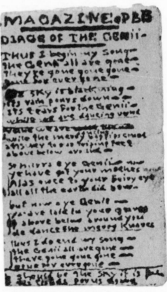

Cover and First Page of Branwell's Blackwoods Magazine for
June, 1829. (Actual Size 2″ x 1½″)

Chapter V

STIRRINGS OF LIFE

C HARLOTTE, early in 1830, bored perhaps with the Young Men's Play, made a feeble effort to break away from its machinery. "The Adventures of Mon. Edouard de Crack," [1] a diminutive volume of more than 2,500 minute words, has no connection with the Glass Town cycle. In a preface more interesting than the story itself the author records her astonishing speed in composition and handprinting:

I began this Book on the 22 of February 1830 and finished it on the 23 of February 1830 doing 3 pages on the first day and 11 on the second. On the first day I wrote an hour and a half in the morning, and an hour & a half in the evening. On the third day I wrote a quarter of an hour in the morning 2 hours in the afternoon & a quarter of an hour in the evening making in the whole 5 hours & a half. C.B.

Another story, "Ernest Alembert," [2] departs even further from the Glass Town tradition, being a pure fairy tale of exotic richness set down in ordinary script, without title-page or other evidence of Captain Tree's hand.

But Charlotte soon found she could not do without the old game. Her unaided imagination was inadequate to the demands of her hungry pen. Two weeks after "Ernest Alembert," she, in the person of Lord Charles, was deep in a scandal on Captain Tree,[3] introducing

[1] Charlotte Brontë: "The Adventures of Mon. Edouard de Crack." By Lord Charles Wellesley. February 22, 1830. 21 pp., 3,000 words. 2½" x 2". (Amy Lowell Collection.)

[2] Charlotte Brontë: "The Adventures of Ernest Alembert: a Fairy Tale." Privately printed by Thomas J. Wise. 1895.

[3] Charlotte Brontë: "An Interesting Passage in the Lives of Some Eminent Men of the Present Time." By Lord Charles Wellesley. June 18, 1830. 16 pp., 4,300 words. 1⅞" x 1⅛". (Amy Lowell Collection.)

a theme developed at length in an untitled story of ten years later—the wickedness of the aristocracy, exposed in the gossip of servants:

I believe that in great houses few know more of family concerns than servants & even in middling establishments the case is the same. As I am generally kind to grooms, valets, footmen, lackeys, &c &c they often make me there confidante entrusting me with many important secrets which by degrees has enabled me to amass such a quantity of information respecting almost every grandee in the Glass Town that if I chose I could unveil a scene of murders, thefts, hypocrisy, perjury & so forth which can scarcely be paralleled in the annals of any other city.

More significant than the theme of the story itself is the radical and unexplained change in the character and personality of the author since "Characters of Great Men." From the admirable youth of six months before Lord Charles has degenerated into an idle mischief-maker, prying into and rejoicing in the sins of his fellowmen.

Charlotte, not content to outdistance Branwell in ease and skill, was now habitually making literary capital out of his weaknesses. His awkward verse inspired her, in June, to a satrical drama in two midget volumes called, "The Poetaster. By Lord Charles Wellesley." [4] Young Soult, the Rhymer, is discovered alone in the agony of composition. He writes:

> Silver moon, how sweet thou shinest
>   In the midnight sky
> Hollow wind, how wild thou whinest
>   Through the vault on high.
>
> The heavens, how beautiful they are
>   Majestically dark
> They are bedecked with many a star.

Here he stops, struggling for a word to rhyme with *dark:*

> stark, clark, hark, lark—Ah that'll do—
>   Fit sojourn for the lark.
> Capital! How lucky to find it out! It came quite apropos.

Infatuated with his own genius, the Rhymer seeks an interview with the Marquis of Douro and Lord Charles, bringing with him a

[4] Vol. I. July 6, 1830. 18 pp., 2,275 words. 1½″ x 1¼″. (Amy Lowell Collection.) Vol. II. July 12, 1830. 14 pp., 2,200 words. 1½″ x 1¼″. (Bonnell Collection, Philadelphia.)

roll of his verses, hoping to gain their patronage. The Marquis asks the poet his name, a question which sets the Rhymer off into a frenzy of meaningless words: "Princes, forgive me. The wings of poesy are ever expanded, and they often bear this unbending spirit to a sudden involuntary flight afar into the wild realms of imagination, and there for a while I bask amid the shadows of unearthly groves or lights of super-human vales, utterly forgetful of all that belongs to this external work-a-day world till some biped's voice calls me again to these dark-some regions to converse among those I dwell with in body, but not in mind. And now, most noble Marquis, I will reply to your interrogation. My name is Henry Reumer, corrupted into Rhymer."

The young nobles read his verse, and dismiss him with the admonition to seek other employment, whether honest or dishonest, and think no more of blotting white paper with meaningless hierglyphics. Rhymer interprets their advice as evidence of jealousy, and rushes out in a passion to seek consolation from Captain Tree.

Tree receives him with cool condescension, reads his rhymes, and kicks him out of the room, exclaiming, "Oh, how our noble profession is dishonored! I could weep for very misery."

The last scene of the play shows Rhymer about to be hanged for the murder of Tree. He is taken to the scaffold and the rope adjusted about his neck. At the last moment the execution is stayed by the appearance of Lord Charles with word that Tree has come to life. The noble messenger intercedes for Rhymer on condition that the culprit write no more and take some useful employment. Rhymer joyfully meets these terms, accepting Lord Charles's offer of a secretaryship "which post is a perfect sinecure with a salary of 200 £ a year."

In August, 1830, Charlotte revived the Young Men's Magazine,[5] after a lapse of seven months. By bringing out two numbers for December, she achieved six issues before the end of the year, all actually written within the three weeks between August 12 and September 9.

---

[5] "Young Men's Magazine." Second Series. August, 1830. 20 pp., 3,500 words plus 40 ll. 2⅛" x 1½". (Bonnell Collection.)
——— October, 1830. 20 pp., 2,900 words plus 88 ll. 2⅛" x 1¾₆". (Bonnell Collection.)
——— December (1), 1830. 20 pp. 2" x 1⅜". (Law Collection.)
——— December (2), 1830. 20 pp., 3,550 words plus 7¾ ll. 2¼" x 1½". (Bonnell Collection.)

The October number, for instance, states its date of composition as August 23 and its publication as August 25. It also announces that "this Second Series . . . is conducted on like principles with the first; the same eminent authors are also engaged to contribute for it."

The marked improvement in the new issue over the original magazine measures Charlotte's growth in creative power and constructive skill through the intervening months. The format has undergone no essential change; most of the features of the earlier series, such as "Conversations" in Bravey's Inn, are continued. Immediately noticeable, however, are changes in the characters of the Marquis of Douro and Lord Charles and their relations to each other. The Marquis has added to his youthful Byronic romanticism a touch of Byronic sophistication and cynicism, while his brother, continuing the metamorphosis noticed in an earlier story, has become a mere child of ten years, a mischievous, prankish, omnipresent elf whom the Marquis now looks upon as a spoiled, conceited, meddlesome brat, always in his way. Lord Charles, on the other hand, considers his brother a "conceited ninny," whose morals are as questionable as his wits.

It develops in course of the revived magazine that Branwell was not alone among the Parsonage children in furnishing Charlotte with copy. October "Conversations" records that Lord Charles, when asked for an account of his recent trip into Parrysland (Emily's kingdom), refused, "being in a taciturn disposition of mind," whereupon Young Soult, volunteering to give it for him, worked himself into such a frenzy of poetic inspiration that he fell into a fit, from which he was revived by "the application of hartshorne, cold water, vinegar, sal-volatile, and sal-everything else." A few days later Lord Charles came out of his taciturnity to write his own proper account of his journey for the magazine, painting an unflattering picture of Emily's hero and his country.

Accustomed to the lordly grandeur of her own creation, Charlotte has only pitying contempt for the Caledonian poverty of her sister's domain. Crossing the borders into Parrysland, Lord Charles relates, he was immediately struck with the changed aspect of everything. "Instead of strong, tall, muscular men, going about seeking whom they might devour, with guns on their shoulders or in their hands, he saw only shiftless little milk-and-water beings in clean blue linen jackets and white aprons. All the houses were arranged in formal rows, and they contained four rooms, each with a little garden in front. No castle or splendid palace towered insultingly over the cottages around. No high-born noble claimed allegiance of his vassals or swayed his broad lands with hereditary pride, and every inch of ground was enclosed with stone walls. Here and there a few regularly planted rows of trees, generally poplars, appeared, but no hoary woods or nodding groves were suffered to intrude on the scene. . . . Nasty factories with tall black chimneys breathing thick columns of almost tangible smoke discoloured not that sky of dull, hazy hue."

Parry's palace, a poor enough dwelling in Lord Charles's eye, was a square building of stone, surrounded by blue slates and some round stone pumpkins. "All the convenient affairs, such as wash-house, back kitchen, stable, and coal house were built in line and backed by a row of trees. In a paddock behind the house were feeding one cow to give milk for the family and butter for the dairy and cheese for the table; one horse to draw the gig, to carry their Majesties, and bring home provisions from the market, together with a calf and foal as companions for both."

Sir Edward and Lady Emily Parry came out to welcome their newly arrived guest. Tea was on the table, and they invited him to partake of it, but before sitting down Parry took a napkin from the cupboard directing his guest to pin it before his clothes, lest he dirty them, saying in scarcely intelligible jargon that he supposed they were the visitor's best, and his mother would be angry if he stained them. Lord Charles thanked him politely, but declined the napkin.

For dinner the next day the guest was served roast beef, Yorkshire pudding, mashed potatoes, apple pie, and preserved cucumbers. All at table ate as if they had not seen a meal for three weeks. About an hour after dinner, Rose, another guest, was taken extremely sick. No doctor being at hand, death was momentarily expected but was prevented by the arrival of Chief Genius Emily at the most opportune moment. She cured with an incantation and vanished. Lord Charles remained at Parry's palace only till the morrow, when he departed, having found his visit intolerably dull.

Across the tiny pages of this Second Series of the Young Men's Magazine fall with increasing frequency prophetic shadows of coming triumphs, in sentences and passages which hold in germ several of Charlotte's greatest scenes. "Liffey Castle," Lord Charles's account of a "pedestrian excursion" into the south of Ireland contains a sentence which strikes response in the memory of everyone who has read *Jane Eyre:* "That night all the dogs of the country-side howled as if the gitrash [gytrash] was abroad, and a sound like a funeral cry was heard at midnight in every house." Again, "An Extraordinary Dream," brings an incident of unmistakable kinship to Lucy Snowe's nerve-racking insomnia and excruciating dream in *Villette.* Even more startling is the story of "The Silver Cup" by Captain Tree, introducing in clear outline the Reed family of *Jane Eyre.*

Over and above all other interests in Charlotte's Young Men's Magazine towers a story in the December number called "Strange Events," the second of her habitual end-of-the-year milestones. A puzzled and awe-struck Pygmalion, she tries in Lord Charles's ruminations to formulate her own wonder and bewilderment at the strange and mysterious life movement discerned in her creation, the first soul emanations from the wooden soldiers:

Taking down Brandart's "Finished Lawyer" I placed myself on a sofa in the ingle-nook. Whilst I was listlessly turning over the huge leaves of that most ponderous volume, I fell into the strangest train of thought that ever visited even my mind, eccentric and unstable as it is said by some insolent puppies to be.

It seemed as if I was a non-existent shadow—that I neither spoke, ate, imagined, or lived of myself, but I was the mere idea of some other creature's brain. The Glass Town seemed so likewise. My father, Arthur, and everyone with whom I am acquainted, passed into a state of annihilation; but suddenly I thought again that I and my relatives did exist and yet not us but our minds, and our bodies without ourselves. Then this supposition—the oddest of any—followed the former quickly, namely, that WE without US were shadows; also, but at the end of a long vista, as it were, appeared dimly and indistinctly, beings that really lived in a tangible shape, that were called by our names and were US from whom WE had been copied by something— I could not tell what.

Another world formed part of this reverie in which was no Glass Town or

British Realm in Africa except Hindoustan, India, Calcutta. England was there but totally different in manners, law, customs, inhabitants—governed by a sailor—my father Prime Minister—I and Arthur young noblemen living at Strathaye, or something with a name like that. Visionary Fairies, Elves, Brownies, the East Wind and wild Arab-broken horses—shooting in moors with a fat man who was a great book. But I am lost, I cannot get on.

For hours I continued in this state, striving to fathom a bottomless ocean of Mystery, till at length I was roused by a loud noise above my head. I looked up and thick obscurity was before my eyes. Voices—one like my own but larger and dimmer (if sound may be characterized by such epithets) and another, which sounded familiar, yet I had never, that I could remember, heard it before—murmuring unceasingly in my ears.

I saw books removing from the top shelves and returning, apparently of their own accord. By degrees the mistiness cleared off. I felt myself raised suddenly to the ceiling, and ere I was aware, beheld two immense sparkling bright blue globes within a few yards of me. I was in a hand wide enough almost to grasp the Tower of All Nations, and when it lowered me to the floor I saw a huge personification of myself—hundreds of feet high—standing against the great Oriel.

This filled me with a weight of astonishment greater than the mind of man ever before had to endure, and I was now perfectly convinced of my non-existence except in another corporeal frame which dwelt in the real world, for ours I thought was nothing but idea.

Whatever evidence Charlotte's magazine gives of her growing maturity, its advertisements reflect the nonsensical fun still pervading the Parsonage play:

An immense crystal ink glass to be sold full of exquisite black wine by Private Layman in Corner Table after Making the Beds.

To be sold 100 pair of excellent shoes by Monsieur Let him walk 20 miles an hour.

A
BOOK AGAINST
ALL FASHION OF LIMNERS
AND DRAUGHTSMEN BY
CAPTAIN HE CAN HANDLE
A SWORD
BUT NOTHING
ELSE.

TO BE SOLD
The 9 Quart Tavern
Tipstaff Lane Chief
Glasstown
By Corporal drink soup.

Young Man Naughty Will instruct
6 pupils in the elegant art of assassination.

BOOKS
PUBLISHED BY SERGEANT TREE

THE ELEMENTS OF LYING BY LORD CHARLES WELLESLEY
in one vol. duodecimo.   Price 2s 6d with
some account of those who practice it.

ORION & ARTHURIUS a Poem by Lord Wellesley.
Recommendation: This is the most beautiful poem that ever flowed from the
pen of man. The sentiments are wholly original. Nothing is borrowed. Glass
T. Review.

AN ESSAY ON CONVERSATION by the Marquis of Douro. 1 vol. Price 5s.

SOLITUDE By the same. Price 10d.

THE PROUD MAN By Captain Tree. Price 30s. 3d.

"Concluding Address" of the revived magazine is worthy of "U. T."
at their worst:

> Reader, farewell.
> Hark my notes of triumph swell,
> My labour finished,
> Though 'twas tedious and long
> Here's my last
> Concluding
> song.

Chapter VI

THE DESTRUCTION OF GLASS TOWN

Having completed her magazine and postdated it to run through the year, Charlotte turned to a series of character sketches, grouped under a typical title-page:

VISITS IN VERREOPOLIS [1]

BY

LORD CHARLES WELLESLEY

IN

Two Volumes

Volume

First

Published by Sergeant Tree

And Sold

By

All Other Booksellers in

The

Chief Glass Town, the Duke

of Welling-

Ton's

Glass Town,

Parry's Glass Town, Ross's Glass Town, Paris &c.,

I began this volume on the 7th of December

1830, & finished it on the 11th of December, 1830

Charlotte

Brontë

December 11th, 1830 Anno Domini.

---

[1] Charlotte Brontë: "Visits in Verreopolis." Volume I. By Lord Charles Wellesley.
———— "Visits in Verreopolis." Volume II. By the Honorable Charles Albert Florian Wellesley, Aged 10 years. December 18, 1830.
32 pp., 6,000 words. 3″ x 2″. (Law Collection.)

A preface announces that "Verreopolis means the Glass Town, being compounded of a Greek word and a French word to that effect." The hybrid proved unsatisfactory, however, and was immediately changed to the more common form, Verdopolis, a name which gradually replaces Glass Town.

In these sketches, Lord Charles, dismissed from his lessons, is ordered by his supercilious and sarcastic brother Arthur to take Lady Zenobia Ellrington a package of his poems for correction. Lady Zenobia, herself a "bluestocking of deepest dye," is the daughter of Lord Ellrington and Lady Pauline Louisada Ellrington, a famous beauty of Latin blood and morals of the worst sort.

Lord Charles finds Zenobia in her boudoir, "sitting on a sofa, attired in a morning costume, reading Herodotus in the original." When she deigns to notice him, it is to ask a question about Marian Hume, Arthur's betrothed. Charles's pert answer excites her to one of her frequent bursts of fury. "She sprang up," he writes, "in a transport of passion, and, raising her dexter foot, kindly assisted me therewith in my passage downstairs, sending forth at the same time a tremendous yell of ungovernable rage."

The boy, picked up by his friend Bud, is taken to Bud's home, where the older man reads to him a drama depicting "Zenobia's mad jealousy of Marian Hume." The climax shows Zenobia in a maniacal rage about to kill her rival with a knife when the Marquis interposes.

Promising to return for tea with Bud, Lord Charles starts on a round of calls, in course of which he drops in on Young Soult, and is unwise enough to ask the poet if he has seen the rainbow, a question which throws "the Rhymer" into an effusion of nine stanzas celebrating the beauty of this phenomenon, "uttered in a strange variety of tones—first speaking, which gradually changed to recitative, then chanting, and last to regular singing." Taking his departure, Lord Charles wanders through the streets until he comes to "that gorgeous and apparently everlasting building, Bravey's Inn," from the portals of which issue "the usual murmur of conversation."

In return for the indignities suffered at "the dexter foot" of the Lady Zenobia, Charlotte, in the person of Lord Charles, composed her first love story: "Albion and Marina," [2] built on the call-and-answer motif familiar to all readers of *Jane Eyre*. Albion is a romantic name for the Marquis of Douro, and Marina, a variant of Marian Hume.

Separated temporarily from his beloved, so runs the love story, Albion comes under the charms of Lady Zenobia and is about to forget Marina when his wandering affections are recalled by the whispering of a "soft but mournful voice," "Albion, do not forget me; I shall be happy when you return." Albion, astonished, makes a memorandum of the day and hour, namely, the 18th of June, 1815, twelve o'clock at night."

This vision plunges the youth into melancholy so deep he immediately sets out for his sweetheart's home. He is met at the gate by a child who offers to lead him to Marina's new abode. Passing down a long avenue of tall, dark trees, they enter a churchyard. There the child vanishes, leaving Albion beside a white marble tombstone on which is chiseled:

Marina Angus
She Died
18th of June 1815
at
12 o'clock midnight

Returning to the mood in which she began the story, Charlotte relieves its melancholy ending with Lord Charles's confession, "I wrote it out of malignity for the injuries that have lately been done me. The conclusion is wholly destitute of any foundation in truth, and I did it out of revenge. Albion and Marina are both alive and well, for ought I know." Thus Charlotte retains and rationalizes her old power of resuscitation.

Published in the magazine or brought out in more ambitious volumes, Charlotte's verse kept pace with her prose. That in the early issues of the Second Series is doggerel celebrating events of the Young Men's Play, such as a poem "written upon the occasion of a dinner

[2] Charlotte Brontë: "Albion and Marina: A Tale by Lord Charles Wellesley." October 12, 1830. 16 pp., 4,000 words plus 53 ll. 2¾" x 1½". (Palmer Collection, Wellesley College Library.)

given to the *literati* of the Glass Town, which was attended by all the
great men of the present time: soldier, sailor, poet, painter, architect,
politician, novelist, and romancer":

> . . . The atmosphere around is one continuous flow
> Of streaming lustre, brilliant light and liquid topaz glow.

But poems of later months, particularly those signed by the Marquis
of Douro, show considerable advance in thought and technique.

The title-page of one of her more ambitious volumes, measuring
3¾ x 2¼ inches, reveals in full splendor the romantic halo surrounding its Byronic author:

The Violet [3] A Poem with Several Smaller Pieces By the Marquis of Douro
Member of the Society of Antiquarians; President for 1830 of the Literary
Club; Honorary Member of the Academy of Artists & Treasurer to the So-
ciety for the Spread of Classical Knowledge; Chief Secretary of the Confed-
erate Hundred for Promoting Gymnastic Exercises &c., &c., &c. Published by
Sergeant Tree and Sold by All other Booksellers in the Chief Glass Town,
the Duke Of Wellington's Glass Town, Paris, Parry's Glass Town, Ross's
Glass Town, &c., &c., &c., &c., &c. November the 14th, 1830.

The title poem follows the pattern of the eighteenth-century "progress piece." The Marquis in the midst of a vast desert falls to dreaming

> Of those who in long ages past
> Attuned the muse's hallowed shell;

and reviews in his mind the progress of "the holy nine" who flourished
first in Greece, then in Italy,

> And now in fair Britannia shine.

He pours out his prayer to Nature that he, too, may march in "the
army of immortals, sons of Albion . . . crowned with honours they
have won." His prayer reaches the "mighty Mother's ear," and she
"condescendingly" answers that the laurel is "for the more exalted

---

[3] This ambitious title-page, now in the Howe Library, was reproduced in Hatfield's
The Complete Poems of Charlotte Brontë, 1923.

mind," and the "lowly violet" must be his coronet. Echoes of Byron run throughout the poem, such as:

> Greece, thy fair skies have flung their light
>   On mightiest of this sunlit world;
> Genius, enthroned in glory bright,
>   O'er thee her banner hath unfurled.
>
> Now desolate, by time decayed,
>   Thy solemn temples mouldering lie:
> While black groves throw Cimmerian shade
>   Beneath a still transparent sky.
>
> Degenerate are thy sons, and slaves;
>   Athens and Sparta are no more;
> Unswept by swans, Eurotas laves
>   As yet its laurel-shaded shore.

The remaining four poems of the volume are dedicated to Marian Hume, whom the lover-poet addresses as

> Thou whom I love, my soul's most fair delight.

One of these, "Lines on Seeing the Portrait of ——— [Marian Hume] Painted by De Lisle," seems to have been suggested by Wordsworth's "She was a Phantom of Delight":

> Are thou then of spirit birth
> And not a denizen of earth?
> No! thou'rt but a child of clay,
> Simply robed in white array;
> Not a gem is gleaming there;
> All is spotless snow so fair,
> Symbol of thy angel-mind—
> Meek, benevolent, and kind;
> Sprightly as the beauteous fawn
> Springing up at the break of dawn,
> Graceful, bounding o'er the hills
> To the music of the rills!

The companion pieces, "Vesper" and "Matin," strike a note somewhat new in Charlotte's poetry. The first echoes faintly of Keats, and more of Wordsworth's "Resolution and Independence."

Then I will sit and listen: not a voice
    Disturbs the unbroken stillness of this hour;
No nestling bird, with faintly rustling noise,
    Raises the leaflets of the vernal bower,
    Or bends the spray where blooms the fruit-betokening flower.

Even the chorister of night is still!
    Sweet Philomel restrains her 'customed song;
Hushed are the murmurs of the unseen rill
    Creeping through matted grass and weeds along;
    And silence soon will reign these solemn shades among!

And the second, Marian calling to her lover, breathes a bit of the passion
of Charlotte's later years:

I hear thy voice, I see thy figure nightly;
    Thou comest to me in midnight slumbers deep!
And through the dark thy blue eyes, glimmering brightly,
    Beam down upon my restless, spirit-haunted sleep.

.   .   .   .

Oh! still I hope for thy long-wished returning:
    Come swiftly o'er the dark and raging sea!
Come, for my soul with hope deferred is burning;
    Then will I sing a song worthy of morn and thee!

In the last poem of this group, "A Serenade" addressed to Marian,
Charlotte goes back to her old theme of moon-illumined summer
glades where

The morrice-dancing fairy train in other times was seen.

To her group of supernatural beings she now adds "the maiden of
the sea that sings within her cell," and the "still, sad music" of the
maiden's song is a distant echo of Wordsworth's immortal line,

The still, sad music of humanity.

Charlotte at fourteen was steeped in eighteenth-century and Romantic poetry . . . but the predominating influence of Byron continued
to shape her meters, as it did the emotions and actions of her characters.
Towards the end of 1830, her god-mother offered to bear the ex-

penses of sending her to school—except for the few tragic months at Cowan Bridge this precocious young authoress had never been inside a formal school room—and the choice fell on the Misses Wooler, at Roe Head, near Mirfield. The effect of her going upon the play was a subject of anxious discussion among the four children. They decided at last to take leave of the game in a grand spectacular finale. A year later, while at home for the Christmas holidays, Charlotte wrote a characteristic account [4] of the splendid conclave of the four chief genii before the kitchen fire and the execution of their decree upon the Glass Town. It was Chief Genius Brannii, as the "Ruler of Spirits," who called his compeers to council:

> The trumpet hath sounded, its voice is gone forth
> From the plains of the south to the seas of the north;
> The great ocean groaned, and the firm mountains shook,
> And the rivers in terror their channels forsook.
> The proud eagle quailed in her aerial dome,
> And the gentle dove flew to her bowery home,
> The antelope trembled as onward she sprang,
> When hollow and death-like the trumpet-blast rang.
>
> It was midnight, deep midnight, and shrouded in sleep
> Men heard not the roar of the terror-struck deep
> Nor the peal of the trumpet still sounding on high;
> They saw not the flashes that brightened the sky.
> All silent and tomb-like the great city lay,
> And fair rose her towers in their moonlight array;
> 'Twas the Ruler of Spirits that sent forth the sound
> To call his dread legions in myriads around.

In answer the genii's armies gathered "from dim green ocean cave," flinging thousands of gems in their path; from the forests of the west, a "giant host of winged forms," and "from the chill and ice-bound north, . . . sailing in tempest clouds."

> The Hall where they sat was the heart of the sky,
> And the stars to give light stooped their lamps from on high.

---

[4] Charlotte Brontë: "The Trumpet Hath Sounded." December 11, 1831. 2½″ pp., 84 ll. 3¾″ x 2⅜″.

This is as far as the poet's revelations may go:

> No mortal may further the vision reveal;
> Human eye cannot pierce what a spirit would seal.
> The secrets of genii my tongue may not tell,
> But hoarsely they murmured: "Bright city farewell!"

Byron's "Destruction of Sennacherib," which suggested the meter of the poem, gave also the formula for executing the genii's decree:

> The morning rose over the far distant hill,
> And yet the great city lay silent and still.
> No chariot rode thunderous adown the wide street,
> No horse of Arabia, impetuous and fleet.
> The river flowed on to the foam-crested sea,
> But unburdened by vessel, its waves murmured free.
> The silence is dreadful. O city, arise!
> The sound is ascending the arch of the skies.
> Mute, mute are the mighty, and chilled is their breath,
> For at midnight passed o'er them the Angel of Death!
> The king and the peasant, the lord and the slave,
> Lie entombed in the depth of one wide solemn grave.

This wholesale wiping out of the machinery of the Young Men's Play, though soon retracted, had a marked effect on Charlotte's development—deeper perhaps, than the adventure into the world which occasioned the cataclysm—for though she retained most of the play's conceptions and characters for years to come, she ever after treated them in a spirit of creative freedom. The tyranny of Chief Genius Charlotte, venting itself in this final gesture of destruction, came to find a more refined pleasure in the arbitrary powers of authorship.

Chapter VII

INTERREGNUM

CHIEF GENIUS TALLI, ruler of spirits, who created and destroyed worlds by the power of her word, traveled to Roe Head in a covered cart as plain Charlotte Brontë, arriving very cold and miserable. To the girls watching and taking stock of her, she appeared a little old woman, shy and nervous, speaking with a strong Irish accent. Extreme nearsightedness accentuated the strangeness of her appearance. She was, in fact, so shortsighted that she seemed always to be seeking something and moving her head from side to side to catch sight of it. When she took a book in hand, she dropped her head over it until her nose almost touched the page. If she were admonished to hold her head up, up went the book with it, provoking the girls to laughter.

Her schoolmates found her as different from themselves in her mental equipment as in her clothes. To those who had gone to school regularly she appeared very ignorant, though they acknowledged her superior knowledge of literature, history, current politics, art, and the Bible. Occasionally she broke her habitual reserve to speak of the family at Haworth, sometimes to speak of Maria and Elizabeth. When a girl expressed surprise that she should remember so much about her sisters who had died when she was but nine years old, Charlotte replied that she had begun to analyze character when she was five. To another who wondered at her "habit of writing in Italics" (minute hand printing), she confessed she acquired it by writing in a magazine written and read only by herself and her brother and sisters. She even told this girl a tale out of the periodical, and promised to show her one of the issues, but retracted the promise and could never be persuaded to bring forth the little volume. She admitted that Branwell, Emily, and Anne, as well as herself, "made out" histories and invented characters and events, evoking from Mary Taylor the blunt comment: "You are just like growing potatoes in a cellar."

In the meanwhile, even in the leader's absence, the "making out" in Haworth Parsonage went on, broken by ripples of dissension among the remaining genii. When Branwell, on Charlotte's departure, eagerly reasserted his claim to leadership on the family stage, he was met by determined resistance from Emily—a practical demonstration of his own doctrine of revolution. Resentful of the domination of the older children and heartily tired of their meaningless wars, she took advantage of the opportunity to set up a play of her own with Anne.

Branwell, thus deserted at home, turned hungrily to long-distance companionship with Charlotte. In May he paid her a visit at Roe Head, and after his return had a letter from her referring to their common interest, the Glass Town Play: "As usual I address my weekly letter to you, because to you I find most to say. . . . After you were gone many questions and subjects of conversation occurred to me which I had intended to mention to you but quite forgot them in the agitation I felt in the totally unexpected pleasure of seeing you." In his loneliness the boy sought, naturally enough, the forbidden company of rough village lads, whose admiration for his mental accomplishments flattered his vanity, while a sense of his own physical inferiority incited him to imitate their wild habits. Long hours, however, went into his now solitary writing. "Letters from an Englishman," begun in September before his sister went away, was continued through the eighteen months of her absence, running into six diminutive volumes, aggregating about 25,000 words. An Englishman, out to see for himself the wonders of the new nation whose fame filled the earth, visits the four kingdoms of the Glass Town Confederacy and describes with encyclopedic completeness of detail their physical features and the manners and customs of their people, adding for good measure full-length word portraits of their leading citizens, rogues, and villains, as well as statesmen and capitalists. Branwell was void of the sense of selection and proportion which is one of the distinguishing marks of genius in Charlotte's work.

Another long treatise begun before Charlotte's departure he finished in May:

THE

HISTORY OF

THE

YOUNG MEN

FROM

Their First Settlement

TO

The Present Time

COMPREHENDING AN ACCOUNT OF

ASHANTEE FROM THE EARLIEST

PERIOD TO THEIR ARRIVAL

By   By

John Bud Esq'r

Captain in the:

10 Regt of Hussars

Vice President of the Antiquarian Society

Fellow of the Literary Society:

Fellow of the Association for

The Reward of Learning

Chief Librarian To

The Royal Glass-

Town Library

&c. &c. &c. &c.

IN VOLUMES

VOL. I.

"It is my Task

To explore the dark recesses of the past

And bring to light the deeds of former ages."

Marquis Douro's

School of Learning v. 139

1831

Great Glass Town   Printed and Sold by Sergeant Tree

Like "The Twelve Adventurers," Charlotte's companion piece of two years earlier, "The History of the Young Men" narrates the origin and growth of the Young Men's Play through its early stages, supplying a wealth of literal details discarded by Charlotte or transformed by her artistry into miracles of the genii. It also carries a folding map of the Glass Town or Verdopolitan Confederacy and a

plate showing monuments and buildings of the capital city. Meticulously literal in its introduction and footnotes, it is the key to the
Brontë *juvenilia,* which means that it is the key to the secret of
Haworth Parsonage.[For previous guesses it gives us an explicit statement of how the Brontë dream world came into existence:

> It was some time in the summer of the year A.D. 1824 when I, being
> desirious to possess a box of soldiers, asked Papa to buy me one, which shortly
> after he procured me from Bradford. They were 12 in number, price 1s. 6d.,
> and were the best I ever have had. Soon after this, I got from Keighley an-
> other set of the same number. These soldiers I kept for about a year, until
> either maimed, lost, burnt, or destroyed by various casualties, they
>
> "departed and left not a wreck behind!" *
>
> Now, therefore, not satisfied with what I had formerly got, I purchased
> at Keighley a band of Turkish musicians which I continued to keep till
> the summer of A.D. 1825, when Charlotte and Emily returned from school
> [Cowan Bridge] where they had been during the days of my former sets.
> I remained for 10 months after they had returned without any soldiers, when
> on June the 5th A.D. 1826, Papa procured me from Leeds another set (these
> were the 12s) which I kept for two years, though 2 or 3 of them are in
> being at the time of my writing this (Dec. 15 A.D. 1830). Sometime in
> 1827 I bought another set of Turkish musicians at Halifax, and in 1828 I
> purchased the last box, a band of Indians, at Haworth. Both these I still
> keep. Here now ends the catalogue of soldiers bought by or for me. And I
> must now conclude this Introduction, already too long, with saying that
> what is contained in this History is a statement of what myself, Charlotte,
> Emily, and Ann really pretended did happen among the "Young Men"
> (that being the name we gave them) during the period of nearly 6 years,
> though in some places slightly altered according to the form and taste of
> the aforesaid Young Men. It is written by Captain John Bud, the greatest
> prose writer they have among them.
>
> P. B. Brontë
> Haworth, December 15 A.D. 1930

Footnotes continue the revelation. Following a grandiose description
of the Young Men as heroes, comes, for instance, the note: "The state
dress here spoken of was what my first soldiers (i. e. the 12s) were
really carved and painted in; the curious shoe was the little stand
which each soldier had to keep him from falling." The first king of
the Twelves, Frederick Guelph, Duke of York, was killed in a battle

with the blacks at Rosendale Hill. The story of his death is accompanied by a note: "The reason why we let Guelph be killed so as he could not be got alive at this battle is that at the time in which we let this battle take place (i. e. in the beginning of A. D. 1827) the real Duke of York died of mortification and therefore [we] determined that he should die so he could not be got alive, the which however, was unusual among us." A similar note explains the election of Stumps to succeed Guelph: "The reason why we really let Stumps be king was he was the same wooden soldier which the Duke of York had been." Branwell omits, however, the salient point that resuscitation could not be practiced in this case because the soldier in question was lost for a time, and hence could not be subjected to the potent remedies of the genii.

Invaluable as a source document, "The History of the Young Men" lacks the literary merits that characterize Charlotte's companion volume, "The Twelve Adventurers." Devoid of unity and form, egotistical, verbose, and pedantic, its saving grace is an unconscious humor resulting from a heterogeneity of detail gathered from wide reading.

School left Charlotte little time for games of imagination played alone or in letters to Branwell, but at home for the summer vacation she returned with avidity to the story of the Marquis of Douro and Marian Hume, celebrating their marriage in a poem called "The Bridal":

> I knew 'twas a bridal, for under a bower
> Of roses and the myrtle and the fair lily flower
> Stood that stately noble in pluméd pride,
> And the sweet, fair lady, his plighted bride.
>
> With the mystic ring on her finger fair,
> And the nuptial wreath in her radiant hair,
> They are joined—and forever the mingled name
> of Marina and Albion is hallowed to fame.

Chapter VIII

GLASS TOWN RESUSCITATED

IN JULY, 1832, Charlotte returned to Haworth to stay, having learned in three half years all the Misses Wooler had to teach her. Immediately, to requote her own quotation of herself in the person of Lord Charles Albert Florian Wellesley,

> The creature was at his dirty work again,

stories of Verdopolis and its people.

Branwell, overjoyed at having her back, joined with her in their old pastime of bookmaking. Feeling keenly the disadvantage to which her enlarged experience and developing powers put him, he tried all the more desperately to keep pace with her through his only media, the conventions of the Young Men's Play. One of his earliest compositions after her return was a long poem in celebration of the African Biennial Games,[1] a fixed institution of Verdopolis, borrowed from the ancient Greeks. His theme is still the tyranny of the genii, depicted as demons of destruction, and the heroic resistance of the Twelves:

> I see, I see appear
> Awful Brannii, gloomy giant,
> Shaking o'er earth his blazing spear.
> Brooding on blood with drear and vengeful soul,
> He sits enthroned in clouds to hear his thunders roll.

---

[1] Branwell Brontë: Poems (in longhand): (1) "The Fate of Regina," May, 1832 (incomplete); (2) "Ode on the Celebration of the Great African Games," June 26, 1832, 177 ll.; (3) "The Pass of Thermopylae," March 3, 1833, 56 ll.; (4) "An Hour's Musing," by Alexander Percy, November 16, 1834. (Brontë Museum and Library.)

Dread Tallii next like a dire eagle flies
And on our mortal miseries feasts her bloody eyes.
Emii and Annii last, with boding cry,
Famine and war foretell, and mortal misery.

. . . .

Then where, oh where, must Mortals turn their eyes?
Not to the Genii-throning hills or tempest-giving skies.
No,—to the Twelves, O Fathers of our Fame!
O Fathers, founders of our glorious name,
To you we look, our latest hope,
Our great Defenders, and our common prop.

Charlotte, in contrast to her brother, wrote with fresh assurance under the inspiration of recent experiences, her imagination seething with new conceptions. Unembarrassed by incongruity of elements, she plunged into a tale, finished August 20,[2] representing Zenobia Ellrington in the madness of unrequited love for the Marquis of Douro, the original out of which, modified from other sources, grew the mad wife of *Jane Eyre:*

One evening about dusk, as the Marquis of Douro was returning from a shooting excursion into the country, he heard suddenly a rustling noise in a deep ditch on the roadside. . . . The form of Lady Ellrington started up before him. Her head was bare, her tall person was enveloped in the tattered remnants of a dark velvet mantle. Her dishevelled hair hung in wild elf-locks over her face, neck and shoulders, almost concealing her features, which were emaciated and pale as death. He stepped back a few paces, started at the sudden and ghastly apparition. She threw herself on her knees before him, exclaiming in wild, maniacal accents: "My lord, tell me truly . . . where you have been. . . . Have you seen that wretch, Marian Hume? Have you spoken to her? Viper! Viper! Oh, that I could sheathe this weapon in her heart!"
Here she stopped for want of breath, and drawing a long, sharp, glittering knife from under her cloak, brandished it wildly in the air.

The unity of this story is broken by a digression projecting into the ever-widening web, tales of industrial disturbances heard from Miss Wooler, which after twenty years of Glass Town incubation reappear in *Shirley:*

[2] Printed by C. W. Hatfield under the title "Love and Jealousy," in *The Twelve Adventurers and Other Stories*, pp. 19–25.

Unequivocal symptoms of dissatisfaction began to appear at the same time among the lower orders in Verdopolis. The workmen at the principal mills and furnaces struck for an advance of wages, and the masters refusing to comply with their exorbitant demands, they all turned out simultaneously. Shortly after, Colonel Grenville, one of the great mill owners, was shot. His assassins, being quickly discovered and delivered up to justice, were interrogated by torture, but they remained inflexible, not a single satisfactory answer being elicited from them. The police were now doubled. Bands of soldiers were stationed in the more suspicious parts of the city, and orders were issued that no citizen should walk abroad unarmed.

The role of agitator, in this, as in all other social and political disturbances in Verdopolis, Charlotte assigns to the wooden soldier-villain, Rogue. Law and order found a champion in her beloved Arthur Wellesley, Marquis of Douro, who fearlessly denounces the demagogue to his face in a speech before Parliament.

Branwell, true to habit, turned the situation into another war, known in the history of Verdopolis as "the Great Rebellion raised by Alexander Rogue," belonging in the category with his "Rebellion in My Army" and the rebellion of the Young Men against the genii. The conflict is developed at length in "Letters to an Englishman," which concludes with Alexander Rogue's capture by the Marquis of Douro and his execution before a firing squad, but, in accordance with custom, Rogue was resuscitated and allowed to continue his progress toward the refined villain he becomes in later days.

The writing was interrupted in September, when Charlotte paid a visit to Ellen Nussey, a school friend living at Rydings, near Birstall. Here she had her first intimate sight of a gentleman's country estate. The house, with its battlements, rookery, and other romantic embellishments, set in many acres of ground, found its way immediately into Charlotte's stories, coming out years later, it is said, as Thornfield Hall in *Jane Eyre*.

Branwell escorted her on this trip, the two traveling in a gig, the only conveyance to be had in Haworth except the covered cart which had taken Charlotte away to school. The boy was in wild ecstasy with all he saw at Rydings, walking about in unrestrained enthusiasm. He enjoyed from every direction the turret-roofed house, the full chestnut trees on the lawn, and the large rookery. He told his sister that he was leaving her in Paradise and if she were not happy on this visit she would never be happy anywhere.

Early in February, 1833, Branwell injected a new element into the Verdopolitan situation by raising Alexander Rogue to the position of a leading character. His story "The Pirate," [3] written under the pseudonym Captain John Flower, presents Rogue as a bloody and highly successful buccaneer, preying alike on the commerce of the Duke of Wellington and that of Napoleon—"L'Empereur, the terror of Europe." Among Rogue's prizes is a merchantman carrying the Earl of Elrington—Branwell spells the name with one *l*, Charlotte with two—and his family on a visit to Stumps Island. The observing Captain Flower is amazed to see the two vessels, captor and captured, "tack round and sail to the Glass Town, side by side."

There Rogue confesses his piracies to the Duke of Wellington and makes restitution to all whose ships he has captured. In return he receives full pardon for his offenses, and wins the Lady Zenobia's hand in marriage—a sudden attachment for that eccentric lady, now restored to full health of mind, being the inciting force in his reformation. "This morning," Captain Flower concludes, "I attended the wedding. . . . I have to attend this evening at a grand feast at Elrington Place . . . where will attend all the nobility and gentry of the Glass Town."

The "grand feast at Elrington Place," as reported by Branwell in the Glass Town "Monthly Intelligencer," [4] proved to be little more than a knock-down, drag-out scuffle, despite its elegant setting, sumptuous feast, and the presence of the "four Kings of Ashantee: Sneaky, Wel-

[3] Branwell Brontë: "The Pirate: a Tale by Captain John Flower." February 8, 1833. 15 pp., 5,250 words. (Bonnell Collection.)

[4] Branwell Brontë: "The Monthly Intelligencer," No. 1. March 27–April 26, 1833. 4 pp. 9" x 3¾". Printed in four columns to the page. (Brontë Museum and Library.)
This seems to be the only number issued; its contents are as follows:
(1) A Few Words to the Chief Genii;
(2) A Visit to Elrington Hall;
(3) Parliamentary Intelligence, Great Glass Town, March 20—Meeting of General Senate—The House of Commons, March 20, 1833—House of Commons, April 25, 1833.
(4) Leading Article.
(5) Rogue in Public and Rogue in Private. By the author of "Letters from an Englishman."
(6) Song Applicable to the Present Crisis by Young Soult, the Rhymer.

lington, Parry, and Ross." "Little Charlie Wellesley," hiding himself under the dining table, starts the fracas by sending an immense pin into Captain Tree's leg, a trick which drew from the victim "such a piercing scream that all thought his soul was leaving its clay," and brought from its perpetrator "peals of eldritch laughter."

By virtue of his marriage, Rogue, in accordance with Glass Town custom, becomes Lord Ellrington.

The same newspaper carries an account of the opening of the Verdopolitan Parliament, a ceremonial occasion which Branwell elaborates at length, under the pen of Captain Flower. Crashey's benediction concluding the session savors amusingly of the Book of Common Prayer:

Here the whole assembly knelt, while Crashey, standing up and stretching his hands over them, cried: "Now may the awful Genii, the Guardians of our kingdom and sole disposers of Mortal Man, continue to protect you heretofore as they have done hitherto. O Mysterious Beings, shine upon these, thy servants; stretch your hands over your favorite city; give strength to our arms; wisdom to our councils; show us the path of happiness, shield us from harm."

All now rose, standing in reverential silence, while the venerable Patriarch, led by the four Kings, departed from the Hall, and, mounting his chariot, proceeded to his hall in the Tower of Nations. The Senate then adjourned, to meet again on Wednesday, the 20th of March.

Charlotte follows Branwell's innovation with a story giving plausibility to Rogue's sudden appearance in the role of pirate, assigning him a romantic family background implied in the name Alexander Percy. She takes as her model for his reshaping Varney, the villain of Scott's *Kenilworth,* though she borrows most of the characters of her story and its plot incidents from *Ivanhoe.* This novel, "The Green Dwarf,[5] a Tale of the Perfect Tense," Charlotte lists on the title-page of another book, "The Foundling," among the works of Captain Tree; but its own title-page declares it the work of Lord Charles Albert Florian Wellesley. Did she for once confuse her two imaginary identities?

"The Green Dwarf," reminiscent of the early days of Glass Town, is told by the antiquarian Captain Bud for the amusement of Lord

---

[5] Charlotte Brontë: "The Green Dwarf: a Tale of the Perfect Tense." By Lord Charles Albert Florian Wellesley. September 2, 1833. 25 pp., 34,000 words. $4\frac{11}{16}'' \times 3\frac{3}{4}''$. (Stark Collection, University of Texas Library.)

Alexander Percy Esqre M.P.
Ætat 21.

An Undated Portrait of Alexander Percy, Drawn by Branwell Brontë

Charles just out from a long illness. Under license of old times, Charlotte relapses into delicious pictures of the Young Men's Play in its prime:

Twenty years since, or thereabouts, there stood in what is now the middle of Verdopolis, but which was then the extremity, a huge, irregular building called the Genii's Inn. It contained more than five hundred apartments, all comfortably and some splendidly fitted up for the accommodation of travellers, who were entertained in this vast hostelry free of expense. It became, in consequence of this generous regulation, the almost exclusive resort of wayfarers of every nation, who in spite of the equivocal character of the host and hostesses, being the four Chief Genii: Talli, Brani, Emi, and Anni, and the despicable villany of the waiters and other attendants, which noble offices were filled by subordinate spirits of the same species, continually flocked thither in prodigious multitudes. . . .

On the evening of the fourth of June, 1814, it offered a rather different appearance. There had been during that day a greater influx of guests than usual, which circumstance was owing to a grand fête to be held on the morrow. The great hall looked like a motley masquerade. In one part sat cross-legged on the pavement a group of Turkish merchants [Branwell's set of Turkish musicians]. . . . Near them a few dark, sunburnt Spaniards strutted with the grave, proud air of a peacock. . . . Not far from those lords of creation sat a company of round, rosy-faced, curly-pated, straight-legged, one-shoed beings from Stumps' Island. . . . More than a dozen genii were employed in furnishing them with melons and rice pudding, for which they roared incessantly. At the opposite extremity of the hall, five or six sallow, billious Englishmen were conversing over a cup of green tea. Behind them a band of withered monsieurs sat presenting each other with fine white bread.

The fete which brought together this motley throng was the African Olympic Games, celebrated in Branwell's recent poem. Chief among the contestants was Rogue called by his new name, Percy. His countenance was handsome, says Charlotte, his features regularly formed; and "his forehead was loftly though not very open. But there was in the expression of his blue, sparkling, but sinister eyes and of the smile that played round his deceitful looking mouth a spirit of deep, restless villainy which warned the penetrating observer that all was not as fair within as without, while his pallid cheek and somewhat haggard air bespoke at once the profligate, the gambler, and, perhaps, the drunkard."

Interesting as the change in Rogue's status may be, the critical significance of "The Green Dwarf" centers, not in Rogue as Percy, but in the character of Bertha, the old hag of a deserted castle to which Percy carries Lady Emily Charlesworth when he abducts her on the eve of her marriage to the hero, Lord St. Clair. Bertha is a direct adaptation of the Saxon Ulrica of Front de Bœuf's castle in *Ivanhoe*. Commonplace and childish as the plagiarism seems in itself, it fixed in Charlotte's mind an image which under the heat of her imagination fused in the course of years with Lady Zenobia Ellrington to become Bertha Mason, the mad wife of *Jane Eyre*.

Into this grotesque adaptation of Scott's romance to the Glass Town setting, Charlotte again brings—this time as joint villain with Percy— the African Prince Quashia, son of one of the Ashantee chiefs (the ninepins) killed in the conquest of the country. Earlier Lord Charles told the story of Prince Quashia's adoption by the Duke of Wellington as he had it from his father.[6] The Duke of Wellington relates that as he walked along the banks of the river Sahala one sultry afternoon, his attention was caught by the sound of distant singing. "The tune were [was] exceedingly wild and plaintive, and as it rose and sank at intervals in the breeze," he recognized the music as "a requiem for the dead, or a song which it is the custom in some African nations to chant over the dying." He followed the sound to a grove of palm trees where he saw "a handsome black woman, richly dressed, reclining in their shade." A little child three or four years old was stretched on the ground beside her in a deep sleep. The dying woman's song, rendered into English by Lord Charles, runs to fourteen stanzas of four lines each, beginning,

> Last branch of murdered royalty
> How calmly thou are sleeping
> While the storm that bowed thy parent tree
> Is still around thee sweeping.

On the reverse of the same page is a companion poem of sixteen lines, possibly written as an alternate, indicating that Charlotte had recently read Byron's *Hebrew Melodies*:

[6] Charlotte Brontë: "The African Queen's Lament." February 12, 1833. 16 l. plus 350 words (longhand), plus 56 ll., plus 69 words. (Bonnell Collection.)

Oh Hyle! Thy waves are like Babylon's streams
  When the daughters of Zion hung o'er them in woe;
When the sad exiles wept in their desolate dreams
  And sighed for the sound of calm Kedron's flow.

Her naïvete saw no incongruity in an African primitive singing an Hebraic melody in Byronic quatrains.

The Duke of Wellington, so goes the story, took the child into his house and brought him up as a son, although between him and the Marquis of Douro there was bitter hatred and constant strife. The black boy was evil tempered and rebellious, the cause of many troubles to both his foster-father and foster-brother. Possibly Quashia, fully developed in the family play before Emily seceded from it, contributed something toward the making of Heathcliff in *Wuthering Heights*.

All this vivid, imaginative life the outward Charlotte tacitly denied to her closest friend:

An account of one day is an account of all. In the morning, from 9 o'clock till half past 12, I instruct my sisters and draw; then we walk till dinner. After dinner I sew till tea-time, and after tea I either read, write or do a little fancy-work, or draw, as I please. Thus, in one delightful, though somewhat monotonous course, my life is passed.

Yearning after art as a means of expression, evident in the colored illustrations of Charlotte and Branwell's first small volumes, speaks through all the stories of the Glass Town cycle. In the highly cultivated society of the Young Men's world, according to these stories, artists receive equal honor and emoluments with poets, dramatists, and novelists, all enjoying alike the generous patronage of the Marquis of Douro. De Lisle, for instance, is one of the most sought after men of the nation, and his portraits are the pride of city palaces and country houses.

In the summer of Charlotte's return from school, the Parsonage group spent long eye-straining hours trying to teach themselves drawing by copying with detailed exactness the prints and engravings that came into their hands. Their father realizing the futility of such effort, employed a teacher to come from Leeds at two guineas a visit.

Chapter IX

EMILY CREATES GONDAL

CHARLOTTE's return did not bring the younger girls back into the group play. Emily at fifteen, just emerging from her aunt's supervision into self-direction, was grown the tallest person in the Parsonage, except her father, and was fast blooming into lithesome grace of figure and beauty of face set by "kind, kindling grey-blue eyes." She and Anne—the prettiest of the family, with soft brown curls, violet-blue eyes, and clear, delicate complexion, gentle natured and amiable—were inseparable companions, like twins in unanimity of action. Emily, the potential "great navigator," and "discoverer of new spheres," to whom Nature was an appetite, a passion, and a love, led Anne into many a hardy adventure her own timid nature would never have suggested. Together, or in company with Charlotte and Branwell—though Charlotte thought herself too old to join in their more tomboyish behavior —they tramped the moors back of the Parsonage, explored glens and ravines that broke the purplish-dun monotony, and waded rippling brooks. In a far nook called "The Meeting of the Waters," shut off from the rest of the world by miles of heather and open only to the blue of the sky and the brightness of the sun, Emily built a world of her own, mixing fancy with philosophy, moralizing in such simple games as chasing tadpoles in the brook and judging them strong or weak, brave or cowardly according to their frightened dartings and wrigglings.

The failure of all persuasion to draw the seceding girls back into the family union incited Branwell to an editorial in "The Monthly

Intelligencer" of Glass Town, scoring the absconding chief genii for heartless desertion of their Young Men:

A Few Words to the Chief Genii

When a parent leaves his children, young and inexperienced, and without cause absconds, never more troubling himself about them, those children, according to received notions among men, if they by good fortune should happen to survive this neglect and become of repute in society, are by no means bound to believe that he has done his duty to them as a parent merely because they have risen, nor are they indeed required to own or treat him as a parent. This is all very plain, and we believe that four of our readers will understand our aim in thus speaking.

A child of the G—ii.

Abandoned by their natural and rightful guardians, Emily's hero, now the Marquis of Ardrah, degenerated into the only inglorious character of the Glass Town cycle, and Anne's one-time favorite, John Ross, never very distinctly realized, was allowed to fade from the picture.

From this time on the four Brontës played and wrote in pairs: Charlotte and Branwell, Emily and Anne, each knowing the others' inventions but never overlapping.

Emily, following the dictates of her own integrity, kept her new world free of the contradictions that make the Young Men's Play ridiculous in the eyes of realism and logic. Her setting was Gondal, a large island in the North Pacific, a country of snow-capped mountains, moors, and wide-spreading lakes. Its capital was Regina on Lake Elderno in the province, or kingdom, of Angora. Like Haworth in climate, Gondal was in winter a land

> . . . of mists and moorlands drear,
> And sleet and frozen gloom,

yet it was more beautiful in the eyes of its far-ranging mariners than the flower-strewn southern isles of their farthest sailings.

The people of this northern continent were a bold, hardy, elemental race to whom loyalty was the highest virtue and treachery the darkest crime; freedom was their dearest blessing and prison their deepest hell. Cathedrals and palaces loomed dim in the shadowy background

—Emily was as impatient of Charlotte's religious pageants, council boards, and drawing-room scenes as of Branwell's battles—but Gondal homes were close in view, real and vivid, and warm with life. Gondal's chief stage of action, however, was the wide expanse of earth and sea. It was the cool, shady bower of the forest or the white, moonlit beach that heard the vows of lovers; the mountain glen that gave a death retreat to the wounded outlaw; and the wild waste of the moor that drank the blood of the suicide and assassin's victim— Earth was mother and nurse to Emily's Gondalians.

There was war in Gondal, too, but unlike Branwell's military parades, it was motivated by stark, elemental passions and was shorn of pomp and glory. It brought broken bodies, death, and captivity and left in its wake devastated cities and ruined countrysides. Resuscitation was not practiced in Gondal, nor had it genii to direct its heroes and interpose in their behalf.

Not a scrap has survived of direct information concerning the Gondal creation before 1834. If Emily wrote it out, her manuscripts have been lost. The story must be coaxed from her poems with the help of a few later fragments of prose, all written after June, 1836.

Chapter X

ENTER MARY PERCY

CHARLOTTE at seventeen was turning out books with astonishing rapidity—1833 was probably the most prolific year of her life—but no longer in size to match the wooden soldiers. The toys were gone and she was an author in her own right, though still claiming the license of old pseudonyms. Her volumes of this period, measuring in general 4½ x 3¼ inches, run to an average length of 20,000 words or more and are so finely printed that they average about 1,200 words to the page. Four such novels are still extant, and titles of eight others are known from her own lists, twelve volumes, aggregating, at the least probable estimate, a thousand pages if transcribed in typing. Those that have survived are surprisingly juvenile in theme for a girl of seventeen, though they show an enviable fluency of expression and power of realization. Having as yet no experience of her own of which to write, she still must needs fall back upon conventional fairy tales, oriental magic, and ghostly adventures from gothic romances. To relieve her embarrassment at the childishness of some of her conceptions, she borrows from Scott, as in "The Green Dwarf," the suggestion of antiquity, cloaking the absurdities of the wooden toys under the pretense of "olden days" and "past times," and enjoying fully her own conceits. Charlotte's sense of humor is the saving grace of these otherwise dull productions.

The longest and most informing of the novels in this year is one retained by Mr. Wise for his own library: "The Foundling.[1] A Tale of

[1] Its title-page is reproduced in *Catalogue of the Ashley Library*. Vol. I, p. 70.

Our Own Times by Captain Tree Author of the Incorporeal Watcher, The Green Dwarf, The Wizard's Cave, Alphonse Howard, A Year of Horrors, The Forgotten Ring, The * Pledge, &c., &c." "This book," the title-page continues, "was begun May 31st, 1833, and finished June 27th." It contains about 34,000 words of minute hand printing covering twenty pages which measure 7⁵⁄₁₆ x 4⁹⁄₁₆ inches. Its picture of Glass Town in its glory as the capital of "Twelves' Land" is the best that has survived:

It was a lovely day in the beginning of summer when his [the hero's] foot touched Africa's shore, and his eye rested on the Tower of All Nations, whose vast outline stood in mighty relief against a deep, unclouded sky. For an instant he paused on the quay and glanced around. Far before him stretched the sea into which two huge arms branched out from the land and, embracing a portion of its waters, formed the harbour where lay upwards of a thousand vessels of war and merchandise, resting in safe anchorage on its long, rolling waves. The greater part of these ships displayed the Lion Flag of England, but banners of almost every empire under heaven streamed promiscuously from their mastheads. . . . Far above him the city walls and ramparts rose to a tremendous height, frowning terribly on the foam-white waves which rushed roaring to their feet. . . . Bells were at this instant announcing the hour of noon, and high above the rest the great cathedral bell sent forth its solemn toll, sonorous as a trumpet's voice heard among lutes and harps. Verdopolis lay at the mouth of a wide valley which was embosomed in long, low hills, rich in hanging groves and gardens, vineyards, cornfield, meadows, etc., etc. The background was closed by lofty, peaked mountains, whose azure tint almost melted into the serene horizon, and all was faintly seen through a mellowing veil of mist, which enhanced instead of depreciating the charms of this earthly paradise.

From the wharf the hero took his way up the main street of Verdopolis, which was "nearly a quarter of a mile broad and apparently of interminable length."

The population of this street was various, consisting chiefly of tall banditti-like men whose muscular frames and weather-beaten brows spoke of active and constant exercise in the open air. Smart, jaunty personages, attired in military costume, passed among these with the dashing step and bearing peculiar to their profession. Now and then a superior-looking cavalry officer galloped by on horse-back. A tolerable sprinkling of bucks and bloods were also observable strutting up and down. But the portion of this motley assembly which most attracted Sydney's attention was some odd little specimens of humanity averaging about four feet in height, whereof those who appeared to be of the male gender were dressed in black three-cornered hats, blue coats, red waist-coats ornamented with large white buttons, black breeches, white stockings, and one great, round wooden shoe on which they scuffled about with marvelous rapidity. The women wore blue gowns, red jackets, white aprons, and little white caps without a border or any other decoration other than a narrow red ribbon. Their shoes were similar in construction to the men's. These strange beings were seated at low stalls which they had raised on the pavement and which were filled with stockings and mittens of lambswool, spun linen, towels, and napkins, eggs, salt butter and fish, watermelons, dried herbs, &c., &c. They called out to every passenger, and occasionally some of the men when unemployed amused themselves by singing the following exquisite stanzas:

> Eamala is a gurt bellaring bull.
> Shoo swilled and swilled till shoo drank her full;
> > Then shoo rolled abaât
> > Wi' screeäm and shaât,
> And aât of her pocket a knoife did pull.
>
> And wi' that knoife shoo'd a cut her throit
> If I hadn't gean her a strait waist-coit;
> > Then shoo flang an' jumped
> > And girned and grumped,
> But I didn't caâre for her a doit.
>
> A' sooin shoo'd doffed her mantle of red,
> An' shoo went an' shoo ligged her daân aën't bed.
> > An' theare shoo slept
> > Till th' hease wor swept,
> An' all the gooid liquor wor gooan fro her head.

Who was the supposed author of these "exquisite stanzas" and whether or not "Eamala" has any reference to Emily does not appear.

A long and involved incident of this novel, reminiscent of the school for children of nobles on the Island of Dreams, gives evidence that Charlotte had read Byron's "Manfred":

At a distance of nearly six hundred miles from the continent of Africa there lies an island called the Philosophers' Island. . . . Embosomed in . . . a valley . . . the only building on the Island stands . . . a sort of college or university for the instruction of the rising generation. Here the most learned philosophers of the world have their residences, and to this place all the noble youths of Verdopolis are sent for their education. There has lately been formed amongst the professors and tutors of the University a secret society of which many of the principal characters in our city are members. This association is said to have dived deeply into the mysteries of nature and to have revealed many of her hidden and unthought-of secrets.

The president of this Philosophical Association was no other than the "venerable Crashie" (earlier written Crashey), now dividing his honors and his magical powers with his "wonderful brother Manfred." After long and arduous effort, Crashie had "succeeded in compounding a fluid so pure, so refined, so ethereal, that one drop of it distilled in our mortal clay penetrated to the soul, freed it from all grosser particles, raised it far above worldly troubles, rendered it capable of enjoying the calm of heaven amid the turmoil of the earth, and . . . forever warded off the darts of death." But those high and unseen spirits, to whom even the potent Crashie must yield, observed his beneficent work and controverted it, so that his liquid changed its nature, and "instead of dispensing immortality and holy delight, it would bring the horrors, the darkness of inevitable death."

The great magician had taken every precaution to prevent the use of this baneful fluid, but Rogue, now Lord Ellrington, breaking his oath sworn, "by names and things ineffable," and braving Crashie's inexorable wrath, obtained a portion of the liquid and used it against the great master's favorite disciple, Arthur, Marquis of Douro. By decree of the council of the Philosophers' Society, the murderer and his accomplices were meted the fate of their victim: death by the magic fumes, "which wrenched and distorted their countenances into the most fearful semblances that death can assume." The grief and wailing that rose up from the Philosophers' Isle for the loss of the Marquis of Douro, writes Lord Charles, so moved "the four chief genii who rule the destinies of our world" that they consented that the cold corpse in the grave should breathe again, first exacting a solemn oath that neither he nor his relatives should take revenge on those who slew him, for it was the "mighty Brannii's will to revivify the murderers also."

Charlotte's most significant book of this prolific year is "Arthuri-

ana," [2] made up, as the title-page says, of "odds and ends" concerning the Marquis of Douro as seen through the critical eyes of his
younger brother. The increasing antagonism between the two reflects
a growing conflict within Charlotte herself, as her conscience condemns while her romantic imagination rejoices in the moral lapses of
her hero. To satisfy conscience she shapes Lord Charles into a yet
more precise instrument of censure through which she roundly denounces the sins that made her hero glorious.

One of the titbits of "Arthuriana," headed "The Tragedy and the
Essay," is based on a knowledge of the drama and stage history of the
eighteenth and early nineteenth centuries not to be expected in a rural
clergyman's daughter, drawn, perhaps, from the library of Ponden
House, whose sale catalogue lists a dramatic collection that might well
excite the envy of a specialist. The story illustrates the ease with which
Charlotte assimilated her diverse reading, as contrasted to her brother's awkward borrowings.

Edwin Hamilton, according to this story, is a young architect enjoying the patronage of the Marquis of Douro—"one of my brother's
numerous toadies." Yielding to a sudden literary inspiration, he writes
a play which he brings for his patron's inspection—here Charlotte had
in mind Byron as a member of the sub-committee of Drury Lane Theatre. The Marquis receives it sarcastically and begins to read it with
sneers, but in the end he pronounces it "Admirable!"

"I advise you," he says to Hamilton, "to offer this play without loss
of time to Mr. Price of the Theatre Royal [Stephen Price was manager
of Drury Lane at this time]. I will write a few lines in favor of it
to him, and I do not doubt but that my recommendation will be sufficient to secure you handsome treatment in that quarter."

Price accepts the play for production and soon announces:

> This evening will be performed at the Theatre Royal
> PETUS AND ARIA,
> an entirely new tragedy by Edwin Hamilton, Esq.
> under the patronage of the Marquis of Douro.

---

[2] Charlotte Brontë: "Arthuriana, or Odds and Ends: Being a Miscellaneous Collection
of Pieces in Prose and Verse By Lord Charles A. F. Wellesley." September 27–November
20, 1833. 18,600 words plus 278 ll. (J. Pierpont Morgan Library.)

The character of Aria to be performed by Mrs. Siddons;
That of Petus by Garry David.

The section of the story describing Mrs. Siddon's acting before the
royalty and nobility of Verdopolis is prophetic of the famous picture
of Rachel as Vashti before the court of Labassecour, in *Villette:*

> Never before was there such a crowded house: pit, box, and gallery over-
> flowed . . . Certainly there are few sights more animated and inspiring than
> a crowded theatre. The brilliant lights, the ceaseless hum of voices, the busy
> and visionary stage, all conspire to raise feelings indescribable in the soul.
> This evening there appeared no fewer than four monarchs in the royal box,
> and, what was more attractive, because more rare, tnree queens graced it
> with their presence. More than a thousand of the loveliest women on earth
> sparkled in the dress-circle, where the waving of plumes, the rustling of
> robes, the glitter of diamonds, and the light-bright eyes were perfectly daz-
> zling. . . .
> The first scene now came on, in the course of which Mrs. Siddons dis-
> played all her finest powers and even excelled herself. Peals of applause again
> shook the theatre to its foundations.

Lord Charles, viewed both audience and performance from an ad-
vantageous "station among the branches of the mighty golden chan-
delier which hangs from the center of the dome."

"Arthuriana" includes the announcement of the birth of a son to the
Marquis and Marchioness of Douro. The sight of the child moves Lord
Charles to a passage of unprecedented tenderness:

> Arthur was standing near the hearth with something little and white
> clasped in his arms, on which he gazed with a smile of such unutterable
> fondness as I never saw beaming on his countenance either before or since.
> . . . I approached and stood on tip-toes to get a look at his tiny burden. It was
> a "wee bairnee" wrapped in a white garment so long that it fell down to
> Arthur's feet; a cap of costliest lace covered its head, from under whose
> borders peeped out a few curls of very light brown hair. Its eyelids were
> closed when I first looked at it, but on a sudden it opened them. I almost
> started when I saw the full, large, dark, perfectly Arthurian eyes which
> beamed from under its little forehead. In fact all over the small, slight fea-
> tures of its face there dwelt a certain mysterious resemblance to that tall,
> magnificent youth in whose paternal embrace it now lay. It seemed as if
> the metamorphosis to a father had imparted to my brotner some touch
> of human feeling. He gently consigned his child to my arms. . . . I eagerly
> accepted the precious burden and kissed it with a transport of affection.

But Branwell could not let the Glass Town story remain long in *status quo*. While Charlotte, as yet unconscious of the revolutionary possibilities inherent in "The Pirate," was turning out adolescent romances of the "sweet little Marchioness Marian," the adored and adoring wife and mother, he was preparing the death blow to that heroine's happiness. In "Politics in Verdopolis [3] by Captain John Flower," he presents full grown a brand-new heroine, Rogue's daughter, Maria Henrietta Percy (more familiarly, Mary Percy), whose advent changes the aspect of Verdopolitan politics and society and infuses a new, life-giving element into Charlotte's writing.

This new heroine, reared by her grandmother on the family estate in Wellingtonsland, knows nothing of the society her father adorns. On the eve of marriage to Sir Robert Pelham she asks permission of her father, now Lord Ellrington, to visit "that vast emporium of the universe, the great Glasstown," which she has never seen, explaining the request by desire to see and converse with the Marquis of Douro, whose poems have quite won her heart. Her father willingly consents, and when he returns she is with him. On this visit, according to Branwell's chronicle, she meets for the first time her stepmother, Lady Zenobia Ellrington, who has been "cautioned against haughtiness or disrespect" and who "accordingly receives her with the utmost courtesy and kindness mingled with pride and distance, which Miss Percy is not slow to return." The heroine's conquest of the capital is complete, and the leading newspaper of the city announces: "Miss Percy has been eagerly received. . . . All the city speaks of her, admires her for her beauty, good-nature, pride, reserve, cheerfulness, gaiety, freedom from sophistication, and elegant mind. Sir Robert Weaver Pelham by sheer force of his ability has at once seated himself as a principal Glasstowner. His approaching marriage with Maria Henrietta Percy is publicly known, and vast preparations are making to celebrate it in a style of splendour worthy of himself and her great father. The Marquis of Douro will give the bride away."

But Sir Robert Pelham's marriage to Mary Percy is never celebrated in the style suggested, for the Marquis of Douro, despite his obligation

[3] Branwell Brontë: "The Politics in Verdopolis: A Tale by Captain John Flower, M.P." November 15, 1833. 18 pp., 16,900 words. 7½" x 4½". (Bonnell Collection.)

to his wife, Marian, and their infant son, conceived and declared a grand passion for the new beauty, which she, notwithstanding her announced engagement to Sir Robert, returned and acknowledged. In a still later story it develops that the Marquis, having told his wife of his new passion, spent a long night, gently and kindly, with Shelley-like logic, pointing out to her the suffering that will be hers if his affection turns to hate, as it surely will if she stands in the way of his desire. To avoid this insupportable calamity, Marian consents to step aside for her rival, but before the blow of separation from her adored lord falls, she dies of consumption and a broken heart. Her infant is given into the keeping of Mina Laury, Douro's earliest love and most faithful mistress.

More and more Charlotte's imagination was finding release from the fetters of the Young Men's Play through the Marquis of Douro, a happy, continuous development keeping pace with her growing understanding of Byron's character. But for Douro's wife, the Marchioness Marian, the great poet provided no model, and Marian remained as she came into being, a green-and-white maiden of snowdrop purity, a childish ideal conceived as a perfect companion for a high-minded and gifted youth, such as Charlotte's innocence at that time pictured Arthur Wellesley, the youthful Byron. She was certainly no suitable mate for the selfish, cynical, and rakish, but glorious Douro of later days, whose morals and personality were at once the scandal and the fascination of Verdopolitan society.

Mary Percy, introduced by Branwell at a moment when Charlotte was beginning to feel the incongruity between her hero and his wife, was eagerly given a fair share of the affectionate attention which hitherto she had reserved for the Marquis alone. Disregarding restraints of moral judgment, Charlotte, vivifying and humanizing her brother's puppet, fashioned her with one thought in mind: to suit in every particular Douro's exacting and fastidious taste. Like every other woman who came under his resistless and deadly spell, Mary was to know the suffering incident to his inconstant love; yet to retain his affection more consistently than any other upon whom he set his mark of possession.

Despite its dramatic staging, Marian's death is as devoid of tragedy as her love for the Marquis of Douro is innocent of passion. And Charlotte did not give her up any more than she had given up the wooden soldiers who fell in battle; she merely resorted to a new form of resuscitation, and continued to write about her in retrospect, adding new traits of character from time to time and new incidents to her life, until Marian Hume dead grows into a vastly different person from Marian Hume living, gradually merging into Mary Percy, and through her into Paulina Mary Home of *Villette*.

Chapter XI

ANGRIA AND THE ANGRIANS

THE METAMORPHOSIS of Rogue into Alexander Percy, now raised to the Earldom of Northangerland, and the marriage of his daughter Mary to the Marquis of Douro ended for a time the long political antagonism between the two principal characters of the Glass Town cycle. Ere long father and son-in-law formed a coalition for their mutual aggrandizement by which Douro, under Branwell's inspiration, effected the greatest coup of his life, thus initiating a new phase of the complex story the two older Brontës were weaving.

When, in the course of Branwell's wars, Napoleon invaded the vast stretch of uncivilized jungleland lying to the east and southeast of the Young Men's capital, it was Arthur Wellesley, Marquis of Douro, rather than his father, the Duke of Wellington, who, at the head of an army, engaged him in a struggle patterned after the actual Duke's Peninsular campaign, for in Glass Town annals the son had long since superseded the father on the battlefield as well as in literature and politics. It irritated Charlotte, however, that, while the original favorites of the play—Wellington, Ross, Parry, and Sneachi—held thrones and ruled kingdoms, her newer and greater hero was only a prince, heir apparent to Wellingtonsland. To correct this unjust and unsatisfactory state of affairs, Branwell now agreed to form the eastern wilderness into a proper kingdom for the young Marquis.

Accordingly, Douro, having saved his country in this crisis, is made to demand through his father-in-law his fields of battle, the large and sparsely populated but very fertile province to the east, which he received after a bitter fight in Parliament and named Angria. In keeping with his latest exploits and his new dignity, he took to himself in rapid succession the titles, Duke of Zamorna, King of Angria, and Emperor Adrian. Arthur Augustus Adrian Wellesley is now his full name, but it is as Duke of Zamorna that he is commonly known hereafter.

Charlotte's and Branwell's stories for the remainder of 1834 and 1835 have to do with the creation of the new kingdom and its fortunes. Which of the two originated these innovations is uncertain; all are implied in Charlotte's early stories of 1834, though usually it is Branwell who records the details. His is the only connected account we have of the actual beginning of Angria, set forth in a volume announcing on its title-page the elevation of Captain Flower to the peerage: "The Wool Is Rising. Or The Angrian Adventurer.[1] A Narrative of the Proceedings of the Foundation of the Kingdom of Angria By the Right Honourable John Baron Flower and Viscount Richton Secretary of State for Foreign Affairs Ambassador to the Court of Angria F L S, &c, &c. . . ." Though Captain Flower's account is tedious and ungrateful reading, displaying in exaggerated degree Branwell's worst faults, it is the foundation stone of Angrian history, and as such is a tremendously important Brontë document.

In this narrative the Earl of Northangerland is discovered sitting alone, analyzing his own character aloud in terms intended to emphasize his Lucifer-like ambition, pride, and bitterness, for Charlotte and Branwell, since reading Milton's *Paradise Lost* and Byron's *Cain,* were redrawing Percy after their common hero:

I know that in all that party, in all this city, in all this country, there is not one man whom I feel a friendship for, not one for whom on the score of feeling alone I should feel very grieved did I hear the cathedral bell just now tolling for his funeral. There is one of them, that fiery young Duke, for whom I sometimes catch myself fancying a friendship . . . I feel solicitous about him because my present fortunes are bound up with him. I do heartily wish him well, because as he is so must I be. I like to see him exhibit all his pride and splendor and prosperity, because, even if I may be a tool in his hands for his ends, I know that he, too, is a tool, in my hand for mine—mine. . . . Though Northangerland appear a freezing, cheerless nobleman, yet he himself can declare that he is a fiery, ardent ambitionist. Aye, that's the word! And can ambition exist without youth, without the principle of youth? I

---

[1] June 26, 1834. 24 pp., 30,000 words. 7⅜″ x 4⁹⁄₁₆″. (Ashley Library.)

don't know how a coal can give warmth without fire. Tonight, this night, in the House of Peers, while in the act of doing what others, what all others, would be ashamed to do, in the act, in the very act of vindicating injustice, of holding a shield of brass, of robbing my benefactors of—hah—of doing an act of benevolence, of benefiting a fellow man!!! Fah! of proving myself a tool of Zamorna, of proving Zamorna a tool of me. . . .

That night in Parliament, in the presence of the members and crowded galleries, Northangerland makes a wild, impassioned, and contradictory speech out of which, by repeated readings, one gathers that in the recent war Arthur Wellesley, Duke of Zamorna, "defeated," "crushed," and "dissipated" "all the plans of Napoleon," thus saving the country from utter destruction. In return for this patriotic service, he demands the cession of the Province of Angria to himself with the title of king. Percy couples his astonishing demand with a veiled threat of civil war if it is refused: "I will present your sentence to your country, and before the judgment of that authority where will you and your mandates fall? Take then to yourself the credit of a good action, for well you know how a forced favor looks from the wretch who bestows it."

He is followed by the Duke of Zamorna urging his own claims in long, literal enumerations that characterize all Branwell's writings:

Hear me, Kings and Nobles of Verdopolis! I have rejoined a shattered government; I have conciliated a divided army; I have ransomed a kingdom from its captors; I have utterly defeated two hundred thousand foes; to your majesties I have brought booty into the exchequer 5,000,000 of pounds sterling! Ha! Now for all this I demand my fields of battle; I demand the provinces of Angria, Calabar, and Zamorna to be yielded up to me in uncontrolled sovereignty, in just right for myself and my heirs, now and forever more, and to this effect I move that tomorrow night, February 4, A.D. 1834, a bill be brought forward in the Commons House of Parliament, for the direct conferring of the kingdom of Angria upon Field-Marshal the most noble Arthur Augustus Adrian Wellesley, Duke of Zamorna, Marquis of Douro, and Lieutenant of the Verdopolitan Armies.

The bill is passed against the judgment of the wiser and more patriotic peers, but with their consent, lest its refusal be the signal for the referendum threatened by Northangerland.

Branwell gives the metes and bounds of this, the newest kingdom of the Verdopolitan Confederacy, carefully setting the stage for the most tremendous war of his career:

All that country . . . stretching in a broad, fertile region from the Gordon mountains in the north to the mouths of the Calabar in the south, bounded on the west by the long ridge of the Glass Town Valley and the eastern skirts of Verdopolis and on the east by the rapid Nowrhene and the huge wastes of Eastern Africa—all this wide stretch of country forming the whole eastern portion of the Great Glass Town Country and measuring about 400 miles in length and nearly 300 in breadth, was now by one sweeping act of Parliament given into the hands of the young Duke of Zamorna as his due and rightful kingdom.

At every step, Branwell continues, the founders of this kingdom, Zamorna and Northangerland, have "to face a hundred difficulties and a thousand cares." With the exception of the Duke of Wellington, every one of the seven kings is determinedly opposed to them; all the ministry of Verdopolis, including the old and long-vested aristocracy, is against them. The popular and powerful John Duke of Fidena frowns upon them. "Quashia, the awful and tremendous Quashia . . . with all his innumerable myriads of expatriated and ferocious negroes, occupies all the mighty and unexplored territory horrid with heat and desolation which lies along all the unprotected east of Angria." There the young lion crouches, watching his opportunity "to rush down upon the unsettled country, overwhelm all the powers of his intensely hated foster-brother, Zamorna, and from thence rush down on Verdopolis and regain his long-occupied throne."

In the months following the creation of Angria, Branwell was in his element, directing the new monarch and his lieutenants in framing a constitution, dividing the country into administrative provinces, forming a ministry and government; organizing a vigorous army; fixing the site of a huge metropolis; "receiving all the unfailing tide of in-flocking adherents"; strengthening Angria's position in the Verdopolitan Union; "laying hold of the huge machine, the public press"; filling, so far as they were able, Parliament with their adherents; "and in a thousand other ways, laying the basis of a firm and despotic sway."

The new capital, laid out on the Calabar, they called Adrianopolis after its emperor, Adrian—Arthur Augustus Adrian Wellesley—who is not able, however, long to sustain the character of Eastern potentate implied in his new name and title. For the most part he remains to the end Zamorna in name and Byron in character.

In the building of the new city the energy and resourcefulness of Northangerland proved an effective substitute for the magic that reared Verdopolis. Zamorna himself, "the young and glorious, the god-like," was on the very pinnacle of splendor. He was adored wherever he appeared, cheered by an applauding populace, surrounded by a resistless young nobility, "worshipped, fairly and decidedly worshipped, by a mighty and heavenly galaxy of all the titled and untitled beauty of Verdopolis." "His strange and unfathomable right hand companion, the dark, deep, treacherous, but unconquerable Northangerland, controlled all the movements, regulated all the marching of the swelling tide of a victorious faction without one solitary smile of pleasure, without a word or gleam of triumph. But with cold and sceptic brow and languid and bitter and melancholy aspect this immortal nobleman devoted, day and night, all his hours and thoughts and choicest imaginings to the advancement and perfection of this, his latest and dearest plan of ambition."

Scrupulously statistical, Branwell lists the provinces of Angria with their capitals, lords lieutenant, and population: [2]

> ZAMORNA. 170 miles long, 112 miles broad.
> Capital. The City of Zamorna.
> Lord Lieutenant. Lord Viscount Castlereagh.
> Population 1,986,000
>
> ANGRIA. 80 miles long, 180 miles broad.
> Capital. The City of Angria.
> Lord Lieutenant. W. H. Warner, Esqr.
> Population 1,492,000
>
> ARUNDEL. 165 miles long, 90 broad.
> Capital. The City of Seaton.
> Lord Lieutenant. The Earl of Arundel.
> Population 971,000
>
> NORTHANGERLAND. 200 miles long, 270 broad.
> Capital. The City of Pequene.

---

[2] Transcript received from C. W. Hatfield.

Lord Lieutenant. The Earl of Northangerland.
Population 376,000

DOURO. 130 miles long, 100 broad.
Capital. The City of Douro.
Lord Lieutenant. The Earl of Jordan.
Population 71,000.

CALABAR. Length 190 miles, breadth 130 miles.
Capital. The City of Gazemba.
Lord Lieutenant. Wilkin Thornton, Esq.
Population 59,000

ETREI. Length 120 miles, breadth 95 miles.
Capital. The City of Dongola.
Lord Lieutenant. Henri Fernando di Enara.
Population 4,000

Total population of Angria 4,959,000

Charlotte shows little interest in the geography of the new country, its political organization, and its financial resources, concerning herself solely with the spirit of its people. Instead of listing the "Angrian Adventurers," she describes, through Lord Charles's disapproving pen, their spectacular exodus from Verdopolis:[3]

The children of Israel are gone up from amongst us, and a mixed multitude went up with them, and flocks and herds and very much *cattle*. They went by way of Baal-Zephon, and are camped in the wilderness of Sin (I believe the original orthography is Zin, but that signifies little). . . . And in their departure they spoiled the Egyptians; they have not slain our firstborn, but they have enticed them away, saying, "Cast in your lot with us, and we will do you good." Hallelujah should now be the watchword throughout Verdopolis, but, alas! some there be who scruple not to cry "Ichabod! Ichabod! the glory is departed."

With that love of ostentatious pomp and flashy display which circulates through the veins of every Angrian as unceasingly as his blood, the grand emigration was so contrived that at one day, almost at one hour, the carriage of each oriental noble stood at the door of his Verdopolitan residence, and in splendid cortege the gathered host of vehicles with their attendant outriders went pouring from sunrise to sunset in a tide of thunder along the Eastern Highway. . . .

---

[3] Charlotte Brontë: "My Angria and the Angrians." By Lord Charles Albert Florian Wellesley. October 14, 1834. 17½ pp., 22,000 words. (Law Collection.)

It was hard for a steady, sober Glass-towner (to say nothing of an irritable old aristocrat) to endure the swaggering effrontery of those latter days. . . . To hear these fellows, I say, alluding with such a puppyish air of scorn to the old city where they dwelt so long, the home of their fathers, the Queen of the Earth, who looks down on her majestic face mirrored in the noble Niger, and sees the far reflection of her valley and her turrets caught by the flashing Guadima and flung with beauty unimaginable on the glass that her harbour gives her; to hear them prefer the marble toy-shop of Adrianopolis, the mushroom of the Calabar, to a Babylon so steadfastly founded, an oak, whose roots have struck so deep as the City of the Guinea Coast, is most hateful, most maddening, to any man cursed with a tithe less folly than themselves.

While Branwell compiles a census of the seven provinces of Angria, his sister sings "A National Ode for the Angrians," [4] reflecting the spirit of these same provinces:

> Zamorna lifts her fruitful hills like Eden's to the
>   sky,
> And fair as Enna's fields of flowers her golden
>   prairies lie;
> And Angria calls from mount and vale, from wood
>   and heather-dell,
> A song of joy and thankfulness on rushing winds
>   to swell.

When invasion threatens the land, Charlotte is not, like her brother, concerned with the number of troops in the field and the alliances of the various factions, but sees in her mind's eye a pageant of mobilization that sets her heart throbbing: Enara gathering his serfs on Douro's bank; Warner calling his clan "from hut and hall on Highland heath"; Moray marching at the head of his vassals; Arundel setting his horsemen in motion; Young Stewart's "lofty flame" waving the signal for advance to his men; Roslyn's men bounding from the depths of the mountain glens—all singing the great Angrian chorus:

> We'll sheathe not the avenging sword till earth
>   and sea and skies
> Through all God's mighty universe shout back,
>   "Arise! Arise!"

---

[4] Charlotte Brontë: "A National Ode for the Angrians." By Arthur Augustus Adrian Wellesley. July 17, 1834. 66 lines. (Bonnell Collection.)

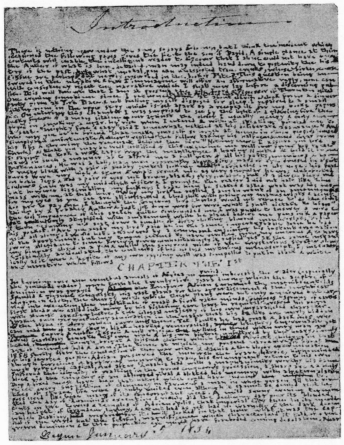

Page (Exact Size) from a "A Leaf from an Unopened Volume"
by Charlotte Brontë

Till Angria reigns Lord Paramount wherever
human tongue
The "Slaves Lament," the "Emperor's Hymn"
in woe or bliss hath sung.

For Captain Flower's detailed statements of the building of Adrianopolis, Charlotte allows us to overhear Zamorna's enthusiastic report
to the Queen: [5]

"Mary, Mary," said the Duke, drawing himself quickly up to the height
of his stately stature and passing his hand over his brow, "Adrianopolis is rising, soaring (not so, either, or it may soar away!) but the buildings spring
like magic, and I and Warner see that they are solidly put together. Men
gather in my kingdom as if they gathered at beat of drum. . . . My subjects
want to have another sight of their sweet Queen, too."

In the midst of the development of Angria, Charlotte wrote a friend
visiting in London: "Will you be kind enough to inform me of the
number of performers in the King's military band? Branwell wishes
for this information." Branwell was preparing for the coronation of
Angria's emperor and, as usual, wished to outdo reality.

Charlotte's expressions of interest in the newly created kingdom
lagged behind her brother's. It was not until fairly late in 1834 that
Angria took full possession of her writing. Earlier stories of that year
betray the restlessness of a growing mind seeking a satisfying theme
for development. "A Leaf from an Unopened Volume," [6] dated
January 17, strikingly out of character, illustrates her unbounded literary curiosity. The most melodramatic and unpleasant of all her writing, it is a confused medley of intrigue, licentiousness, and fraternal
hate, with illegitimate or disowned children, dwarfs, and Negroes playing leading parts. As none of the events which make up its long,
loosely woven plot become an accepted part of Angrian history, it is
interesting chiefly in contrast to her admonition in a letter to a friend
to "adhere to standard authors and avoid novelty." Sage advice while
she herself was exploring the slums of literature!

In this same letter, dated July 4, 1834, Charlotte now eighteen, re-

[5] "Corner Dishes" Chap. III.
[6] Charlotte Brontë: "A Leaf from an Unopened Volume." Edited by Lord Charles
Albert Florian Wellesley. Preface by Sergeant Tree, January 17, 1834. 20,000 words.
(Library of A. Edward Newton.)

ports to her friend, Ellen Nussey: "I am not grown a bit, but [am] as short and dumpy as ever."

She completed within this period "High Life in Verdopolis," [7] a delightful orgy of Byronism. The text, "which treats principally of lords, ladies, knights, and squires of high degree," is introduced by a paraphrase of a familiar passage from *Childe Harold*:

> A gladder day usurped the place of night,
> For Africa's capital had gathered then,
> Her beauty and her chivalry, and bright
> The lamps shone o'er fair women and brave men.

One of its scenes shows Mary Percy, the three months bride of Zamorna, experiencing the agony which was the inevitable penalty any woman paid for his love. He, while torturing his young wife by flirtations with Maria Sneachi, is insanely jealous of her slightest notice of her old lover, Sir Robert Pelham. Misunderstanding an incident which occurs in the course of a grand reception at the Palace, he shows his displeasure in such a manner as to send Mary into a near swoon. Coldly placing her in a chair near the window, he proceeds to lead forth in a dance "the charming and brilliant" Maria Sneachi, "whose cheeks glowed with the brightest of pleasure as the irresistible Zamorna whirled her away to the giddy and wheeling waltz with a cavalier-like unceremoniousness that none but his omnipotent and audacious self dared have used toward a princess of the blood."

The sight of Mary's miserable face, "so like Marian's in its despair," at last moved Douro to tenderness. Crossing to her "with his lightest tread, he folded his arms and rested them on the back of her chair, then bending down till his lips almost touched hers, recited in that beguiling undertone of his, which was given him to entice," a poem of inquiry as to the reason of her sadness:

> My lady turned her from the light
>   Which filled her castle halls
> To where through veil and shade of night,
>   The driven moon-beam falls.

---

[7] Charlotte Brontë: "High Life in Verdopolis, or The Difficulties of Annexing a Suitable Title to a Work Practically Illustrated." In six chapters. By Lord C. A. F. Wellesley. February 20–March 20, 1834. 22 pp., 38,000 words. (British Museum.)

> Why does she leave the dance and song;
>   The sweet harp's stirring tone?
> Why turns she from the glittering throng,
>   To sigh and mourn alone?

Mary turns round, takes the hand which was now laid on her shoulder, kisses it fondly, and replies with admirable tact:

> She dreamt she saw a glance of fire
>   Shot forth from princely eyes,
> And viewed the scarlet flush of ire
>   To brow of marble rise.
> The troubling dream is past and o'er;
>   Beloved, *thy* love will sigh no more.

Joy restored, Zamorna leads Mary away to dance, stopping her attempted explanation with, "Hush, Love, don't attempt to extenuate. Leave your husband, Mary, to find out his own faults if he has done wrong, and never, either by inference or direct assertion, show him where they lie."

Soon after completing "High Life in Verdopolis," Charlotte attempted in "The Spell" [8] to weave around the Duke of Zamorna a legend of dual personality, suggested, perhaps, by a current story of Byron, but the theme was beyond her ability, and was dropped from the Angrian canon.

"The Spell" left its trace, however, on later writings, for Lord Charles's "six Seymour cousins" here paraded come out in *The Professor* as the six Seacombe cousins, and in *Shirley* they appear as the six Misses Sykes.

Of the several new characters introduced in "The Spell," only one, a mystery child called Ernest, retains his place of prominence in the Angrian story. To explain his presence, Charlotte in later narratives, names him Edward Ernest Gordon, and adds to Zamorna's already complicated marital adventures a boyhood alliance antedating his marriage to Marian Hume:

Ernest . . . was born in seclusion. The deep and solemn woodlands of the West gave him a sequestered home and his ill-fated mother an obscure grave. Helen Victorina, the young and beautiful Lily of Lock Sunart, died in the

---

[8] Charlotte Brontë: "The Spell, an Extravaganza." By Lord Charles Albert Florian Wellesley. June 21–July 21, 1834. 26 pp., 42,000 words. (British Museum.)

sickness of hope deferred on the same day that the Duke of Zamorna's first-born son entered a world which I fear is not destined to be a bright or blissful one to him.[9]

Into her characterization of the child Charlotte injects her newly acquired knowledge of Byron's "cutthroat" Gordon ancestors: "It is not to be supposed . . . that Ernest is all placid goodness. . . . No; Zamorna is his father, and the Gordons, the dark, malignant, scowling Gordons, are his blood relatives."

At this point, as if fearing that her hypothetical reader may become lost in the complicated maze she is weaving, Charlotte pauses for one of her useful periodical summaries, recommended as "Corner Dishes, Being a Small Collection of Mixed and Unsubstantiated Trifles in Prose and Verse. . . . Begun, May 28th, 1834. Finished June 16th, 1834." [10] The title is followed by the cryptic introduction:

The frail bark which I now launch onto the boisterous tide of public opinion is freighted purely with a dish of syllabub. I say no more. *Verbum sap,* &c.

In the first of its three pieces, "A Peep into a Picture Book," [11] Lord Charles, who is doing the peeping, "reads the characters" of Charlotte's favorite Angrians, whose portraits are before him. His first comment is for Percy, Earl of Northangerland, emphasizing his Luciferian nature:

In my opinion this head embodies the most vivid ideas we can conceive of Lucifer, the rebellious archangel; there is such a total absence of human feeling and sympathy; such a cold frozen pride; such a fathomless power of intellect; such passionless yet perfect beauty—not breathing and burning, full of lightning blood and fiery thought and feeling like that of some others whom our readers will recollect—but severely studied, faultlessly refined, as cold and hard and polished and perfect as the most priceless brilliant. And then in his eye there is a shade of something, words cannot express what. . . . A gleam, scarcely human, dark and fiend-like, it steals away under the lash, quivers sometimes with the mysterious tremor of a northern light, fixes steadfastly on some luckless bystander, who shrinks from the supernatural aspect, and then is all at once quenched. Once that marvelous light

[9] Charlotte Brontë: "The Scrap-Book: A Mingling of Many Things." Compiled by Lord C. A. F. Wellesley. March 17, 1835. 31 pp., 53,000 words. (British Museum Library.)
[10] 19,100 words plus 282 ll. (Henry E. Huntington Library.)
[11] Printed by C. W. Hatfield in *The Twelve Adventures and Other Stories.*

fell on me; and long after I beheld it vanish, its memory haunted me like a spirit. The sensation which it excited was very singular. I felt as if he could read my soul; and, strange to tell, there was no fear lest he should find sinful thoughts and recollections there, but a harassing dread lest anything good might arise which would awake the tremendous power of sarcasm that I saw lurking in every feature of his face.

Percy's portrait is followed, as is fitting, by that of "his Countess . . . the lady of Ellrington House, . . . the prima donna of the Angrian Court, the most learned woman of her age, the modern Cleopatra, the Verdopolitan de Staël," an Amazon in physical strength and a maniac in temper:

Who would think that that grand form of feminine majesty could launch out into the unbridled excesses of passion which her ladyship not infrequently indulges? . . . It would seem as if neither fire nor pride nor imperiousness could awaken the towering fits of ungoverned and frantic rage that often deform her beauty. . . . Is it natural that such hands should inflict the blows that sometimes tingle from them? . . . She can spar, I verily believe, with her own husband, one of the best boxers on record.

Lord Charles begins his portrait study with the second volume of the set; presently, he takes up the first, which opens with Zamorna and his queen: "The originals of these two engraved portraits," he states, "hang in the grand refectory at Wellesley House. Five hundred guineas was the sum paid for each. They are De Lisle's, and rank amongst his most perfect *chefs-d'œuvre*." He rhapsodizes:

Fire! Light! What have we here? Zamorna's self blazing in the frontispiece like the sun on his own standard. . . . Keen, glorious being! tempered and bright and sharp and rapid as the scimitar at his side when whirled by the delicate yet vigorous hand that now grasps the bridle of a horse to all appearances as viciously beautiful as himself. O Zamorna! what eyes those are glancing under the deep shadow of that raven crest! They bode no good. Man nor woman could ever gather more than a troubled, fitful happiness from their kindest light. . . . All here is passion and fire unquenchable. Impetuous sin, stormy pride, diving and soaring enthusiasm, war and poetry are kindling their fires in all his veins, and his wild blood boils from his heart and back again like a torrent of new-spring lava.

Among the "unsubstantiated trifles" of this volume, is one headed "Stanzas on the Fate of Henry Percy," a poem in *Childe Harold* verse stanzas, which marks Charlotte's awakening to a new conception of romantic love. The argument reveals that Marian Hume, like Zamorna, experienced a child marriage before they two met, her posthumous husband—shall we say?—being Henry Percy, son of Alexander Percy. Percy, so the story goes in retrospect, displeased at the marriage, sends his son on a voyage to the South Seas where he is murdered by command. Just before the fatal blow is struck, the sleeping Henry sees in a dream his child bride yielding to the wooing of Zamorna,

> . . . she who was his bride
> Ere thirteen summer suns had flung their ray
> With gentlest glow on her youth's springing pride.

He perceives the difference between her innocent affection for himself and her awakening passion for Zamorna, a distinction which was just dawning in Charlotte's own consciousness:

> Yes, it is love, but not such love as thine:
>   Not that pure, young affection of the breast
> That used to breathe of peace and bliss divine,
>   And o'er her white brow fling a shade of rest.
> Oft with his hand in hers in transport pressed
> Henry had watched that calm fall on her cheek,
>   And while his own heart felt most deeply blessed
> Has wished a blush of bashfulness to break
> What seemed to him too still, too sisterly, too meek.
>
>   . . . .
>
> Now passion's waves of conflict o'er her rush:
>   The sob, the tear, the pallid brow reveal
> How wildly strong the love her heart and spirit feel.

This belated invention of Marian's marriage to Henry Percy, coming into existence more than a year after the story that records the heroine's death, persists through the remainder of the cycle and is the occasion for an utterance by Marian, again in retrospect, having the ring of Jane Eyre's passionate declaration to Rochester in the garden:

"The fact is that I have far keener feelings than any other human being I ever knew. I have seen a hundred times beautiful women round me, compared with whom I was in appearance only a puppet, and in mind, in imagination,

I knew them dull, apathetic, cold, to me . . . and if Lord Douro ever thinks to be loved again with half the burning intensity with which I *have* loved him, with which I *do* love him, with which, if he were torturing me, I *should* love him, he is deluded."

Marian in eclipse is a step in the direction of Charlotte's favorite theme of later years: passionate devotion over against fortunate situations.

Chapter XII

PATRICK BENJAMIN WIGGINS

The second of the "Corner Dishes" has a strange, un-Charlotte-like flavor suggesting that the ingredients were brought from the Black Bull Inn. The reader is, therefore, the more impressed with her skill in dressing them into the merry dish she sets before her imaginary public.

Interest in pugilism, popularized by high society, had reached even remote Haworth. At the village boxing club, an extension of the groups that haunted the Black Bull Inn, Branwell through the sporting columns of *Bell's Life in London* became familiar with the names and attainments of the better known boxers and professional trainers of the metropolis, enjoying vicariously a glory peculiarly dazzling to a youth of his own slight physique and sensitive nerves. At the same time his easily acquired knowledge attracted the soothing and flattering deference of his rude associates. Maurice Flanagan, of "Corner Dishes," Zamorna's pugilistic protégé, is at once a reflection of Branwell's interest in the ring and an adaptation of Byron's friend and boxing master, "Gentleman Jackson."

In this story is presented for the second time a character brought into the cycle with the creation of Angria, Warner Howard Warner, head of the clan of Howards, Agars, and Warners, who established themselves in Angria several generations before the country was ceded to Zamorna. The new monarch was wise enough to invite Warner to take the portfolio of home secretary in his government, thereby attaching to himself an efficient statesman and loyal friend. First introduced in "High Life in Verdopolis," as he sought among the Angrian ladies for a wife, "young, rich, handsome, graceful, accomplished, and good tempered," Warner appears utterly commonplace and uninteresting except for his gift of second sight, but as he comes and goes through succeeding stories, the reader begins to recognize the hero of *Villette* in the making.

Early one morning—so runs this scene of "Corner Dishes"—Lord Charles, tempted by the brilliance of the weather to make a series of calls in Verdopolis, seeks out his cat "Groby, the brother of Muzzle," and tucking him under his arm for company, "leaves Thornton Hotel and proceeds in the direction of Howard Square." Much pleased by the picture he makes, he walks bareheaded, threading his way through the crowd of pedestrians with his cat pressed by his elbow to his side, flourishing a slight rattan cane in his right hand, to "Warner's splendid residence in the square above mentioned." On the steps of "Warner Hotel" he finds two men in hot discussion. The first is Henry Warner, brother to Warner Howard Warner, a clergyman who foreshadows the curates of *Shirley*. This reverend gentleman has been summoned by his brother to appear before him and answer for behavior which shames his priestly office and threatens the interests of the family. The other is Arthur O'Connor, one-time boon companion and partner of Rogue, trying to encourage the worried and hesitating churchman, who grumbles:

"I'd as leave go to breakfast on sulphur and brimstone in company with one whose name I seldom mention except on Sunday as enter the door of the house we're now besieging like starved rats around the entrance of a dairy; but 'needs must when the devil drives' so there's no help for it."

"Help for it?" replied the other in a tone of braggadocian swagger, "Yes, there's me, and am not I help enough to defend a reverend gentleman in trouble against all the whey-faced hermaphrodites in the world?"

"Ay," was the reply, uttered with a disconsolate groan, "you don't know Howard, O'Connor. He's no hermaphrodite, unless that long word means a creature half horse, half alligator. He has a tongue that would outring a woman's, and that's saying a great deal."

"A tongue!" shouted O'Connor, "What care I for that? . . . Zounds! I promise you if I could have been done up with words, I should have been nestling side by side with Darn and Carem before this. Rogue used to give us enough of them. My word! I've heard him swear many a time till questionable company has been raised like a cock in the very midst of us." . . .

With these words, he delivered a loud and thundering rap on the door. On its being opened, we were all three shown upstairs.

They are passed into a splendid breakfast room, where above twenty gentlemen are assembled, all bearing the names of Howard, Warner, or Agar. Each has a taunting or teasing remark for the clergyman who occasioned their being called together, until the object of this bantering is at length worried completely out of patience.

"Hang our head!" he exclaimed, reddening with passion, "and hang Angria, and behead the Duke and Duchess, and drown the Primacy, and break Stanhope on the wheel! Zounds, gentlemen! Am I to be treated in this way merely because I happen to be a parson? That circumstance is my misfortune and not my fault. Nature never cut me out for such a thing any more than the rest of you. I was born to drink claret, shuffle cards, and throw dice; to hunt hares, shoot partridges, and ply a knife and fork; and because I follow my destiny, I'm to be called up every now and then to be rated and abused before all the family. But I'll stand it no longer, I'm de-termined——"

He is interrupted by "the well-known silver voice" of his dreaded brother, ordering the group to breakfast. The sudden solemnity of the seated company, looking "as grave as the devout congregation of a country church," is too much for young Mrs. Warner. "At length her keen sense of the ludicrous prevailed. . . . She could hold out no longer, but pushing back her seat and covering her blushing face with her hands, she gave way at once to the laughter which had been con-vulsing her internally."

Her mirth precipitates the reproof that all have been dreading. Her husband looks at her, but addresses his offending brother:

Henry Warner (I dare not add the epithet "Reverend"), when your shame-ful irregularities begin to bear upon the interests of the family generally, when you are depriving the house, whose head I am, of accessions of power and consequence which would dignify it and ultimately benefit all Angria . . . when you are herding with associates too low and degraded to merit even the reproof of a respectable member of society . . . it would be a crime in me to remain any longer silent. Sir, it is my way to act, as well as to speak, and be assured, if I do not see an instant and serious and radical reform in all your habits, and an immediate abandonment of everything unbecoming a clergyman, and a sincere assumption of correct and orderly manners, I will myself write to his Grace the Primate of Verdopolis, and request your dismissal from the church.

O'Connor too drunk to heed the snubs he has received in the Warner house, here rises to resent the implications of the speaker's reference to Henry Warner's associates. His host's only notice of his impudence is to order him from the room and the house.

"Aye, is that the chat?" roared O'Connor, "you little epitome of the leavings of nature's workshop, you compound of all sorts and sexes, do you think I'll stir a foot's breadth for you? No, my little hermaphrodite! . . . He . . . who has overcome the wildest moods of Alexander Rogue; he who has stood against Northangerland, drunk or sober, bond or free, shot or hanged; he who has cheated that blackguard Gordon, fought with the giant Montmorency, out-argued the Countess Zenobia, beguiled suckling-doves, bullied half Verdopolis, and finally broken stones on the road; the hero who has done all this may well make light of that which is only part of a man."

Warner Howard Warner meets the situation by asking O'Connor, "Are you not head-supervisor of the Angrian Excise? . . . Say that you *were,* from this moment. I, as Home Secretary, dismiss you in disgrace from the office."

This dire pronouncement effectively sobers O'Connor, who takes hurried leave of Warner Hotel to lay his appeal before the Queen of Angria, the King being in far-off Adrianopolis. Lord Charles, after more leisurely and friendly good-bys, follows him.

Whether or not Charlotte in her practical family relations yet saw the ruinous tendencies of her brother's village associations, she, as Lord Charles, in their completely amoral world of Angria, paints his weaknesses with peculiar clarity, but without condemnation, in the good-natured, teasing, satirical portrait of Patrick Benjamin Wiggins—Patrick Branwell Brontë—discovered in the Queen's waiting room:

His form was that of a lad of sixteen, his face that of a man of twenty-five, his hair red, his features not bad, for he had a Roman nose, small mouth, and well-turned chin; his figure, too, though diminutive, was perfectly symmetrical, and of this he seemed not unconscious from the frequent complacent looks he cast down on his nether man. A pair of spectacles garnished his nose, and through these he was constantly gazing at Flanagan [Zamorna's boxing master], whose breadth of shoulder appeared to attract his sincere admiration, as every now and then he touched his own with the tip of his fore-finger, and pushed out his small contracted chest to make it appear broader.

Of course by this time my readers will have recognized Patrick Benjamin Wiggins, that quizzical little personage whose *outre* manners and almost insane devotion to all the celebrated characters in Verdopolis, whose "lick-spittle general" he openly professed himself to be, have of late absorbed so much of the public attention. I addressed him, "Well, Mr. Wiggins, what can possibly be your business here today?"

"My business, Lord Charles? Oh, nothing at all, that is, nothing of any consequence. I'm just here with Mr. Greenwood who is now in her Grace's boudoir. . . . Do you know, my Lord, Mr. Greenwood is going to England? I thought of following him, but last night Dragonetti spoke to me, and so—"

"You'll toady for him, I suppose?"

"Yes, if your lordship thinks proper to say so; that is, I'll do anything Mr. Dragonetti tells me to. But, my Lord, who is the gentleman just opposite to us with red hair and a splendid pair of arms and shoulders?"

"That's Flanagan, the famous boxer."

"Is it? Is it? You'll excuse me, my Lord, for going away, but—but, in short, I want to see whether he would look at me, if I went a little nearer. A fine man! Beautiful hair! Flanagan the great boxer! He *has* a chest."

So saying, Wiggins edged away from me on towards Pratee [nickname for Flanagan]. I would have stayed on to watch his manoeuvers, but just then a rich burst of music arose from the inner room, and while it transfixed him, for the creature has considerable taste in all relating to the fine arts, ir-resistibly drew *me* in the direction whence it proceeded.

The music came from the Queen at her lesson with the great master, Greenwood. When the lesson is finished and the master is departing, Mary says: 'Next time you come to Wellesley House . . . bring with you that *rara avis* Mr. Patrick Wiggins. I have heard a good deal of him lately and I wish to see him."

Upon being told that the person she wishes to see is in the anteroom, she directs that he be shown in immediately.

"Come forward, sir," said she, extending her small, snowy hand (the exact miniature resemblance of her father's) toward a chair which stood near her, "be seated; I wish to cultivate your acquaintance if you will allow me."

"I—I, my lady, I am a dog, that is, a toad. I would rather stand, if you please, or sit down on the carpet, or walk three yards on my head, or anything you think proper to bid me."

"You are very gallant, Mr. Wiggins, quite a knight of the old stamp, but I will not be so harsh as the dames of *their* devotion were. My present mandate shall only consist in requesting your acceptance of the seat at my right hand."

Wiggins still hesitated, but Greenwood who was standing behind, laid hold of the back of his neck, and so pushed him forwards. At length the young gentleman established himself on the offered chair, occupying, however, only the extreme edge of the cushion, and thereby giving an undue prominence to his knees which were bashfully protruded forward, while his feet were drawn in under, the toes only on the ground and the heels in the air.

"I beg that you will make yourself comfortable," said the Duchess. "Don't be under any restraint on my account."

"Oh, I'm quite comfortable, my Lady; the edge of the chair is too much for a villain, a rascal like me. But—but, my Lady," he continued, suddenly poking his nose and sharp spectacled face up into Mary's, "you have got such a—such a—in short, the fact is,—I mean—rogue, scoundrel, beast that I am—I would say you have got such a beautiful nose!"

With these audacious words, he bent forward, raised his hand, and actually laid hold of the beautiful and sacred feature, which I verily believe was never before desecrated by mortal touch, except once or twice when I have seen Zamorna's fingers lightly and playfully passed down the polished ivory line from brow to under lip, and the result of the experiment when performed by him was, I think, very soothing and agreeable.

Wiggins's effrontery did not remain unpunished. The very chair he sat on rose in rebellion against him. In stooping to commit the sacrilege, he lost the slight balance that had before supported him; the cushion slipped, the chair kicked up, and prone he came, prostrate as a felled calf before the indignant Duchess, who pushed him rather passionately with her little foot, started up, brow, cheek, and neck glowing with one flush of crimson, and moved off toward the window.

"Curse the idiot, the born natural!" exclaimed Greenwood. . . . "Didn't you know, Sir, that her Grace's nose was not to be mentioned or even looked at, much less touched? Touched! The very flesh creeps on my bones! Touched! Tremendous! Handel's choruses will become jigs, and Mozart's masses turned to Wesleyan psalm-tunes. Touched! What will his Grace say? . . . Stir yourself!"

Charlotte continues her exaggerated portrait of Branwell as Wiggins in "My Angria and the Angrians,"[1] written in October of this same year (1834). Lord Charles, having scornfully refused to join in

[1] See Note 3 (p. 81).

the Angrian exodus from Verdopolis, lest his so doing imply submission to his brother, now sets out alone on foot for the new capital, stating his choice thus: "I who might have commanded a carriage and a *posse* of attendants chose to set out on a journey of one hundred miles with no other aid but such as my own bodily limbs afforded me, and the prospective chance of a rest in the carts and wagons I might meet by the way." Presently he is joined by Patrick Benjamin Wiggins, whom he describes as "a low, slightly-built man, attired in a black vest and raven-gray trousers, his hat placed nearly at the back of his head, revealing a bunch of carroty hair so arranged that at the sides it projected almost like two spread hands, a pair of spectacles placed across a prominent Roman nose, black neckerchief adjusted with no great attention or precision, and, to complete the picture, a little black rattan flourished in the hand. His bearing as he walked was tolerably upright, and marked with that indescribable swing always assumed by those who pride themselves on being good pedestrians."

His response to Lord Charles's greeting suggests that Charlotte was getting even for her brother's patronizing:

"An uncommonly fine morning, Lord Charles. I'm excessively glad to see you; hope you are going a good way along the road; shall be glad of your company, that is, if you can keep up with me. . . . I don't think of walking much farther than Zamorna. I came to Edwardston last night and slept there. . . . The distance, you know, Lord Charles, is forty miles, and I did it all in twelve hours. Indeed it is more than forty—nearer fifty, I believe—oh, yes, and above sixty, I dare say, or sixty-five. Now, sir, what do you say to a man's walking sixty-five miles in one day?"

Their conversation was interrupted by the approach of Edward Percy "riding at a rapid trot on a splendid bay horse." Lord Charles watched him down the road and then turned back to Wiggins. "Lo! he was fallen upon his face, flat as a fluke, motionless as a dead herring, prostrated towards the east like a Parsee worshipping the new-risen sun." The deafening rush and rattle of the Angrian coach on the road made him "spring up pretty actively," but no sooner was he on his feet than he broke out with:

"Base dunghill cock that I am! I, super-annuated, doting, blind worm, deformed mongrel, turnspit, wretch, thief, highwayman, assassin, murderer, pick-pocket, petty larcenist, dog-stealer, essence of plague, pestilence, and famine! . . . I, that I should live after having seen Percy, the son of Northangerland, pass by without either shooting or spitting at me! Why didn't I throw myself under the wheels of that coach, like a Hindoo beneath the car of Juggernaut? And I dare say there were great men contained in it, too! . . . But, dear me! What am I saying? How can I think, talk, or dream about anybody except Mr. Edward Percy riding along on that grand horse, which must be worth five hundred guineas, that is, eight hundred or else a thousand, at such an early hour, and without either footman or page or any such trash trailing after him. He's determined to reach Zamorna first and order all things according to his own will. I hope he'll command abundance of accommodation to be provided for the bands of music. . . . There are to be five brass bands, each consisting of two trumpets, three bombardones, four cyclopedes, five serpents, six bugles, seven French-horns, eight gongs, nine kettle-drums, and ten ramgalongtinas, a new kind of instrument that's never been blown in Africa before. And then the five wood bands will contain eleven flutes, . . . twelve clarionets, thirteen piccolos—"

Lord Charles interrupts this tirade to question Wiggins as to his private history. His answer is Charlotte's opportunity for a bit of family fun, in which Thorncliffe stands for Thornton, where the four little Brontës were born, and Howard for Haworth:

"Why, Lord Charles, I was born partly at Thorncliffe, that is, after a fashion, but then I always account myself a native of Howard a great city among the Warner hills under the domination of that wonderful and super-human gentleman, WARNER HOWARD WARNER, Esqre. (here he took off his hat and bowed low). It had four churches and above twenty grand hotels, and a street called the Tarn Gate, far wider than Bridgenorth in Free Town."

"None of your humbug, Wiggins," said I, "I know well enough that Howard is only a miserable little village, buried in dreary moors, and moss-hags, and marshes. I question whether it has one church, or anything nearer an hotel than that way-side ale-house you are now eyeing so longingly."

"I'm rather thirsty," replied he, "and I think I'll call for a pot of porter or a tumbler of brandy and water at the public yonder."

What Wiggins actually got was "two or three cups of tea, with a due quantity of bread and butter very rapidly discussed," but he came back boasting:

"I feel like a lion now, at any rate. Two bottles of Sneachi's Glass-town ale, and a double quart of porter, with cheese, bread, and cold beef, have I devoured since I left you, Lord Charles . . . and I'm not a bit touched, only

light and smart and active. I'd defy all the ganders in Christendom now
—that I would! and a hundred goslings to boot. . . . What were you asking me, sir?"

"I asked you where you were born, sir, and now I ask you what relations you have?"

"Why, in a way, I may be said to have no relations. I can't tell you who
my father and mother were, no more than that stone. I've some people who
call themselves akin to me in the shape of three girls. They are honoured
by possessing me as a brother, but I deny that they are my sisters. . . ."

"What are your sisters' names?"

"Charlotte Wiggins, [Emily] Jane Wiggins, and Anne Wiggins."

"Are they as queer as you?"

"Oh, they are miserable, silly creatures, not worth talking about. Charlotte's
eighteen years old, a broad dumpy thing, whose head does not come higher
than my elbow. Emily's sixteen, lean and scant, with a face about the size of a
penny, and Anne's nothing, absolutely nothing."

"What! Is she an idiot?"

"Next door to it."

"Humph! you're a pretty set."

Wiggins's answer to Lord Charles's next question bespeaks Branwell's ambition to try his talents in London:

"But pray, Master Wiggins, what first induced you to leave Howard and
come to Verdopolis?"

"Why, you see, Lord Charles, my mind was always looking above my
station. I wasn't satisfied with being a sign-painter at Howard, as Charlotte
and them things were with being sempstresses. I set before myself the grand
plain of Africa, and I traced a path for my own feet through it, which terminated at the door of a splendid palace situated on Cock Hill, whose portal
bore inscribed, 'Residence of the Duke of Thorncliffe,' and beyond that, a
tomb under the oaks of my own park, showing to the passengers such words
as these, 'Erected to the memory of Patrick Benjamin Wiggins, Duke of
Thorncliffe and Viscount Howard. As a musician, he was greater than
Bach; as a poet, he surpassed Byron; as a painter, Claude Lorrain yielded to
him; as a rebel, he snatched the realm from Alexander Rogue; as a mer-
chant, Edward Percy was his inferior; as a mill-owner, Granville came not
near him; as a traveller, De Humboldt, Ledyard, Mungo Park, etc., etc.,
never braved half his dangers, or overcame half his difficulties. He civilized
Australia, he founded the city of Wigginopolis in New Zealand; he erected
the obelisk of Baralitius in Otaheite, to which country he also introduced
the arts and sciences which now flourish there in such perfection; and
last and greatest of his mighty acts, he built the stupendous organ called

rollrogthunderandsqueakandotheroreimus now glorifying the Cathedral of St. Northangerland in his native place of Howard. Having earned all this meed of renown and attained his four hundred and sixth year, this *summum bonum* of human grandeur was at length rapt to Heaven in a fiery chariot, which miraculous event took place about the year two thousand two hundred and forty.' "

While Charlotte was writing this picture of her brother as Wiggins, he, seventeen years old and still playing a game of wooden soldiers at their wars, set in motion all the earlier enumerated forces of opposition to the new kingdom of Angria. But more dangerous than outside foes are jealousies and dissensions within, engendered and fostered by Zamorna's powerful coadjutor, Northangerland, mouthpiece for Branwell's rebellion complex and agent for his spirit of destruction. That strange nobleman, unable long to submit to the leadership of any man or to keep faith with any friend, is ready to wreck his own structure rather than acknowledge allegiance to another. By devious and subtle means he tries to rouse in the king jealousy of his ministers, and to plant in the hearts of the people fear and distrust of their monarch, his son-in-law, Zamorna, whom he represents as a voluptuary with brain and will shattered by dissipation. In a final treasonable move, he joins with the Marquis of Ardrah—Emily's deserted favorite—in a Verdopolitan plot against Angria.

The gathering storm gave both Charlotte and Branwell the theme for many pages of wearisome and absurd newspaper and platform oratory. Charlotte's effusions are grouped together in a volume called "The Scrap Book [2] A Mingling of Many Things. Compiled by Lord C. A. F. Wellesley." Its first piece, "Address to the Angrians by His Grace The Duke of Zamorna," throws down the gauntlet to Northangerland. A fragment by Branwell [3] recounts the dismay of Lord Richton in Verdopolis as he reads it the following morning in "The Heart of Angria." The next day the lords lieutenant of the several provinces of Angria, issue handbills calling mass meetings in their respective capitals to take action on their king's challenge.

The theme and tone of Zamorna's "Address" are continued by Charlotte in a "Speech at the opening of the first Angrian Parlia-

---

[2] See Note 8 (p. 86).   [3] Transcript received from C. W. Hatfield.

ment," another of her futile attempts to analyze Percy's satanic character:

The letter before alluded to . . . is like hemlock. . . . Its qualities contain a mixture of good and evil. There is a tone of subdued tranquil sadness pervading it. . . . Its very sound might beguile a listener, but . . . in its pages there is often conveyed, through a strain of language which might befit a weary, persecuted saint . . . sentiments which a demon's heart alone could have engendered.

This speech is followed by the "Opposition's" picture of the king as an Eastern voluptuary, "extracted from the last number of the Northern Review." Its anonymous author, the Marquis of Ardrah, pictures Zamorna as a "poor insane being," about to fling himself and his people into a war through a personal whim. Zamorna retaliates in a "Letter to the Right Honourable Arthur, Marquis of Ardrah," dated December 6, 1834. There the quarrel rests until March 16, 1835, when, according to the "Verdopolitan Intelligencer," Zamorna drags his grievances before the General Parliament on the night of its opening session, serving notice to his fellow sovereigns and peers that no advice from them would be heard. He addresses himself to Percy:

What I hate most in all your conduct . . . is the tone of pretended candour and partiality you have chosen to assume towards me. Am I not aware, my Lord, that the man never breathed whom you could regard with one feeling of friendship? Do I not know that you are unable to tolerate your fellow creatures, that your soul is too cold and vitiated for sympathy with them? Have I yet to learn that the conformation of your strange nervous system obliges you to hate that man worst whom by a stretch of dissimulation you have pretended to admire, and that, consequently, I, of all living men, am the most utterly abominable to you? Happily this has been taught me by sharp experience. . . .
You know that selfish weakness in my character which prevents me from ever thoroughly hating or seriously injuring those who I am certain are attached to myself personally, however iniquitous they may be in other respects, so you imagine that by taking due advantage of this unguarded point, by managing it with your own super-human skill, by playing the candid Lucifer with that exquisite tact which none possess save yourself, you might make a few flattering words pass on me, the Royal Idiot, as a sufficient panacea for all the following crimes. . . . Percy, I have made up the catalogue of your crimes: you have hated my friends and you have loved my enemies.

Pencil Drawing by Charlotte Brontë Probably Representing
the Duchess of Zamorna.

Can we then any longer act together? Impossible! Yet it grieves me to part. . . . When we combatted together last year I would have stabbed the man to the heart who should have told me you were so black, so hollow a traitor as I now find you to be. . . . My Lord, I demand the seals of office in your possession. You have ceased to be the Premier of Angria.

All this was said in the hearing of the assembled kings and peers. At its conclusion, the Duke was silent a moment. He then drew quite close to Lord Northangerland, and taking the Earl's hand in both of his, recommenced speaking in a very low but emphatic tone, threatening that if Percy did not immediately sever connection with Ardrah he would strike him to the heart through the only living creature whom he loved—his daughter, Zamorna's wife. Regardless of his own suffering, he (Zamorna) would put her away, and that, Percy knew as well as himself, would kill her. "Take the warning," he urged, "I *will* do as I have said; if eternal death were the immediate consequence my resolution would remain unshaken."

"The Scrap Book," completed March 16, 1835, was, for Charlotte, the final act in the Young Men's Play. With it ended her happy, irresponsible youth.

Chapter XIII

THE INTERIOR OF GAALDINE

WHILE BRANWELL, now seventeen years old, lapsed further into games of war, and Charlotte turned his absurdities into copy for herself, Emily, with Anne, continued the development of Gondal, matching Angria character for character and expansion for expansion. Moving along parallels of contrast, free of basic contradictions and false sentimentality, Emily adhered undeviatingly to eternal principles of morality and human psychology. Thanks to the early influence of the genii, Angria was a completely amoral world where sin was shorn of its natural consequences, and such suffering as had to be admitted for romantic effect was an arbitrary visitation. Its people were good or bad, heroes, or traitors, according to their attitude toward the Byronic egotist, Zamorna. But in Emily's Gondal sin was real, paid for with Old Testament certainty in fixed wages of suffering—real suffering—and death. And Emily admitted no arbitrary force for good or evil; her Gondals were free moral agents following their own wills in accordance with circumstances.

For Angria's glorious, love-compelling Zamorna, whose straying fancy sent susceptible women into pleasurable decline or romantic graves, Emily gave Gondal a beautiful and richly endowed queen, a generous, joy-giving girl, hardening through indulgence of her ardent nature into a selfish, cruel woman ruthlessly feeding her vanity on the souls of men. And in place of sin-haloed Percy, raised by pride above human emotions, Emily envisioned darkly unhappy Douglas, a wronged youth grown into an embittered, conscience-tortured murderer.

To match the expansion of Glass Town into Angria, Emily had her Gondal vikings discover Gaaldine, an island in the South Pacific—

> . . . tropic prairies bright with flowers
> And rivers wandering free—

explore, conquer, and partition it into kingdoms and provinces ruled by representatives of the great Gondalan families. Only two prose records of this conquest have survived, and these, apparently, by accident. On November 24, 1834, Emily, sixteen, set down on paper a series of childish household commonplaces [1] illuminated by one brilliant sentence:

> Taby said just now   Come Anne pilloputate (i. e. pill a potato)   Aunt has come into the kitchen just now and said   Where are your feet Anne   Anne answered   On the floor Aunt. Papa opened the parlour door and gave Branwell a letter saying   Here Branwell read this and show it to your Aunt and Charlotte. The Gondals are discovering the interior of Gaaldine. Sally Mosely is washing in the back kitchen.

And Anne one day pondering over "A Vocabulary of Proper Names" at the end of Goldsmith's *A Grammar of General Geography* [2] inserted alphabetically in pencil a group of Gondalan place names:

> Alexandia [*sic*], A kingdom in Gaaldine.
> Almedore, a kingdom in Gaaldine.
> Elseraden, a kingdom in Gaaldine.
> Gaaldine, a large Island newly discovered in the South Pacific,
> Gondal, a large Island in the North Pacific.
> Regina, the capital of Gondal.
> Ula, a kingdom in Gaaldine, governed by 4 Sovereigns.
> Zelona, a kingdom in Gaaldine.
> Zedora, a large Provence [*sic*] in Gaaldine Governed by a Viceroy.

Chief among the Gondalan *conquistadores* of Gaaldine, was Prince Julius Brenzaida of Angora, who became king of Almedore, and from that position of vantage waged wars of conquest against the neighboring kingdom of Zalona, and finally invaded his native Gondal as claimant to its throne.

By mid-summer 1835 Gondal, like Angria, faced civil war and foreign invasion.

---

[1] Journal fragment. November 24, 1834. 2 pp., 350 words. 4″ x 2½″. (Bonnell Collection.)
[2] See Note 1 (p. 11).

Chapter XIV

CONSCIENCE VERSUS ANGRIA

M ID-SUMMER OF 1835 found Haworth Parsonage in the throes of a family breakup. Branwell's future had become a matter of immediate concern. Low tastes and bad habits acquired from village associates must be broken. The time had come, it was agreed in family council, for him to go into definite training for his long prophesied brilliant career. Ambition pointed toward literature or art, though his strongest passion was for sacred music. He could play the organ after a fashion and knew the works of the great composers. The sound of organ music sent him into raptures. According to one who knew him, "he would walk about the room with measured footsteps, his eyes raised to the ceiling, accompanying the music with his voice in an impassioned manner, and beating time with his hand on the chairs as he passed to and fro."

Charlotte in one of her satires takes notice of her brother's fondness for organ music by having Wiggins stand on his head as an expression of delight in Handel's oratorios:

In the month of May last, a fine and full new organ was opened in Howard Church. At that period John Greenwood, Esqre., the musician and composer, chanced to return from his sojourn in Stumpsland. . . . When I heard of his arrival I stood upon my head for fifteen minutes running. It was news almost too glorious to be believed. . . . I remember the moment when he entered the church, walked up to the organ gallery where I was . . . placed his fingers on the keys, his feet on the pedals, and proceeded to electrify us with "I know that my Redeemer liveth."

Then said I, "This is a god and not a man." As long as the music sounded in my ears I dared neither speak, breathe, or even look up. When it ceased, I glanced furtively at the performer. . . . Instantly I assumed that inverted position which with me is always a mark of highest astonishment, delight, and imagination. In other words, I clapt my pate to the ground and let my heels fly up with a spring.

Mr. Brontë's judgment, however, joyfully acceded to by his son, was that Branwell should become a portrait painter, and Charlotte wrote on July 6, 1835, that he was to enter the Royal Academy at London. She herself seemed predestined to a life of schoolteaching, so when "duty—necessity . . . stern mistresses" spoke in an offer from Miss Wooler of a position in her school, she answered, "Better sune as syne," and wrote with a show of cheerfulness, "Yes! I am going to teach in the very school where I was myself taught." Emily, who had never been inside a schoolroom since Cowan Bridge, almost in her infancy, was to accompany Charlotte as a pupil. The plan worked out but imperfectly.

The girls dreaded the change, though they were grateful that Charlotte's employer was a loved and trusted friend rather than a stranger, while many of her pupils were younger sisters of old schoolmates, and her two closest friends lived within walking distance of the school. Yet Charlotte and Emily, now nineteen and seventeen, were abjectly miserable in their new abode, to the puzzlement of all around them. Truth to tell, they were homesick, suffering from such nostalgia of soul as few persons ever knew, homesick not for Haworth and the moors, nor even for the Parsonage and its family, but for their dream worlds, Angria and Gondal. Deprived in strange surroundings of the only media they had for expressing their creative genius, a natural function of their beings was suspended and they almost died of the suppression.

All this as it pertains to herself, Charlotte pours out in lyrical, passionate, heart-rending pages of her secret journal.[1] "Away from home," she concludes one of these homesick rhapsodies on her dream familiars, "I cannot write of them; except in total solitude, I scarce dare think of them." Years later, trying to interpret Emily to the public, she repeats the story in the more obvious and easily understood terms of ordinary homesickness. "Every morning," she wrote in explanation of Emily's

[1] Diary Fragments, 1835–39. (Bonnell Collection.)

failure to remain at school, "when she awoke, the vision of home and the moors rushed on her, and darkened and saddened the day that lay before her. Soon her white face, attentuated form, and failing strength threatened rapid decline." She concludes with the revealing sentence: "Nobody knew what ailed her but me—I knew only too well." Charlotte knew because she shared her sister's suffering. Convinced that Emily would die if she did not go home, Charlotte arranged for her to return to the Parsonage and for Anne to take her place at Roe Head. Her own greater strength of will enabled her to endure.

Anne fitted well enough into the Roe Head situation; and Charlotte, no longer worried about Emily, had more freedom to consider her own case. Added to exile from Angria was the bitterness of conflict between her two selves. Conscience, long duped by the childish fiction of Lord Charles's railings against his brother, was disillusioned at last and fully roused. Shocked to find the hold the Angrian dream had upon her imagination, and fearing she had fallen into the mortal sin of idolatry, the outward Charlotte was ready to apply rack and torch to extirpate the heresy. A fifteen years war was on.

As an antidote against the blissful, but soul-destroying poison of her imagination, Charlotte sought the comforts of religion and friendship. To a schoolmate, Ellen Nussey, she turned her hysterical cries in letter after letter through three anguished years, never once admitting clearly the true cause of her suffering:

. . . If you knew my thoughts; the dreams that absorb me; and the fiery imagination that at times eats me up and makes me feel society as it *is,* wretchedly insipid, you would pity me and I dare say despise me. But, Ellen, I know the treasures of the Bible, and love and adore them. I can *see* the Well of Life in all its clearness and brightness; but when I stoop down to drink of the pure waters, they fly from my lips as if I were Tantalus. . . . I am in that state of horrid, gloomy uncertainty, that at this moment I would submit to be old, grey-haired, to have passed all my youthful days of enjoyment and be tottering on the verge of the grave, if I could only thereby insure the prospect of reconcilement to God and Redemption through His Son's merits. . . . I am a very coarse, commonplace wretch, Ellen. I have some qualities that make me very miserable, some feelings you can have no participation in, that few, very few people in the world can understand. . . . I read your letter with dismay, Ellen—what shall I do without you? Why are we so to be denied each other's society? It is an unscrutable fatality. . . . Why are we to be divided? Surely, Ellen, it must be because we are in danger of loving each other too well—of losing sight of the *Creator* in idolatry of the *creature*. . . . I go on constantly seeking my own pleasure . . . I forget God, and will not God forget me? . . . You cannot imagine how hard rebellious, and intractable all my feelings are. When I begin to study on the subject, I almost grow blasphemous, atheistical in my sentiments.

But conscience waged a losing battle. While the outward Charlotte poured forth veiled confessions and renunciations to her staid, phlegmatic, and unimaginative friend, the inward Charlotte, writhing under the irritations and tedium of teaching, wooed the Angrian dream. It came first as a fleeting, uncertain memory, adored and tenderly cherished, bringing a degree of comfort into her visionless days. She writes in her journal:

And now once more on a dull Saturday afternoon I sit down to try to summon around me the dim shadows, not of coming events, but of incidents long departed, of feelings, of pleasures, whose exquisite relish I sometimes fear it will never be my lot again to taste. How few would believe that from sources purely imaginary such happiness could be derived! Pen cannot portray the deep interest of the scenes, of the continued train of events, I have witnessed in that little room with the low narrow bed and bare white-washed walls twenty miles away. What a treasure is thought! What a privilege is reverie! I am thankful I have the power of solacing myself with the dream of creations whose reality I shall never behold. May I never lose that power, may I never feel it grow weaker. . . .

Remembrance yields up many fragments of past twilight hours spent in that little unfurnished room. There have I sat on the low bedstead, my eyes fixed on the window, through which appeared no other landscape than a monotonous stretch of moorland and a grey church tower rising from the center of a churchyard so filled with graves that the rank weeds and coarse grass scarce had room to shoot up between the monuments. Over these hangs in the eye of memory a sky of such grey clouds as often veil the chill close of an October day, and low on the horizon glances at intervals through the rack the orb of a lurid and haloed moon. Such was the picture that threw its reflection upon my eye but communicated no impression to my heart. The [mind?] knew but did not feel its existence. It was away; it had launched on a distant voyage, and haply it was nearing the shores of some far and unknown island under whose cliffs no bark had ever before cast anchor. In other words, a long tale was perhaps then evolving itself in my mind, the history of an ancient and aristocratic family, the legendary records of its origin, not preserved in writing but delivered from the lips of old retainers, floating in tradition up and down the woods and vales of Earldom or Dukedom or Barony. . . .

My dream shifted to some distant city, some huge imperial metropolis, where the descendants of the last nobleman, the young lords and ladies, shine in gay circles of patricians, and, dazzled with the brilliancy of courts, . . . sons and daughters have almost forgotten the groves where they were born and grew. As I saw them stately and handsome, gliding through these saloons where many other well-known forms crossed my sight, where there were faces looking up, eyes smiling, and lips moving in audible speech that I knew better almost than my brother and sisters, yet whose voices had never woke an echo in this world, whose eyes had never gazed upon that daylight, what glorious associations crowded upon me, what excitement heated my face and made me clasp my hands in ecstasy! . . .

I am not accustomed to such magnificence as surrounds me. . . . I know nothing of people of rank and distinction, yet there they are before me; in throngs, in crowds they come, they go, they speak, they beckon, and that not like airy phantoms, but as noblemen and ladies of flesh and blood. . . . I know the house, I know the square it stands in. . . . Is it not enjoyment to gaze round upon these changeful countenances, to mark the varied features of those high-born and celebrated guests, some gay and youthful, some proud, cold, and middle-aged, a few bent and venerable; here and there a head throwing the rest into shade? . . . There is one just now crossing, a lady. I will not write her name, though I know it. . . . She is not one of those transcendently fair and inaccessibly sacred beings whose fates are interwoven with the highest of the high. . . . Far from home I cannot write of them; except in total solitude, I scarce dare think of them.

Unable in her exile to continue her creation, she could yet in rare moments lose herself in the emotion of Angria:

Well, here I am at Roe Head. It is seven o'clock at night; the young ladies are all at their lessons; the schoolroom is quiet, the fire is low; a stormy day is at this moment passing off in a murmuring and bleak night. I now assume my own thoughts; my mind relaxes from the stretch on which it has been for the last twelve hours, and falls back onto the rest which nobody in this house knows of but myself. I now, after a day of weary wandering, return to the ark which for me floats alone on the billows of this world's desolate and boundless deluge. It is strange I cannot get used to the ongoings that surround me. I fulfil my duties strictly and well. I, so to speak—if the illustration be not profane,—as God was not in the fire, nor the wind, nor the earthquake, so neither is my heart in the task, the theme, or the exercise, and it is the still small voice alone that comes to me at eventide, that floats like a breeze with a voice in it over the deeply blue hills and out of the now leafless forests and from the cities on distant river banks of a bright and far continent; it is that which takes up my spirit and engrosses all my living feelings, all my energies which are not merely mechanical. . . . Haworth and home wake sensations which lie dormant elsewhere.

Those who stood between her and her dream world were the objects of her smothered resentment:

I am just going to write because I cannot help it. Wiggins [Branwell] might indeed talk of scribblemania if he were to see me just now, encompassed by the bulls (query: calves?) of Bashen all wondering why I write with my eyes shut—staring, gaping—hang their astonishment! E-C-k on one side of me; E-L-r on the other; and Miss W——r in the background, stupidity the atmosphere, school-books the employment, asses the society! What in all this is there to remind me of the divine silent unseen land of thought, dim now, and indefinite as the dream of a dream, the shadow of a shade? . . . That wind, pouring in impetuous current through the air, sounding wildly, unremittingly from hour to hour, deepening its tone as the night advances, coming not in gusts, but with a rapid, gathering stormy swell—that wind I know is heard at this moment far away on the moors of Haworth. Branwell and Emily hear it, and as it sweeps over our house, down the churchyard, and round the old church, they think, perhaps, of me and Anne! Glorious! that blast was mighty; it reminded me of Northangerland; there was something so merciless in the heavier rush that made the very house groan as if it could scarce bear this acceleration of impulse. Oh, it has awakened a feeling that I cannot satisfy. A thousand wishes rise at its call that must die with me, for they will never be fulfilled.

Now I should be agonized if I had not the dream to repose on: its existence, its forms, its scenes do fill a little of the craving vacancy. "Hohenlinden!" "Childe Harold!" "Flodden Field!" "The Burial of Moore!" Why cannot the blood rouse the heart, the heart wake the head, the head prompt the hand to do things like these?

Again she wrote:

Friday August 11th.—All this day I have been in a dream, half-miserable and half-ecstatic,—miserable because I could not follow it out uninterruptedly, ecstatic because it showed almost in the vivid light of reality the ongoings of the infernal world. I had been toiling for nearly an hour with Miss Lister, Miss Marriott, and Ellen Cook, striving to teach them the distinction between an article and a substantive. The parsing lesson was completed; a dead silence had succeeded it in the school room, and I sat sinking from irritation and weariness into a kind of lethargy. The thought came over me: Am I to spend all the best part of my life in this wretched bondage, forcibly suppressing my rage at the idleness, the apathy, and the hyperbolical and most asinine stupidity of these fat-headed oafs, and on compulsion assuming an air of kindness, patience, and assiduity? Must I from day to day sit chained to this chair, prisoned within these four bare walls, while these glorious summer suns are burning in heaven and the year is revolving in its richest glow, and declaring at the close of every summer day, the time I am losing will never come again? Stung to the heart with this reflection, I started up, and mechanically walked to the window. A sweet August morning was smiling without. The dew was not yet dried off the field, the early shadows were stretching cool and dim from the hay-stacks and the roots of the grand old oaks and thorns scattered along the sunk fence. All was still except the murmur of the scrubs about me over their tasks. I flung up the sash. An uncertain sound of inexpressible sweetness came on a dying gale from the south. I looked in that direction. Huddersfield and the hills beyond it were all veiled in blue mist. The woods of Hopton and Heaton Lodge were clouding the water's edge, the Calder, silent but bright, was shooting among them like a silver arrow. I listened—the sound sailed full and liquid down the descent; it was the bells of Huddersfield Parish Church. I shut the window and went back to my seat. Then came on me, rushing impetuously, all the mighty phantasm that this had conjured from nothing,—from nothing to a system strange as some religious creed. I felt as if I could have written gloriously—I longed to write. The spirit of all Verdopolis—of all the mountainous North—of all the woodland West—of all the river-watered East, came crowding into my mind. If I had had time to indulge it I felt that the vague sensations of that moment would have settled down into some narrative better at least than anything I ever produced before. But just then a dolt came up with a lesson.

Even in her ignorance of whither it tended, Charlotte was well aware through suffering of the great awakening going on within her soul. Back at home for the Christmas holidays, she recorded the experience in verse,[2] likening the Young Men's Play to a web woven in childhood, now expanded to all-embracing proportions. The longer the Angrian vision hid its face the more passionately she longed for its return:

When I sat 'neath a strange roof-tree
With naught I knew or loved around me,
Oh, how my heart shrank back to thee!
Then I knew how fast thy ties had bound me.

[2] Charlotte Brontë: "We Wove a Web in Childhood." December 19, 1835. 6 pp., 185 ll. plus 350 words. (Huntington Library.)

In the blackest hour of a stormy day, the cold autumnal twilight, made doubly depressing by the sprinkle of sleet on the window and the wolfish howl of the wind, the vision descended:

> Where was I ere an hour had passed?
> Still listening to that dreary blast?
> Still in that mirthless, lifeless room,
> Cramped, chilled, and deadened by its gloom?
>
> No! thanks to that bright, darling dream!
>   Its power had shot one kindling gleam:
> Its voice had sent one wakening cry,
>   And bade me lay my sorrow by,
> And called me earnestly to come,
>   And borne me to my moorland home.
>
> I heard no more the senseless sound
>   Of task and chat that hummed around:
> I saw no more that grisly night
>   Closing the day's sepulchral light.
> The vision's spell had deepened o'er me;
>   Its lands, its scenes were spread before me.

A free and familiar spirit, she wanders through regal palaces and under lordly domes, listening to well-known footsteps in anteroom and corridor and watching the coming and going of heroic forms that give radiance to the rich halls. From a palatial drawing room she follows the Duke of Zamorna on a midnight ride across a lonely moor "slumbering and still in clear moonlight," to a spot where he dismounts to blow a requiem for a kinsman who lies buried under a "mute marble Victory."

Never shall I, Charlotte Brontë, forget [she concludes] what a voice of wild and wailing music now came thrillingly to my mind's, almost my body's ear, nor how distinctly I, sitting in the schoolroom at Roe Head, saw the Duke of Zamorna leaning against that obelisk. . . . I was quite gone. I had really, utterly, forgot where I was and all the gloom and cheerlessness of my situation. I felt myself breathing quick and short as I beheld the Duke lifting up his sable crest, which undulated as the plume of a hearse waves to the wind, and knew that music which sprang as mournfully triumphant as the scriptural verse,

> O Grave, where is thy sting? O Death
>   where is thy Victory?

was exciting him and quickening his ever-rapid pulse.

"Miss Brontë, what are you thinking about?" said a voice that dissipated all the charm, and Miss Lister thrust her little rough, black head into my face. *Sic transit* &c.

In the course of this same December (1835) Branwell wrote to the editor of *Blackwood's Magazine* a letter voicing in the first person those qualities which he habitually characterized in his heroes as "pride," "independence," and "ability":

sir, read what I write. And would to Heaven you could believe it true, for then you would attend to and act upon it.

I have addressed you twice before, and now I do it again. . . . Now, sir, to you I appear writing with conceited assurance; but I *am not;* for I know myself so far as to believe in my own originality, and on that ground I desire of you admittance into your ranks. And do not wonder that I apply so determinedly: for the remembrances I spoke of have fixed you and your Magazine in such a manner upon my mind that the idea of striving to aid another periodical is *horribly repulsive.* My resolution is to devote my ability to you, and for God's sake, till you see whether or not I can serve you, do not so coldly refuse my aid. . . . In letters previous to this I have perhaps spoken too openly respecting the extent of my powers. But I did so because I determined to say what I believed. I *know* that I am not one of the wretched writers of the day. I know that I possess strength to assist you beyond some of your own contributors; but I wish to make you the judge in this case and give you the benefit of its decision.

Now, sir, do not act like a commonplace person, but like a man willing to examine for himself. Do not turn from the naked truth of my letter, but *prove me;* and if I do not stand the proof, I will not further press myself on you. If I do stand it—why— You have lost an able writer in James Hogg, and God grant you may gain one in Patrick Branwell Brontë.

This appeal, like others that preceded and followed it, was never answered.

The Christmas vacation over, Charlotte returned heavy-hearted to Roe Head, and Branwell continued the *History* which he had begun on January 1, loosing upon Angria civil war and foreign invasion. His story is told in endless detail of numbers, positions, and movements of troops over a terrain which had taken on a realistically local contour, and in many instances local names. At best his chronicles of the next year are but involved repetitions of battles and rapine, yet they gave Charlotte occasions and themes for stories that were carrying her surely toward the triumph of *Jane Eyre.*

The events he chronicled probably were discussed with her in the course of her Christmas vacation at home. Her diary shows that she received through his letters more-or-less regular bulletins of war-torn Angria, which she elaborated into vivid and moving pictures. She writes:

About a week since I got a letter from Branwell containing a most exquisitely characteristic epistle from Northangerland to his daughter. It is astonishing what a soothing and delightful tone that letter seemed to speak. I lived on its contents for days. In every pause of employment it came chiming in like some sweet bar of music, bringing with it agreeable thoughts such as I had for many weeks been a stranger to. . . . A curtain seemed to rise and discover to me the Duchess as she might appear when newly risen and lightly dressed for the morning, discovering her father's letter in the contents of the mail which lies on her breakfast table. There seems nothing in such an idea as that, but the localities of the picture were so graphic, the room so distinct, the clear fire of morning, the window looking upon no object but a cold October sky, except when you draw very near and look down on a terrace far beneath and, at a still dizzier distance, on a green court with a fountain and rows of stately limes—beyond, a wide road and wider river and a vast metropolis— you felt it to be the Zamorna Palace.

Again she hears from Branwell that Zamorna, in retreat, has evacuated and burned Adrianopolis, and that the invaders have taken possession of such buildings as remain. The picture takes a definite and vivid shape in her mind:

Last night I did indeed lean upon the thunder-waking wings of such a stormy blast as I have seldom heard blow, and it whirled me away like heath in the wilderness for five seconds of ecstasy; and as I sat by myself in the dining-room while all the rest were at tea, the trance seemed to descend on a sudden, and verily this foot trod the war-shaken shores of the Calabar, and these eyes saw the defiled and violated Adrianopolis shedding its lights on the river from lattices whence the invader looked out.

Remembering that African Quashia had one time been in love with Mary, she pictures him in drunken slumber upon the Queen's own couch:

Aye, where she had lain imperially robed and decked with pearls, every waft of her garments as she moved diffusing perfume, her beauty slumbering and still glowing as dreams of him for whom she kept herself in such hallowed and shrine-like separation wandered over her soul, on her own silken couch, a swart and sinewy Moor, intoxicated to ferocious insensibility, had stretched his athletic limbs, weary with wassail and stupefied with drunken sleep. I knew it to be Quashia himself, and well could I guess why he had chosen the Queen of Angria's sanctuary for the scene of his solitary revelling. While he was full before my eyes, lying in his black dress on the disordered couch, his sable hair dishevelled on his forehead, his tusk-like teeth gleaming vindictively through his parted lips, his brown complexion flushed with wine, and his broad chest heaving wildly as the breath issued in snorts from his distended nostrils. . . . while this apparition was before me, the dining-room door opened, and Miss W. came in with a plate of butter in her hand. "A stormy night, my dear!" said she.

Branwell's next bulletin brought the story of Zamorna's capture and exile. In a desperate attempt to meet his foes and dash toward Verdopolis, the king suffered a terrible defeat at Edwardston, "losing 18,000 men and [being] forced to fly . . . till all his splendid army dashed in pieces, his generals dispersed . . . and himself flying to Angria was taken alone and exhausted among the Warner Hills."

Then after detention and brutal insult from Simpson, Northangerland bought him and had him conveyed to Verdopolis. . . . But Northangerland was in torment. He visited him and pressed him to assent to the destruction of Angria and in freedom ascend to power with him! Zamorna sternly refused, and Percy—his friend, his father!—had him that night placed in the ROVER, under S'death, who directly set sail to banish him two thousand miles off on the rocks of Ascension Isle.

Branwell went to London, probably in March, 1836, but did not enter the Royal Academy. According to the testimony of a contemporary he remained in the city but a very short time, visiting the principal art galleries and monuments, and conversing in Castle Tavern kept by the famous prize fighter, Tom Spring, where he deeply impressed the group he met with his knowledge of the history of the ring and his familiarity with the streets of the city. His own account runs differently, if we may interpret as autobiographical a story [3] written by him in May, which would clear up the mystery of his failure to make use of his longed-for opportunity. Unfortunately only a short fragment of this story, describing Charles Wentworth's first visit to Verdopolis, survives.

[3] Transcript received from C. W. Hatfield.

Wentworth, the narrative goes, on beholding the great city spread before him, felt the excitement of anticipation change suddenly to intense depression. "His mind being over-strained the lapse was as strong as the spring. . . . Tears came starting into his eyes, and a feeling like a wind seemed to pass across his spirits, because he now felt that not even the flashes of glory which these streets and buildings had struck from his soul . . . could preserve his thoughts from aimless depression."

Passing through the streets, hardly turning his eyes to look at them, he entered a hotel, "stretched himself on a sofa and listlessly dreamed away his time till dark." The next day, too depressed to present his letters of introduction or go about the business that had brought him there, Wentworth walked out alone to view the great buildings he had long dreamed of seeing: The Tower of All Nations (the Tower of London), the two Houses of the Twelves (the Houses of Parliament), and St. Michael's (St. Paul's) Cathedral, "all forming so sublime an assembly of our national glory that none beholding it could be other than constitutional." St. Michael's Cathedral moved him more than all else. Fearing to enter, lest realization shatter the pleasure of anticipation, he remained long gazing at its noble exterior. At last dashing across the entrance, he lost himself in joy of its grandeur and beauty. Standing under the mighty dome, he gazed upward until "to his dimmed eyes it seemed to rise and soar beyond his sight," then, stretching himself on the pavement, he continued to gaze till "he thought it would thunder down in ruins over his head."

Strangely enough, neither the great libraries nor the picture galleries of the city attracted Wentworth. Restless and aimless, he lingered in his hotel, "feeding his feelings with 'little squibs of rum,' " though he was perfectly aware that the drink "would only the more depress him afterwards."

The effort to save Branwell had come too late. Back at Haworth, his hurt pride found in the easy admiration of the Black Bull Inn, a soothing substitute for the respect of his equals. Even without money to spend for drink, he was always welcomed by its frequenters, and he could usually count on finding there a chance traveler willing to share his liquor with the cleverest man in the village. At local gatherings, too, such as singings and "arvills," his varied talents and conversational powers were in great demand. Flattery, added to drink and drugs, stimulated his already inflated egotism to dreams amounting almost to delusions of grandeur.

Within a few months of his return from London, he began to rewrite the old "History of the Young Men," again treating the nonsensical escapades of the wooden soldiers with all the pretentious seriousness of authentic history. Following the conquest of Ashanteeland under the leadership of Arthur Wellesley, so runs the revised narrative,[4] the little group of Englishmen pushed their boundaries to the Senegal and the Etrei, where "speedily they began the business of founding towns in various eligible situations, exploring lands, and shooting negroes." Meanwhile "shiploads of emigrants filled the harbor of Verdopolis with the seed of something mighty to come." An elaborate treatise on the constitution of the Verdopolitan Confederacy concludes with the summary: "Verdopolis its capital, Nigritia its nucleus, its kingdoms four, but its nation one."

At the end of the Napoleonic Wars, the new version continues, when "Europe certainly was falling rapidly into decay, the boldest, noblest, and most daring of her sons" embarked for Verdopolis. "Spain and Italy furnished thousands, but England and Ireland and Scotland almost millions." The French discovered an island lying south of Nigritia, "large in size, European, and cultivable," and named it France, "whither all true Parisians flocked with eager wing." Here too the exiled Napoleon found refuge, "whereupon his devout soldiers, commanders, and people crowded after him, till France was literally drained into this island; and here transplanted it has since grown unshaken."

In February of 1836, Branwell became a freemason, serving in the course of the next two years as secretary, organist, and junior warden of the Lodge of the Three Graces, which held its meetings in the Black Bull Inn. In 1838 he set up as a portrait painter in a studio in Fountain Street, Bradford, alternating between that place and Haworth for about a year. One who knew him at this period wrote,[5] years later, a

[4] Transcript received from C. W. Hatfield.

[5] Francis A. Leyland: The Brontë Family, with Special Reference to Patrick Branwell Brontë. 1886.

description of him, probably highly idealized, which explains his easy popularity:

His complexion was fair and his features handsome; his mouth and his chin were well-shaped; his nose was prominent and of the Roman type; his eyes sparkled and danced with delight, and his fine forehead made up a face of oval form which gave an irresistible charm to its possessor, and attracted the admiration of those who knew him. Added to this, his address was simple and unadorned, yet polished; but being familiar with the English language in its highest form of expression, and with the Yorkshire and Hibernian *patois* also, he could easily make use of the quaintest and broadest terms when occasion called for them. It was indeed amazing how suddenly he could pass from the discussion of a grave and lofty subject . . . to one of his light-hearted and amusing Irish or Yorkshire sallies. He could be sad and joyful almost at the same time.

Tragically enough, he was never able to infuse his personal charm into his writing. His gesture at portrait painting failed, as was inevitable, because of his lack of skill, and in the spring of 1839, he gave up the studio and returned to the Parsonage.

Chapter XV

DUAL PERSONALITIES

THE YEARS that saw Branwell's precocious adolescence lost in degenerate manhood were for Charlotte a period of substantial growth, rooted in true genius and cultivated by suffering. While presenting the orthodox Victorian lady's repertoire of "ill health" and "low spirits," she was in her inner imagination, working her habitual miracle of raising to life her brother's wilderness of dry bones. Emily, at home and happy, thanks to Charlotte, watched in understanding sympathy her sister's practical demonstration of dual personality, a theme she recurrently failed to master in her stories.

The order of Charlotte's days did not permit of long narratives such as she had delighted in at Haworth. The single scene or incident or emotion, vividly realized, was the limit of her present indulgence. And because, perhaps, of this curtailment in length, as well as because of her awakened sensibilities, her vignettes are quickened by a power that marks them as belonging to a new order of creation, high and above her earlier romances. Over and over she evinces the quality that Miss Sinclair cites as the essence of her genius: ability to convey a poignant impression of surroundings, of things seen and heard, of the earth and sky; of weather; of the aspect of houses and rooms, suggesting a positive exaltation of the sense of sound and light, an ecstasy, an enchantment before the visible, tangible world, an almost supernatural intentness raised to the *nth* power.

On her twentieth birthday, April 21, 1836, she began a series of such sketches, which she finished eight days later, giving to the whole the fitting title, "Passing Events." [1] In these she was writing of persons and places known only in her imagination, yet one finishes reading them with a sharp impression of the characters and personalities of Angrian statesmen, soldiers, and poets, and the world they represent. This power, belonging so peculiarly to herself, she attributes to Lord Richton and Captain Hastings, both representing her brother, though she must long since have realized his total lack of it. Was she so lost in realization of the Angrian world that Branwell was forgotten and Lord Richton and Captain Hastings become real men to her?

Every man to his trade; [she writes] the blacksmith to his anvil, the tailor to his needle. Let Richton take his seat at the council board of war or peace. Let him paint to the life the members gathering round that table of heavy and dark Honduras, whose large circle groans under the piled documents of state. . . . Let him write so well that each separate voice shall speak out of the page in changeful tone the word passing from mouth to mouth, the flexible lip and rapid tongue of Edward Percy answering in raised bass the energetic, silver dictum of Howard Warner. . . .

Let Richton do this and astonish us, and let Hastings familiarize us with the terms and tactics of war. Let him stir us up with the sweet and war-like national airs of Angria. Let him lead us along her many and splendid streams . . . through the haunts of herons and curlews and water ouzels and lamenting bitterns, fringed with sedges and canes and long-jointed dog-grass. Let him reveal to us the Calabar or the Etrei (the wild eerie Etrei, a battle stream whose pitchy billows evermore carry a vein of negro blood to the ocean) by moonlight.

Let Hastings speak of Gazemba, show the armed household of bandit vassalage of Enara, the rendezvous of regiments, the headquarters of general officers, polished, brave, intriguing, ambitious, scoundrelly, sagacious men. . . .

Let the Earl and the Major, I say, dilate on these things. Let them rush upon that noble quarry; they are eagles. Let them travel that broad road; they are mounted on chargers of the Ukraine. For me, I am but a crow, so I must dwell content in the rookeries that shade Africa's ancestral halls. I have but my own shanks to go on, therefore, I can travel no further than the grounds and park gates of the magnates.

True to the limitations she set herself, Charlotte attempts no inventions in plot and no grand scenes, leaving such effort to her more ambitious brother.

[1] Charlotte Brontë: "Passing Events." By Charles Townshend. April 21, 1836. 20,000 words. (Morgan Library.)

The best sketch of this series, following up Zamorna's threat to punish Percy through his daughter, portrays the effort of Mary Percy, Duchess of Zamorna and Queen of Angria, to hold her husband against his purpose of revenge. The Queen is in Verdopolis, her husband in Angria. She is pining away for news of him. Warner arrives from Adrianopolis to get from her a state document left in her keeping. This business done, the Queen asks the question that she cannot suppress: What effect has the news of her father's coalition with Ardrah had upon Zamorna?

Warner knitted his brows. "I would have avoided this subject," returned he, "but since your Majesty commands me, I must speak. The Duke says nothing."

"But what does he think?" pursued Mary, eargerly following up the path into which she had struck. "How does he look? You can read his countenance, surely; at least I could."

"His countenance is paler than when your Grace last saw him, and it expresses thought and mental disquietude."

"And—and—" continued the Duchess, throwing off restraint and writhing with impatience as she spoke, "have you no letter for me, Mr. Warner; do you bring no message, no word of his welfare and no inquiry after mine?"

"My lady, I have not so much as a syllable for you, not so much as a scrap of paper."

"Then his children?" said she, her excitement still increasing, "He must have mentioned their names—Frederick and Julius. He must have spoken of his sons; they are his own flesh and blood. And my little Arthur who was only two months old when he went, he must have wished to know whether he still promises to be as exact a copy as ever?"

"My lady, he did mention his children. He said, 'If you see the boys, tell me how they are,' and he looked as if he would have said something more, but when I stopped to receive further directions he dismissed me hastily. Do not doubt, however, that he was thinking of yourself."

Speaking on a sudden decision, Mary informed Warner that she would return to Adrianopolis with him and refused to listen to his protest.

Back in Adrianopolis, his report to his monarch finished, Warner tries to speak a word for the Duchess, whom the King thinks is still in Verdopolis, but is silenced by his monarch:

"Warner . . . but two living creatures in the world know the nature of the relations that have existed between Alexander Percy and myself. From the beginning, in my inmost soul, while I watched his devious and eccentric course, I swore that if he broke those bonds and so turned to vanity and scattered in the air sacrifices that I had made and words that I had spoken; if he made as dust and nothingness causes for which I have endured jealousies and burning strife and emulations amongst those I loved; if he froze feelings that in me are like living fire, I would have revenge. In all but one quarter he is fortified and garrisoned; he can bid me defiance. But one quarter lies open to my javelin, and, dipped in venom, I will launch it quivering into his very spirit, so help me Hell!"

"Hell will help you," returned Warner quite coolly. . . . "There is a lady in the next room [who] wishes to see you . . . the wife, I think she says, of an officer in the Angrian Army. She seems exceedingly anxious to have an audience. May I admit her here?"

"As you like," replied the Duke, scarcely seeming conscious of what he said.

The woman was, of course, the Duchess. Warner sent her in and fled. When the monarch discovered her identity, he called him back in "the impatient, haughty, terrible accent of a despot driven to desperation."

"How dared you do what you have done?" said he at once. "How dared you bring my wife here when you know I'd rather have an evil spirit given to my arms this night! You must have been conscious, sir, that I had wrought up my resolution with toil and trouble, that I had decided to let her die if her father cut loose, and decided with agony. And what possessed you to ruin it all and set me the whole torturing task over again? . . . You know how I loved Percy and what it is costing me to send him to the D——l! Look at his daughter! I'm to stand her devotion and beauty, am I? But I will, though you've swept away all perception of the reasons why I should. I'll go on the tack of blind obstinacy now. Leave me, Warner. I felt as if I could shoot you five minutes since. I was phrenzied."

A "glance of entreaty from the Duchess prevailed" upon Warner to withdraw. Her tact managed the rest.

"Passing Events" also introduces a new element into the old Percy-Zamorna theme. Dissatisfied with the early unmotivated animosity between the two super-heroes, Charlotte early offered as its *raison d'être* the overwhelming ambition inherent in the Luciferian nature imputed to Percy. To complete the case she now paints in a background of early association, representing Percy as the mentor of Zamorna's youth and the corrupter of his naturally noble nature. To the already complicated relationship between them she here adds the more subtle suggestion of mutual fascination in its true sense implying both love and hate. The same force which drew the two together drove them to bitter quarrels, compelling each to wreck his own happiness in the effort to destroy the other. Absorbing as this theme becomes to Charlotte, she never masters it.

The fictitious narrator of "Passing Events," and of the entire new phase of the Angrian cycle thereby inaugurated, is an old character under a new name and guise—Charles Wellesley now becomes Charles Townshend. Lord Charles, the precocious child-man novelist, belonged peculiarly to the Young Men's Play, and passed from view when Charlotte rang down the curtain on her second departure for Roe Head. Charles Townshend is still Charles Wellesley in that he is the Duke of Wellington's son and Zamorna's brother, enjoying all the privileges of his family connections, though disdaining their life. His break with his family and social station and his assumption of a new name are not explained. His self-portrait is not a flattering one:

All this [the gathering of the revolution] to a single gentleman like me is pleasant. I have no wife, no family to potter me, no stake in commerce, no landed possessions, no property in the funds to bother myself about. I laugh at the anxiety written on the brows of monied men, who in the grand suspense know not whether tomorrow may not behold them bankrupts. What goods I have are portable; two or three suits of clothes, a few shirts, half a dozen dickies; half a dozen cambric handkerchiefs, a cake or two of Windsor soap, a bottle of Macassar oil, a brush and comb, and some other material of the toilette. The few sovereigns I have in ready money may be easily secreted about my person, and, in case of the worst, what is there to which I cannot turn my hand for a livelihood? Not an atom of pride do I possess to check me. I'd as soon be a shoe-black in a merry, jovial servants' hall as heir-apparent to Wellingtonsland. I'm burdened neither by domestic ties, religious scruples, nor political predilections. I never could understand what home pleasures and family affections meant. The sect of which I am a member [the Methodists] is sunk so low that nothing can degrade it further. My political lungs would have the freest play in such a current of air as a hurricane revolution might create. Rogue will never proscribe me; and, if he does, where are the policemen, the bailiffs, the blood-hounds that could catch me? the jail that can hold me? the halter that can hang me? Were the streets of Verdopolis slippery with blood, they'd offer firm enough footing for Charles Townshend. Were each member of society a police-spy and law sleuth-dog upon the other, Charles Townshend would out-do them all in treachery, in double-dealing, in blood-thirsty hypocrisy.

As a matter of fact, the painter's self-denunciation is not to be taken seriously. Charles Townshend is idle, indifferent, and selfish; omnipresent, curious, and gossipy, but neither malicious nor treacherous. In another connection he remarks, "Though I have no friends, I have few particular enemies." In some unexplained manner he has become so closely identified with another familiar character, Sir William Percy, that Charlotte herself occasionally confuses their personalities. Both have renounced their families; both have a cynical, satirical turn of mind and tongue, and both come and go with disconcerting suddenness, having access to places and groups closed to other narrators. They are so much alike in features and dress that a stranger might easily take one for the other. They seek each other's company, and frequently take long walks together, usually carrying on a rapid fire of repartee. Yet they differ widely: Charles is a symbol rather than a real person; Sir William is emphatically a human being, a passionate idealist under his outward mask. He comes out in *The Professor* as Yorke Hunsden, and fuses with Warner Howard Warner to make Paul Emanuel of *Villette*.

Chapter XVI

ANGRIA WINS OUT

IN COURSE of the summer vacation of 1836 Charlotte wove her brother's recent Angrian developments into a long untitled poem in *Don Juan* stanzas,[1] which measures her emotional growth through her year of exile. In some respects the most finished production of the Angrian cycle, this poem, with a later novel called "Caroline Vernon," marks the culmination of the Byronic influence which had dominated her work since she first read *Childe Harold* late in 1829.

The opening scene shows the captive Zamorna on his way to exile, hanging over the rail of the moving ship, in his thoughts addressing Percy:

> How oft we wrung each other's callous hearts,
>   Conscious none else could so effectively
> Waken the pain, or venom the keen darts
>   We shot so thickly, so unsparingly,
> Into those sensitive and tender parts
>   That, veiled from all besides, ourselves could see
> Like eating cankers, pains that heaven had dealt
> On devotees to crime, sworn slaves of guilt.

The vision of his wife, Mary, dying of grief, murdered by him she loved better than life itself, softens his heart to repentance, and he wishes with all his being that he might at that moment envelop her in his love, reviving her spirits and restoring her health:

> She said she'd die for me, and now she's keeping
>   Her word, far off at Alnwick, o'er the sea.

-----
[1] July 19, 1936. 12 pp., 576 ll. 7¼" x 4½". (Bonnell Collection.)

The Duchess of Zamorna at Alnwick. Pencil Drawing by
Charlotte Brontë

What does she dream of lingering all alone
On the vast terrace, o'er that stream impending?
Through all the dim still night no life-like tone
With the soft rush of wind and wave is blending.

The very wind around this vessel sweeping
  Will steal unto her pillow whisperingly
And murmur o'er her form, which shall be sleeping
  Ere long, beneath some quiet, pall-like tree.
I would she were within my reach just now;
Not long that shade should haunt her Grecian brow.

At this point the ship, now in the harbor of Marseilles, is boarded by a French flower girl who offers Zamorna a rosebud. When he would gallantly kiss her for her pitying kindness, he discovers that she is his faithful mistress, Mina Laury, escaped from Angria to join him in exile:

Well, when I lifted up the fruit girl's head
  To give her that salute, the black curls parted,
And the revealed and flashing eye-balls shed
  A ray upon me not unknown. I started,
And, half indignantly, I would have said:
  "This must not be!" but then so broken-hearted,
So full of dying hope was that dark eye,
I could not put its mute petition by.

Thinking of Mary, he refuses to let Mina remain with him, but she persists until the ship is under sail and she cannot be put ashore:

Now for my Mary's sake I have not given
  One smile or glance of love to that poor slave;
And I have seen her woman's feelings riven
  With pangs that made her look down on the wave
As if it were her home, her hope, her heaven,
  Because a semblance of repose it gave.
She sees I do not want her. None can tell
What torments from the chill conviction swell.

He gives her at last the attention she craves, only to hear in choking sobs the cruel murder of his son, the little prince, Edward Ernest Gordon, left in her care when the war broke out:

                . . . all the dreary tale
  Of what has happened, Percy, to my son:
How all her watchful care could naught avail,
  How she has struggled, how her prize was won.
And the departing blood left cold and pale

> The cheek that late it glowed so brightly on,
> As she revealed what floating rumor said:
> That the young Lord of Avondale was dead.

She continues, telling how Warner rescued the body and gave it burial:

> Ere I could speak, the impetuous words came gushing
>   Forth from her lips. "It was by night," she cried,
> "The tryst was on a moor, and there came rushing
>   The thousand serfs to Warner's house allied.
> He stood up in the midst, the red blood flushing
>   His face and brow; his voice rang far and wide
> As in that hour he bade them look upon
> The mangled relics of their monarch's son.
>
>   .   .   .   .
>
> "They buried Gordon on the moor that night.
>   Warner with his own hands the body laid
> Low in its narrow house. No funeral rite,
>   No prayer, no blessing o'er the grave was said,
> Only, as all the hosts their lances bright
>   Reversed in homage to the royal dead,
> Their chief cried solemnly, 'O Lord, how long
> Shall thine elected people suffer wrong!' "

Mina's recital rouses to white heat all Zamorna's half-subdued hatred for Percy, and he screws his purpose of revenge again to the sticking point, though it means the sacrifice of his own beloved wife:

> You would not save him, Percy! Nor will I
>   Save yours from desolation. With wild pleasure
> I'll now call down the doom of the Most High—
>   His curse upon my head in fullest measure.
> I'll fix me for a passage to the sky
>   By heaving overboard my choicest treasure.
> Yes, I'll leave it all, take up my cross and follow—
> All flesh is grass, all joys are vain and hollow!

The poem ends in an effusion of Byronic despair:

>   . . . All words are weak,
>   Tongue cannot utter what the victim feels
> Who lies outstretched upon that burning lake
>   Whose flaming eddy now beneath me reels.

All that breathes happiness seems to forsake
His blighted thoughts; a demon hand unseals
That little well so treasured in man's breast,
Whose drop of hope so sweetens all the rest.

At last Charlotte's pen has turned Branwell's nonsense into literature—almost great literature.

Vacation over, she returned to her Roe Head bondage, and Branwell continued the Angrian wars. Under his dispensation, the Duchess of Zamorna, in exile at Alnwick, dies, a long-drawn-out, unconvincing death. Any suggestion of pathos in the scene, as he draws it, is dispelled by the weakness of Percy's moan, "O, mother, I have too much to bear! Despair without and within! I am plotted against just now so that there can be no time for me to witness the funeral of my child." On November 19, Branwell chronicles:

Now at last Mary is buried, and so let us turn our faces to the approaching awful strife of war; and to this we may turn without difficulty, since as quickly even her miserable father was fired without heart or spirit for it to turn likewise, though from the very brink of the vault which held his buried child, and toward confusions and plots and treacheries which required for their disentanglement the clearest and most disengaged and unoppressed brain.

And Charlotte at Roe Head, heartsick and lonely, wonders if Branwell really has killed the Duchess:

Is she dead? Is she buried? Is she alone in the cold earth on this dreary night, with the ponderous gold coffin-plate on her breast, under the black pavement of a church, in a vault closed up with lime mortar—nobody near where she lies, she who was watched through months of suffering as she lay on her bed of state, now quite forsaken because her eyes are closed, her lips sealed, and her limbs cold and rigid, the stars as they are fitfully revealed through the serried clouds looking in through the church windows on her monument? A set of wretched thoughts are rising in my mind. I hope she's alive still, partly because I can't abide to think how hopelessly and cheerlessly she must have died, and partly because her removal, if it has taken place, must have been to North[angerland] like the quenching of the last spark that averted utter darkness.

Percy was unable to stay the distintegrating process among his allies. By the end of the year Branwell recorded the breakup of the Ardrah-Percy coalition and the flight of Percy, the rallying of the

Angrians under Warner, and the return of Zamorna to power. Charlotte, war-weary, eagerly adjusted her inner world to peace-time conditions, writing in her diary:

The other day I appeared to realize a delicious hot day in the most burning
height of summer. . . . I keep heaping epithets together and I cannot describe what I mean—I mean a day whose rise, progress, and decline seem
made of sunshine . . . a day when fruits visibly ripen, when orchards
appear suddenly to change from green to gold over the distant Sydenham
hills in Hawkscliffe Forest. . . . It seemed to me that the war was over,
that the trumpet had ceased but a short time since, and that its last tones had
been pitched in a triumphant key. It seemed as if exciting events, tidings of
battles, of victories, of treaties, of meetings of mighty powers, had diffused
an enthusiasm over the land that made its pulses beat with feverish quickness.
After months of bloody toil a time of festal rest was now bestowed on Angria.
The noblemen, the generals, and the gentlemen were at their country seats;
the Duke, young but war-worn, was at Hawkscliffe, stupendous still in
influence.

At home for the Christmas vacation, she brought her poem up to
date [2] with Branwell's chronicles, finishing it January 9, 1837. Zamorna's triumph is subdued by the memory of its cost to martyred
Angria:

> I've borne too much to boast. Even now I know
>   While I advance to triumph, all my host
> So sternly reckless to the conflict go
>   Because each charm and joy of life they've lost;
> Because on their invaded thresholds grow
>   Grass from their children's graves; because the cost
> Of their land's red redemption has been blood
> From gallant hearts poured out in lavish flood.

Alone in the dead quiet of night, his mind too much raised for
sleep, Zamorna has time to think "of each event that hath befallen of
late to all below." The thought of Mary pushes all others into the
background, the intelligence of her death having met him at Calais
on his return voyage:

> In a far foreign land with strangers round,
>   Reading a journal of my native West,

---

[2] 439 ll. 7¼″ x 4¾″. (Bonnell Collection.) See also untitled story beginning "Reader,
I'll tell you what." *circa* 1837. 35 pp. 7¼″ x 4½″. (Law Collection.)

Rang from the black-edged funeral page the sound
    Expected and yet dreaded. There the crest,
The arms, the name were blazoned, and the ground
    Marked where the corpse would lie, and all exprest,
Even to the grim procession, hearse and pall,
The grave, the monument to cover all!

He reviews the bitter struggle in his heart between love and revenge:

Watching her thus through many a sleepless night
    I never utterly resolved to slay—
I could not when, all young and soft and bright,
    Trusting, adoring me in dreams she lay,
Her fair cheek pillowed on the locks of light
    That gleamed upon her delicate array,
Veiling with gold her neck and shoulders white
    And varying with their rich and silken flow
    Her forehead's smooth expanse of stainless snow.

Then comes the heart-breaking realization that Mary is gone:

Did I think then she'd die, and that forever
    The grave would hide her from me? Did I deem
That after parting I should never, never
    Behold her save in some delusive dream?
That she would cross death's cold and icy river
    Alone without one hope, one cheering beam
Of bliss to come, all dark, all spectral, dreary?
Was this thy fate, my loved, my sainted Mary?

The revenge that he had sought is his; he addresses Percy:

Am I not well avenged? Struck in her prime
    Dies thy fair daughter, her last look revealing,
Her last word telling, to what hand she owes
Her grave beneath this avalanche of woes.

        .   .   .   .   .

It is finished; now the cloud, the pang, the tear
    Are thine forever. Brow and heart and eye
Shall keep till death thy daughter's legacy.

The poem continues in a burst of Byronic self-pity:

Victory! the plumed, the crowned, I hear her calling
    Again my diadem, my land she flings
Redeemed before me! Glorious sunlight falling

> On the vermillion banner lights its wing
> With the true hue of conquest.
>
> And alone I shall be when the trumpet is sounding
> To tell to the world that my kingdom is free!
> Alone while a thousand brave bosoms are bounding.
> The yoke and the fetter-bolt shivered to see!
>
> Alone in the hall where the last flash is shining
> Of embers that wane in their mid-night decay!
> How shall I feel as the wild gale's repining
> Fitfully whispers and wanders away?

By the end of the Angrian War Charlotte's awakening was complete, and conditions set for the maturing of her genius: fancy had given way to intensity of imagination that carried with it a suggestion of the supernatural; suffering had changed adolescent romanticism to passion so intense as to give the stamp of conviction to the most impossible situations; and mere fluency of expression had developed into a characteristic style. The struggle was not over, but for two critical years the Angrian dream had held its own against the allied forces of conscience, material circumstances, and well-meant advice.

In the course of this same Christmas vacation Charlotte sent the poet-laureate, Robert Southey, a specimen of her verse, asking his opinion of her talents. The title and nature of the poem she submitted are unknown, for her letter of conveyance has not come to light. A second letter thanking the laureate for his "kind and admirable" but "somewhat stringent" answer tells the strange story of the double life she was leading:

My father is a clergyman of limited though competent income, and I am the eldest of his children. He expended quite as much in my education as he could afford in justice to the rest. I thought it therefore my duty, when I left school, to become a governess. In that capacity I find enough to occupy my thoughts all day long, and my head and hands too, without having a moment's time for one dream of the imagination. In the evenings, I confess, I do think, but I never trouble anyone else with my thoughts. I carefully avoid any appearance of preoccupation and eccentricity which might lead those I live amongst to suspect the nature of my pursuits. Following my father's advice—who from my childhood has counselled me, just in the wise and friendly tone of your letter—I have endeavoured not only attentively to observe all the duties a woman ought to fulfill, but to feel deeply interested in them. I don't always succeed, for sometimes when I'm teaching or sewing I would rather be reading or writing; but I try to deny myself; and my father's approbation amply rewarded me for the privation.

Branwell, following suit, submitted to Wordsworth, on January 19th, a portion of a story having to do with his hero Henry Hastings, asking his opinion of its merits:

What I send you is a Prefatory Scene of a much longer subject, in which I have striven to develop strong passions and weak principles struggling with high imagination and acute feelings, till, as youth hardened toward age, evil deeds and short enjoyments end in mental misery and bodily ruin. . . .

Return me an answer; if but one word, telling me whether I should write on, or write no more.

Apparently Wordsworth did not return the desired word, but Branwell continued to write, repeating himself over and over.

Despite the mass carnage of Branwell's Angrian battles and Charlotte's reference to

> . . . blood
> From gallant hearts poured out in lavish flood,

not a single individual death is recorded on the field. A postwar roll call of Angrian soldiers, officers, and men, finds all present. The only named victims of the war are the non-combatants, Edward Ernest Gordon and Mary, Duchess of Zamorna and Queen of Angria. The Duchess was Charlotte's dearest heroine, and though she did indeed find romantic pleasure in her death through portraying the bereaved husband's grief with all the histrionic éclat of Byron parading the pageant of his bleeding heart through Europe, she could not give up her "matchless Henrietta" for good and all—her going left too great a blank. Indeed the war was hardly over and Zamorna back on the throne before the Duchess, too, was in her old place, leading her accustomed life.

The postwar Duchess, however, in common with other Angrian characters, shows a marked advance toward realism. From the proud, aloof, fastidious creature, set aside for the divine honor of being Zamorna's consort, envied of all women, she has become merely an unusually beautiful, tactful woman, exerting all her charms to hold her husband's wayward affection, and suffering as an ordinary wife when she fails.

Zamorna himself, after the Restoration, is less the godlike hero who can do no wrong, glorifying everyone he looks upon either in love or hate, and more the ordinary business man and country squire, indulging in commonplace irregularities of life and adopting the commonplace husband's expedients to hide them. And Percy, from this time on, loses his halo, except upon occasions, and appears a common, broken-down rake and hypochondriac, paying for his dissipations in disease and shattered nerves. Stripped of all political influence, he returns at the close of the war to his accustomed haunts, where Zamorna occasionally visits him, impelled as much by the old fascination as by Mary's pleadings. The two continue to disagree on every possible subject, and quarrel as often as they meet.

In short, Charlotte, heartily tired of the war and its turmoil, sweeps her Angrian stage clean of battle lines, and settles down to the kind of writing she likes best: drawing characters, painting emotions, and etching scenes, all marked by a determination toward realism.

Chapter XVII

AUGUSTA GERALDINE ALMEDA

NOT A WORD from Emily's pen, nor even her name in Charlotte's letters, remains to tell of her activities through the months immediately following her release from Roe Head. Her poems, however, make it clear that back at home she lost herself again in the Gondal-Gaaldine creation, as vividly real to her and as rapturously absorbing as Angria to Charlotte. These two island continents, separated by the length of the Pacific Ocean, she bound together as a complicated social and political entity, recurrently shaken by wars of conquest and political revolution. Her world was more violent than Charlotte's because more individual and elemental.

We do not know whether the Gondal story at this stage was committed to paper or remained in Emily's imagination to be shared orally with Anne, but we do know that the Gondal literature—written or oral—took a new turn in the summer of 1836, with the beginning of a series of poems, which, continued for more than a decade, is the only extant fruit of Emily's genius before *Wuthering Heights*. Still, almost a century after her death, incompletely edited—mutilated in text, stripped of explanatory headings, and their story thread broken by chronological arrangement—these poems have contributed more than any other factor to the popular misunderstanding of their author. Some readers, interpreting them subjectively, profess to find in them confessions of a secret lover and clandestine adventures. But the poems show such an embarrassing abundance of lovers, secret and avowed, true and false, with midnight trysts on the moors, rapturous meetings, heart-rending partings, sublime sacrifice, and dastardly betrayal, that interpreters cannot agree which represents the actual lover in Emily's life. Some, misapplying certain poems to Branwell, have argued abnormal fixations between them. Virginia Moore, by misreading the heading of one of the poems, "Love's Farewell"—added by Charlotte—as "Louis Parensell," even discovered the name of a lover whom Emily betrayed because she was a Lesbian in love with her sister Anne.

Indeed Emily's poems afford ample evidence—judiciously selected—to support any theory.

Out of the mass, utterly unintelligible as a whole, successive generations of readers have extracted a small group of poems more understandable than the rest as an Emily Brontë canon, and from these have created the traditional Emily: "Remembrance," a dirge for a lover fifteen years dead, so moving as to argue an actual experience in her own life; "The Wanderer from the Fold," a lament for a moral derelict identified in the public mind with Branwell; "No Coward Soul is Mine," taken as an expression of her own indomitable nature; "The Visionary" and "The Prisoner," bespeaking the mystic; and a number of poems voicing communion with nature. The multiplied greater number, poems of war and captivity and murder and suicide and betrayal, they ignore because they can make nothing of them.

Emily's manuscripts, with their original heading which name, in many instances, the persons speaking, the person spoken to, and sometimes the place and occasion of the action, make it evident that the majority, at least, of her approximately two hundred poems and verse fragments were written as incidents in a great Gondalan epic having for its central figure a super-heroine, Queen Augusta Geraldine Almeda. Clear presentation of the building of this Gondal epic through a period of ten years is difficult, however, by reason of conflict between composition dates and story sequence, for if the poems are arranged chronologically the narrative is hopelessly confused, while if, on the other hand, the story is kept intact, we have such oddities as two poems recounting the same incident from opposing viewpoints separated by an interval of six years; the lament of the Queen for her husband four years before his death; and the escape of the Queen's assassin from a crime he had not yet committed. The conclusion follows that Emily did not create or evolve the epic as she wrote, but merely gave poetic expression, as her muse moved her, to scenes in a complicated drama always vividly before her imagination. Dates of composition become significant only after the poems have been arranged in epic sequence.

It happens, however, whether by accident or design, that the opening lyric of the series bears the earliest composition date, July 12, 1836, just a week earlier than Charlotte's long poem depicting Zamorna's exile. It celebrates the birth of a girl child under auspices of the planet Venus:

> Cold, clear, and blue the morning heaven
>   Expands its arch on high;
> Cold, clear, and blue Lake Werna's water
>   Reflects that winter's sky:
> The moon has set, but Venus shines
>   A silent, silvery star.

This child's mother, inquiring of a soothsayer the course of her daughter's life, receives the Delphic answer,

> Lady, watch Apollo's journey;
>   Thus thy first born's course shall be.

A group of seven poems, written between 1837 and 1844, reveals that the baby grows into a glorious child, courageous, truthful, generous, affectionate, and joyous, a "being whose very presence blessed, like gladsome summer day." Then comes reverse of fortune, clouding her life until love dawns, bringing radiant happiness again—Venus' gift to her earth-child. In this connection her name appears for the first time, Augusta Geraldine Almeda, commonly indicated in the headings of the manuscript poems by the initials A.G.A.

In September of the opening year of the Gondal epic, Emily wrote a vignette ("The evening sun was sinking down"), which gathers around itself twenty-eight other poems composed between September, 1836, and December, 1844, all having to do with the death of A.G.A.'s lover, Alexander, Lord of Elbë in Gaaldine. Wounded in battle, he dies on the shore of Lake Elnor in Gondal, his head pillowed in her lap. Augusta is taken prisoner and confined in a dungeon, where she is reduced almost to madness before she is released. Back at her old home in Gaaldine, she passes from prostrating grief into renewed health—and a new love adventure.

Written concurrently with the Elbë incident, from July, 1837 to May, 1845 (though again story sequence and chronology of composition do not agree), are sixteen poems having to do with A.G.A.'s second matrimonial venture. This time her charms infatuate Lord Alfred of Aspin Castle, father of a beautiful golden-haired, blue-eyed daughter, named Angelica, who earlier took into her loving care a youth eighteen years of age, a dark and gloomy boy of sorrow. The young people welcome Augusta in wholehearted affection as "a radiant bow in a stormy sky." She proves, on the contrary, a herald of disaster, for—her ardent nature betraying her—she wins the boy to dishonorable love, then, tiring of his devotion, casts him off, sending him into exile. Angelica weeps and pleads for him in vain. Both are scornfully driven to a foreign land, where they plunge into a life of outlawry, "a 'wildering dream of frenzied crime."

From this or perhaps an earlier beginning, Augusta becomes a veritable "Sidonia's deity" in her cruelty to men. Beautiful, impulsive, passionate, speaking noble sentiments, she is irresistible. Fickle, ever craving new conquests, she grows utterly selfish and callous to the suffering of her victims. Yet she remains to the end a poet, clothing her harshest edicts in exalted phrases. Betrayed men die cursing her for her cruelty, yet acknowledging with their latest breath a love that even death cannot kill. In course of time she deserts Lord Alfred for Prince Julius Brenzaida of the Gondalan house of Angora, sending Lord Alfred into exile. On a lonely English moor he takes his own life, gazing on her picture inscribed in her smooth, rapid hand, "Dearest, ever deem me true."

In her love for Julius, now king of Almedore in Gaaldine, A.G.A. finds the great, absorbing, and lasting passion of her life. She urges him on to wars of conquest against the neighboring kingdom of Zalona ruled by the Gondalan house of Exina. Besieging the rival capital, he starves it into surrender and sends its miserable remnant into exile and captivity. Extending the war to Gondal, he invades his native land and forces Gerald Exina to accept him as joint sovereign. The coronation takes place in the great cathedral of Regina before a massed throng. In violation of his oath, Julius soon throws Gerald into prison and usurps full sovereignty over the land. His Gondal triumph is not shared by his queen, called in this connection Rosina of Alcona, who at the critical moment falls ill of brain fever.

A group of Gondalan patriots, joined by Angelica and her foster brother, formulate and carry out a plot for the murder of the new emperor in his own palace. The lot of actual assassin falls to the unhappy dark youth; he strikes the blow, but pays the instant penalty of his own life. Some of his fellow conspirators escape; others are taken and thrown into dungeons. Rosina, regaining consciousness after weeks of wild delirium, hears that her adored Julius is dead and his empire overthrown.

The events which follow are not clear, but there are two poems describing the return of Gondal patriots in mixed sorrow and happiness to homes redeemed by the blood of loved ones. Another group has to do with the fortunes of Rosina, here again called Geraldine. In one poem she nurses her darling child in a rocky cave, rejoicing in the baby's resemblance to Julius; in another she sees her little one freeze to death in a mountain snowstorm; in still others she grieves for her lost darling.

Then comes her coronation as Augusta, Queen of Gondal. Attended by lovers and adored by her subjects, she goes through the dreary years, hiding her aching heart under a proud and gay exterior. Emily's two loveliest poems, "Death, that struck when I was most confiding," and "Cold in the earth, and the deep snow piled above thee," are expressions of her grief for Julius. In his death she is fittingly punished for her cruelty to other men, but lonely and suffering remorse, she yet knows neither repentance nor diminution of ambition.

One day as she wanders over the lea, attended only by Lord Lesley and Fair Surry, lovers absorbed in each other, she lies down to sleep on a sunny bank. There she is discovered by her old enemy, Angelica, changed from a tender, loving girl into a hardened, desperate woman. Angelica steals near, knife in hand. Before she can strike, a bird wakes the sleeping Queen with its song, and she opens her eyes with such a dreary sigh that Angelica decides to let her live on in her misery.

An hour later, however, Angelica is pleading with Douglas, her lover and fellow outlaw, one of the conspirators in the assassination of Julius, to help "send to hell her mortal foe." Lord Lesley and Fair Surry, she says, must die first, that Augusta may "drain a deeper cup of bitterer pain." This preliminary murder done, the assailants lie in ambush beside a fern-bordered spring, knowing the Queen will come there to quench her thirst.

Hours later Lord Eldred, captain of the Queen's Guard, discovers his sovereign there on the earth, "a cold corpse beneath the moon." Detecting drops of blood across the moor, he sends his men in pursuit of the murderer, while he himself keeps the death watch, reviewing in his mind the stormy career of this woman "once so adored, so deified." "Like sudden ghosts to memory came" a long procession of lovers sent to miserable and dishonored graves. Full many such hearts, he thought, might have throbbed again could they but see their idol come to such a fate. He mourns, not for what she has been, but for what she was about to become, her passionate youth almost gone and the quiet sea of later life stretching smooth before her.

In the meantime Douglas's pursuers gain upon him, finally trapping him on a mountain ledge between a high wall on one side and a deep chasm on the other. In desperation he dislodges a giant pine bridging the chasm. Down it crashes, starting an avalanche that engulfs his enemies.

Closing the series, comes Lord Eldred's lament that Augusta's lovers and subjects alike have forgotten her.

Among the many puzzles encountered in reading Emily's poems are the three manuscript headings: "From the D[ungeon] W[all] in the N[orthern] C[ollege]"; "M.A. Written on the Dungeon Wall N[orthern] C[ollege]"; and "From a Dungeon Wall in the Southern College," utterly unintelligible until one remembers the school dungeon in The Play of the Islanders, which Emily has retained through the years practically unchanged.

The Gondal epic was interrupted in its early years by Emily's second venture into the outer world, a term as teacher in Miss Patchett's School at Law Hill, near Halifax, variously fixed by three Brontë authorities as beginning September, 1836, March, 1837, and September, 1837, two of them quoting from the same letter by Charlotte, which one dates October 2, 1836, the other, April 2, 1837—the correct date is October 2, 1837:

My sister Emily is gone into a situation as teacher in a large school of near forty pupils, near Halifax. I have had one letter from her since her departure; it gives an appalling account of her duties—hard labour from six in the morning until near eleven at night, with only one half-hour of exercise between. This is slavery. I fear she will never stand it.

Out of the Law Hill experience came the first of the half-dozen or more subjective Gondal poems, those revealing the importance of the creation in her own life. Dated December 4, 1838, it is a striking companion piece to Charlotte's "We Wove a Web in Childhood" of three years earlier (December 19, 1835), and it shows that Emily at Law Hill, like her sister at Roe Head, found occasional escape from her misery through the dream world:

> A little while, a little while,
>   The noisy crowd are barred away;
> And I can sing and I can smile
>   A little while I've holyday!
>
> Where wilt thou go, my harassed heart?
>   Full many a land invites thee now;
> And places near and far apart
>   Have rest for thee, my weary brow.
>
> There is a spot 'mid barren hills
>   Where winter howls and driving rain,
> But if the dreary tempest chills
>   There is a light that warms again.
>
> The house is old, the trees are bare
>   And moonless bends the misty dome
> But what on earth is half so dear,
>   So longed for as the hearth of home?
>
>   .   .   .   .
>
> Yes, as I mused, the naked room,
>   The flickering firelight died away
> And from the midst of cheerless gloom
>   I passed to bright, unclouded day—

Even as I stood with raptured eye
Absorbed in bliss so deep and dear
My hour of rest had fleeted by
And given me back to weary care.

Despite the exactions of her duties and her suffering from nostalgia, Emily remained at Law Hill for eighteen months or longer, until Miss Patchett announced her intention to marry and give up the school.

Chapter XVIII

REUNION

IN THE summer of 1837 Miss Wooler removed her school to Dewsbury Moor, a less healthy location than Roe Head. In the autumn Anne fell ill. A cough, short breathing, and a pain in her chest alarmed Charlotte. Miss Wooler, according to Charlotte's account, thought her a fool, and by way of proving her opinion treated her with marked coolness. Their difference culminated in a little *éclaircissement* one evening, when Charlotte's warm temper, getting the best of her, rose to a regular passion, and the Brontës departed for Haworth, but not before Miss Wooler made it plain that Charlotte misunderstood her feeling. Mollified, Charlotte consented to return after the Christmas holidays if Miss Wooler wished it. Emily was at home to receive her sisters.

The peace of the visit was broken when, early in the holidays, the old servant Tabby slipped on ice in the street and broke her leg. The girls insisted on nursing her themselves, with only the aid of a woman who dropped in now and then to help with the drudgery. An eagerly anticipated visit from Ellen Nussey had to be canceled, yet Charlotte found time and inspiration to write an after-the-war Angrian story [1] of approximately 18,000 words, which she finished January 17, 1838.

Anne improved so much at home that the opening of February saw Charlotte back in school, but in late spring Charlotte's own health and spirits failed utterly. Acting on a doctor's advice she returned to Haworth, "a shattered wretch," as she describes herself. It was only

[1] Charlotte Brontë: "The last scene in my last book concluded within the walls of Alnwick House." January 17, 1838. 35 pp., 18,000 words plus 14 ll. 7¼" x 4½". (Law Collection.)

"after months of mental and bodily anguish not to be described," that "something like tranquillity and ease began to dawn again."

The four Brontës were now together once more, though Branwell still kept his studio at Bradford. Within a few weeks after her return, Charlotte sketched a gay picture of the home group: "Mary and Martha Taylor . . . have been staying at Haworth for a few days. They are making such a noise about me I cannot write any more. Mary is playing on the piano; Martha is chattering as fast as her little tongue can run; and Branwell is standing before her, laughing at her vivacity."

One month later, on July 7, 1838, she wrote a poem [2] of seventy-eight lines describing Zamorna's grand review of the Angrian army at Gazemba after the victories which restored him to his throne. Within the month she completed a sizable volume of sketches [3] having considerable biographical interest and critical importance. One presents such an astonishing number of new characters mingling in easy familiarity with those who habitually parade her pages, that the reader can but gasp in wonder at the complexity of the society moving always before Charlotte's inner eye. Here again she tries, though as usual without success, to analyze the fatal fascination that draws Percy and Zamorna together, confessing in conclusion: "All this I have written before, but the subject is a strange one and will bear recurring to; and the fact is, when I once get upon the topic of Douro and Ellrington I cannot help running on in the old track at a most unconscionable rate." The most important feature of this volume, however, is the reappearance of an old character in a new semblance: William Percy, now Colonel *Sir* William Percy of the Angrian army, who comes to rival in interest even Zamorna himself, and makes important contributions to three of Charlotte's published novels. William Percy, introduced four years earlier in "Wool Is Rising," Branwell's account of the creation of Angria, is the younger of Percy's (Rogue's) two cast-off sons. Percy, it appears, cherished the conceit that his male children were devils, partaking of his own Satanic nature, while his daughter was the offspring of his pleasant human side. Branwell, at seventeen, tells the story of the Percy brothers crudely but clearly:

[2] Charlotte Brontë: "Review at Gazemba." July 7, 1938. 78 ll. (Bonnell Collection.)

[3] Charlotte Brontë: A volume of stories by Charles Townshend and Sir William Percy. July 21, 1838. 42 pp., 28,000 words. (Law Collection.)

Edward Percy, Esqr., as all know, is the eldest son of the Right Honorable Alexander Earl of Northangerland. But the moment he was born that strange nobleman delivered him to Old S'death, his lieutenant, with strict injunctions for his death instantly and decidedly. Old S'death, for motives known only to himself, did convey him away, but secreted him and caused his life to be preserved. . . . Upon the birth of another son . . . the Earl also gave him to S'death to destroy, but the old fellow also conveyed him away with life.

The course of existence pursued by these two young men I cannot describe, but after a childhood and youth spent in unmitigated hardships, destitution, and wickedness . . . after trying all means to rise, whether robbing, swindling, gambling, or pilfering, they, or rather the oldest, whose firm intellect—alas not united with a spark of goodness—had borne him through every disaster, determined to set up in Verdopolis on his own account, first as a working woolcomber, then to mount, if successful, through every stage, even as his own audacity planned it, to the very highest attainable. . . .

He set up his trade in an obscure hole in partnership with his younger brother, William Percy, and a wretch by the name of Timothy Steaton [Steighton Charlotte spells the name] . . . a fellow young in years but old in wickedness, meanness, treachery, and hypocrisy. The trio, in a month or two, from the mere possession of a wretched combing shop, had mounted to the employment of many hands and a decent floating capital. Ere long they bought a mill, employed workmen, set up a decided merchantile concern, and found themselves working gradually to riches. Edward Percy now, with the audacity and keenness peculiar to himself, claimed the whole management of the concern. Instantly the spirited but weak William and the mean and grovelling Timothy were under him, were subordinates. He was the sole head and director.

Taking up Branwell's crudities, Charlotte began her usual work of refinement, shaping them in course of years into *The Professor*. Edward and William Percy, under her pen, quarrel and separate in violence. William goes into the Angrian army, where his talents, enhanced by his relation to the Queen—he is Mary's brother—obtain him in rapid succession a captain's, a major's, and a colonel's commission. With his marriage to Cecilia, one of the six rich and beautiful Seymour girls, he drops out of the cycle for a time, to reappear—his marriage forgotten—a cynical bachelor, acknowledging none of his relatives except his sister. Between them there is as much friendship as is consistent with the difference in their rearing and their circumstances in life. From a sensitive, neglected, and abused youth, craving affection, though too proud to ask for it, William has become a sophisticated man of the world, quite able to

hold his own in any company. Scoffing in speech and irritating in behavior, he enjoys nothing so much as sowing seeds of mischief among
those he dislikes, dropping words and insinuations where they will
rankle and bring forth trouble. Yet there is a touch of kindliness in him
too, showing itself at unexpected times toward odd persons. On this
side he contributes a recognizable flavor to Paul Emanuel of *Villette*.
Sir William's own importance is accentuated by his close connection, in
this story and elsewhere, with Jane Moore, who becomes Shirley Keeldar.

In such Angrian adventures as this the creative Charlotte lost herself
through a blessed year at home, while the practical Charlotte busied herself with church work, helped with the housekeeping, paid visits to
Ellen Nussey and Mary Taylor, and received these friends in turn at the
Parsonage. In March of 1839 she returned "a decided negative" to a
proposal of marriage from Henry Nussey, Ellen's brother, "an amiable
and well-disposed man," at that time a curate at Donnington in Sussex.
All the while she was quieting her conscience by half-hearted efforts to
find a situation. It was necessary, all knew, for one of the girls to stay at
home to help their aunt with the housekeeping. By common consent,
that privilege went to Emily. Charlotte and Anne, then, must needs find
places as governesses. Anne succeeded first, and on April 8, 1839, departed to begin a nine-months' struggle with the unruly and violent
children of Mrs. Ingham of Blake Hall. A few weeks later Charlotte
went into a similar situation in the Sidgwick family at Stonegappe near
Keighley, but stayed less than three months, returning to Haworth in
July.

About this time Mr. Brontë added a curate to his ecclesiastical establishment, who necessarily came frequently to the Parsonage. He fell into
the habit of bringing his curate friends with him, particularly around
tea-time. These visits, though sometimes a nuisance and a bore, broke
the monotony of Parsonage days and brought variety into the life of
the Brontë girls. Another visiting curate, an Irishman named Pryce, proposed to Charlotte in writing after his first meeting with her. Charlotte,
reporting the incident in a letter, concludes, "I leave you to guess what
my answer would be, convinced that you will not do me the injustice of
guessing wrong."

In the early autumn she passed a fortnight at Easton, enjoying keenly her first sight of the sea. The visit left her well and fat, though much inconvenienced by the loss of her spectacles, for she could "neither read, write, nor draw with comfort in their absence." At home again, she sank back contentedly into the routine described in a letter of December 21, 1839, soothing and satisfying because it left time for dreams of the imagination:

Poor Tabby became so lame that she was at length obliged to leave us. She is residing with her sister, in a little home of her own, which she bought with her savings a year or two since. She is very comfortable, and wants nothing; as she is near we see her very often. In the meantime Emily and I are sufficiently busy, as you may suppose: I manage the ironing, and keep the rooms clean; Emily does the baking, and attends to the kitchen. We are such odd animals that we prefer this mode of contrivance to having a new face among us. Besides, we do not despair of Tabby's return, and she shall not be supplanted by a stranger in her absence. I excited aunt's wrath very much by burning the clothes, the first time I attempted to iron; but I do better now. Human feelings are queer things; I am much happier black-leading the stoves, making the beds, and sweeping the floors at home than I should be living like a fine lady anywhere else. I must indeed drop my subscription to the Jews, because I have no money to keep it up.

House dust did not obscure the Angrian vision, nor kitchen walls shut out Gondal.

Chapter XIX

CHARLOTTE RINGS DOWN A CURTAIN

THIS YEAR at home brought to Charlotte, however, increasing heart-ache and growing uneasiness for her brother, who by now, adding drugs to drink, had become the acknowledged familiar of degraded company and the habitué of low resorts. Her strongest hope of reclaiming him lay in the Angrian game, which she continued to share with him, allowing him, as always, leadership in plot-making, though often his inventions must have sickened her in their reflection of his life outside the Parsonage.

His stories of these days are sorry reading, for profanity and obscenity, introduced as touches of realism, only emphasize the natural feebleness of his style as he repeats chapters of his old chronicles in "lives" of Percy, the archrebel, and Warner Howard Warner, the superstatesman. Much of his attention was devoted to a new dramatization of himself in his degenerate state—Henry Hastings, the warrior poet of Angria, a captain in the Nineteenth Infantry of Lord Hartford's Division of the Angrian army, author of "Sound the Loud Trumpet," "Shine on Us, God," and other national songs, and historian of the bloody campaign against the Negroes of the East that immediately preceded the Great War. His bravery and military genius, in accordance with Branwell's usual exaggeration, attracted the favorable notice of his superiors and won him promotion to the rank of major, while his literary success made him the lion of Angria and Verdopolitan society. Hastings is, in fact, on the literary and social side, an Angrian adaptation of Robert Burns. In a fit of disaffection, Hastings—so the story runs—

shot his colonel and became a fugitive from justice, joining himself to an underworld gang of Percy's erstwhile friends, also in hiding. As their tool he attempted Zamorna's life.

Branwell's Henry Hastings is unconvincing, a hero of low tastes, a traitor without temptation, and a murderer without motive; in later stories he is indecent and revolting in the extreme. But for Charlotte's treatment [1] of him, he would be better ignored. In a story dated June 29, 1837, she takes him up at the height of his popularity and analyzes his character, making it plain how his rise in society reacted upon his peculiarly unhapp[...] his ruin. In a later story she depicts Sir William Perc[...]ing's commission to track Hastings down [...] Sir William, under Charlotte's pen, shrew[...]nal, run to bay, will seek the help of his sist[...] teacher, and foil to brilliant Jane Moore, "t[...]s quite right; Henry succeeds in reaching El[...]ngenuity to hide him from his pursuers, and[...]ther is under sentence of death, she risks eve[...] to intercede for him with the Queen. Sir V[...]onishment the hitherto drab and lifeless Elizab[...]ened and her emotions aroused, falls a victim to the charms of a [...] and soul usually hidden under a plain and colorless exterior. Thus for the first time Charlotte projects herself, her outward self and circumstances and her inner emotions, into her Angrian stories, and thus, in the person of Elizabeth Hastings, there enters that charmed circle of beautiful and fortunate highborn Angrian ladies the first of Charlotte's governess-heroines, the prototype of Jane Eyre and Lucy Snowe.

Other elements in the story show progress toward the greatness of Currer Bell. Sir William Percy, forbidden by rank and pride to ask Elizabeth Hastings to marry him, woos her to be his mistress in a scene that carries a theme already old in Charlotte's mind, very close to its

---

[1] Charlotte Brontë: "There is, reader, a sort of pleasure." June 29, 1837. 36 pp., 15,000 words. (Wrenn Library, University of Texas.)

——— Group of Angrian stories and poems. July 21, 1837. 42 pp., 15,000 words. (Law Collection.)

——— "Henry Hastings." By Charles Townshend. February 22–March 20, 1839. (Harry Elkins Widener Collection, Harvard University Library.)

supreme expression in *Jane Eyre* when Rochester on the evening following the frustrated wedding uses all the force of his compelling personality to take Jane with him to the Continent.

The most interesting feature of "Henry Hastings," from the view-
point of a Brontë biographer, is its dramatic reflection of Charlotte's
sympathy for her brother in his discouragement and depression..Hast-
ings, acknowledged by Branwell as representing himself, is an ugly
character indeed under his pen, without an appealing quality. But
Charlotte's portrayal of him in poignant suffering, a youth of brilliant
talents, ruined by adverse circumstances, raises him to the status of a
tragic hero. Hastings' sister, supposedly representing herself, remains
his only friend in his degradation, aiding him in blind sympathy, with
never a question or word of reproach. When the sentence of death passed
upon him by a court-martial is, through her efforts, commuted to life
sentence in a degraded and despised Angrian regiment, Elizabeth, far
from resenting the disgrace he has brought upon her, is happy that he
has "walked out of jail with the breath of life in his body." "It was
very odd," the narrator observes, "that his sister did not think a pin the
worse of him for all his dishonor. It is private meanness and not public
infamy that disgraces a man in the opinion of his relatives."

One more long story, or novel, has survived from this last year of
Angria, "Caroline Vernon," [2] the final chapter in the life histories of
two characters who reappear in *Jane Eyre* as Rochester's ward Adèle
and her mother Céline Varens, his one-time mistress. An evident adaptation of the Jane Clairmont episode, "Caroline Vernon" is Charlotte's
last Byronic fling.

Unable to see how her destiny was working itself out through the
Angrian creation, Charlotte was inclined to take her inward self severely
to task for lingering so long in a world which, however vivid and dear
to her, would have no meaning for a publisher. By the end of 1839, her
conscience, occasionally silenced, but never convinced, so far gained the
victory as to force her to a formal farewell of Angria, spoken through her
diary in words of such convincing emotion as to place it with "We wove

---

[2] Charlotte Brontë: "Caroline Vernon." March 26, 1839. (Widener Collection.)

a web of childhood," as a confession of her faith, and of such lyrical cadence as to suggest the final passage of *Villette:*

I have now written a great many books and for a long time I have dwelt upon the same characters and scenes and subjects. I have shown my landscapes in every variety of shade and light which morning, noon, and evening —the rising, the meridian and the setting sun can bestow upon them. Sometimes I have filled the air with the whitened tempest of winter: snow has embossed the dark arms of the beech and oak and filled with drifts the parks of the lowlands or the mountain pass of wilder districts. Again, the same mansion with its woods, the same moor with its glens, has been softly coloured with the tints of moonlight in summer, and in the warmest June night the trees have clustered their full-plumed heads over glades flushed with flowers. So it is with persons. My readers have been habituated to one set of features, which they have seen now in profile, now in full face, now in outline, and again in finished painting,—varied but by the change of feeling or temper or age; lit with love, flushed with passion, shaded with grief, kindled with ecstasy; in meditation and mirth, in sorrow and scorn and rapture; with the round outline of childhood, the beauty and fullness of youth, the strength of manhood, the furrows of thoughtful decline;—but we must change, for the eye is tired of the picture so oft recurring and now so familiar.

Yet do not urge me too fast, reader; it is no easy theme to dismiss from my imagination the images which have filled it so long; they were my friends and my intimate acquaintances, and I could with little labour describe to you the faces, the voices, the actions, of those who peopled my thoughts by day, and not seldom stole strangely into my dreams by night. When I depart from these I feel almost as if I stood on the threshold of a home and were bidding farewell to its inmates. When I strive to conjure up new images I feel as if I had got into a distant country where every face was unknown and the character of all the population an enigma which it would take much study to comprehend and much talent to expound. Still, I long to quit for a while that burning clime where we have sojourned too long—its skies flame —the glow of sunset is always upon it—the mind would cease from excitement and turn now to a cooler region where the dawn breaks grey and sober, and the coming day for a time at least is subdued by clouds.

Thus Charlotte at twenty-three emerged from the strangest apprenticeship that ever an author served. Could she then have taken stock of herself in the perspective of years, the plan for establishing a school at the Parsonage would never have been discussed, and there would have been no M. Héger for the imagination of biographers to play with. But the "Farewell to Angria" must not be taken too seriously as a milepost in her career, for it marks no sudden change from one order to another. Her landscapes and social life, always English, had of late taken on a distinctly local cast, and now, conscience propitiated by this gesture of renunciation, she had but to transport her Angrians to the cooler clime of England and continue the process of naturalizations already well under way. Percy, sometimes under his old name, sometimes under a new one; Zamorna as Arthur Ripley West, General Thornton as De Capell, and others of their group continue in their habitual relations to each other across many a transition page.[3]

Between May, 1840, and February, 1841, Charlotte sent one of her Percy-West romances to Wordsworth or Hartley Coleridge asking his criticism of it. His reply can be guessed from her later note of thanks:

It is very edifying and profitable to create a world out of your own brains, and people it with inhabitants, who are so many Melchisedecs, and have no father nor mother but your own imagination. . . . I am sorry I did not exist fifty or sixty years ago, when the "Ladies' Magazine" was flourishing like a green bay tree. In that case, I make no doubt . . . I should have had the pleasure of introducing Messrs. Percy and West into the very best society, and recording all their sayings and doings in double-columned, close-printed pages. . . . I am pleased that you cannot quite decide whether I am an attorney's clerk or a novel-reading dressmaker. I will not help you at all in the discovery; and as to my handwriting, or the ladylike touches in my style and imagery, you must not draw any conclusion from that—I may employ an amanuensis. Seriously, sir, I am very much obliged to you for your kind and candid letter. I almost wonder you took the trouble to read and notice the novelette of an anonymous scribe, who had not even the manners to tell you whether he was a man or a woman, or whether his "C.T." meant Charles Timms or Charlotte Tomkins.

"C.T." stood for her old pseudonym, Charles Townshend.

At this same time Branwell, probably in agreement with Charlotte, was also seeking literary advice. In January of this year (1840) he entered upon his first remunerative work, a tutorship in the family of Mr. Postle-

---

[3] Charlotte Brontë: (Fragment) "Miss Percy and Miss Thornton being both settled in Yorkshire." 2,672 words. (Bonnell Collection.)
——— (Fragment) "Mr. Ashworth." (Widener Collection.)

thwaite at Broughton-in-Furness. From this place he wrote Hartley Coleridge, April 20th:

Since my childhood I have been wont to devote the hours I could spare from other and very different employments to efforts at literary composition, always keeping the result to myself. . . . I like writing too well to fling aside the practice of it without an effort to ascertain whether I could turn it to account, not in *wholly* maintaining myself, but in *aiding* my maintenance. . . . I seek to know, and venture, though with shame, to ask from one whose word I must respect: whether, by periodical or other writing, I could please myself with writing, and make it subservient to living.

Having given up his post and back at Haworth, he again on June 27 addressed Coleridge in a letter revealing that in the course of a day's visit at Ambleside, he had received the older man's promise to read and criticize a translation of Horace that he was making, one book of which he now enclosed, explaining, "I dared not have attempted Horace but that I saw the utter worthlessness of all former translations and thought that a better one, by whomsoever executed, might meet with some little encouragement. I long to clear up my doubts by the judgment of one whose opinion I should revere."

He wished, he said, to inscribe the book to Coleridge, should it prove acceptable to a publisher, adding: "Let me say that my bones would have no rest unless by written agreement a division should be made of the profits (little or much) between myself and him through whom alone I could hope to obtain a hearing with that formidable personage, a London bookseller." With the translation he enclosed a poem of 354 lines ("At dead of midnight—drearily . . .") which he characterized as "the sequel of one striving to depict the fall from unguided passion into neglect, despair and death."

It is doubtful that Coleridge was able to excuse, as the writer asked, the "unintelligibility, haste, and appearance of presumption" of the letter, for with it the correspondence seems to have closed.

In October he went into another position announced by Charlotte, whether in fun or satire, in terms which recall by contrast her earlier high ambition for him: "A distant relative of mine, one Patrick Boanerges, has set off to seek his fortune in the wild, wandering, adventurous, romantic, knight-errant-like capacity of clerk on the Leeds and Manchester Railroad." In the next year he was transferred to a similar position at Luddenden Foot, where, according to his own boast, he spent a year in "grovelling carelessness" and "malignant yet cold debauchery," determined "to find out how far mind could carry body without both being chucked into hell!" The logical result of the experiment was his discharge for drunkenness and dishonesty.

Through most of this year the three girls were at Haworth, for the Christmas holidays of 1839 terminated Anne's connection with the Inghams. The advent of the penny-postage system, flirtations with neighboring curates, occasional visits paid and received, and half-hearted attempts to secure a situation as governess make up Charlotte's letters of 1840. On August 20 she wrote: "I have got another bale of French books . . . containing upward of forty volumes. I have read about half. They are like the rest, clever, sophistical, and immoral. The best of it is, they give one a thorough idea of France and Paris, and are the best substitutes for French conversation that I have met with."

Early in the following March Charlotte tore herself away from home once more to take up the drudgeries of governess in the family of the John Whites at Upperwood House, Rawdon. In taking this place, she wrote, she sacrificed salary in hope of comfort: not "good eating and drinking, or warm fire, or a soft bed, but the society of cheerful faces, and minds and hearts not dug out of a lead mine, or cut from a marble quarry." Her salary, nominally £20 was reduced to £16 by the deduction of laundry expenses.

Her pupils, a girl of eight and a boy of six, were not "such little devils incarnate" as her former charges, but they were overindulged and required the closest attention, so that she was obliged to devote her evenings—which she coveted for writing—to the sewing expected of her in addition to other duties. Though not happy in this position, she was decidedly less miserable than she usually was when away from home. She stood in little awe of her employer, "a good sort of body in spite of all her bouncing and boasting, her bad grammar and worse orthography," and held her own with her to a fair degree, wangling permission to pay and receive visits, and sticking up for three week's vacation instead of one. This vacation began in July, too late to see Anne, who was now governess in the Robinson family at Thorpe Green.

Chapter XX

BIRTHDAY NOTES

Occasionally, if not habitually, Emily and Anne exchanged notes to be opened on Emily's birthday, July 30, several years thence. Happily those of 1841 and 1845 have been preserved.[1] The earlier set, Emily's from Haworth, and Anne's from Scarborough where she had gone with her employers, bring the first direct information of the Gondal play since the joint journal fragment of November 24, 1834, confirming the testimony of Emily's poems that Gondal had come through a war of invasion corresponding to the great Angrian war and was on the verge of a political upheaval suggested by the French Revolution. Emily's note reads:

A PAPER to be opened
when Anne is
25 years old,
or my next birthday after
if
all be well.
Emily Jane Brontë. July the 30th, 1841.

It is Friday evening, near 9 o'clock—wild rainy weather. I am seated in the dining-room, after having just concluded tidying our desk boxes, writing this document. Papa is in the parlour—aunt upstairs in her room. She has been reading Blackwood's Magazine to Papa. Victoria and Adelaide are ensconced in the peat-house. Keeper is in the kitchen—Hero in his cage. We are all stout and hearty, as I hope is the case with Charlotte, Branwell, and Anne, of whom the first is at John White, Esqr.'s, Upperwood House, Raw-

---

[1] Emily and Anne Brontë: Birthday notes. July 30, 1841. 850 words.
——— Birthday notes. July 31, 1845. 1,276 words. (Law Collection, Printed in Clement Shorter: *The Brontës: Life and Letters*, 1908.)

don; the second is at Luddenden Foot; and the third is, I believe, at Scarborough inditing perhaps a paper corresponding to this.

A scheme is at present in agitation for setting us up in a school of our own; as yet nothing is determined, but I hope and trust it may go on and prosper and answer our highest expectations. This day four years I wonder whether we shall still be dragging on in our present condition or established to our heart's content. Time will show.

I guess that at the time appointed for the opening of this paper we i. e. Charlotte, Anne, and I, shall be all merrily seated in our own sitting-room in some pleasant and flourishing seminary, having just gathered in for the midsummer holiday. Our debts will be paid off, and we shall have cash in hand to a considerable amount. Papa, aunt, and Branwell will either have been or be coming to visit us. It will be a fine warm summer evening, very different from this bleak look-out, and Anne and I will perchance slip out into the garden for a few minutes to peruse our papers. I hope either this or something better will be the case.

The Gondalians are at present in a threatening state, but there is no open rupture as yet. All the princes and princesses of the Royalty are at the Palace of Instruction. I have a good many books on hand, but I am sorry to say that as usual I make small progress with any. However, I have just made a new regularity paper! and I mean *verb sap* to do great things. And now I close, sending from far an exhortation, "Courage, boys, courage," to exiled and harassed Anne, wishing she was here.

Anne writes from Scarborough:

July the 30th A.D. 1841.
This is Emily's birthday. She has now completed her 23rd year, and is, I believe, at home. Branwell is a clerk in the railroad station at Luddenden Foot, and I am a governess in the family of Mr. Robinson. I dislike the situation and wish to change it for another. I am now at Scarborough. My pupils are gone to bed and I am hastening to finish this before I follow them.

We are thinking of setting up a school of our own, but nothing definite is settled about it yet, and we do not know whether we shall be able to or not. I hope we shall. And I wonder what will be our condition and how or where we shall all be on this day four years hence; at which time, if all be well, I shall be 25 years and 6 months old, Emily will be 27 years old, Branwell 28 years and 1 month, and Charlotte 29 years and a quarter. We are now all separate and not likely to meet again for many a weary week, but we are none of us ill that I know of, and all are doing something for our own livelihood except Emily, who, however, is as busy as any of us, and in reality earns her food and raiment as much as we do.

How little know we what we are
How less what we may be!

Four years ago I was at school. Since then I have been a governess at Blake Hall, left it, come to Thorpe Green, and seen the sea and York Minster. Emily has been a teacher at Miss Patchet's school, and left it. Charlotte has left Miss Wooler's, been a governess at Mrs. Sidgwick's, left her, and gone to Mrs. White's. Branwell has given up painting, been a tutor in Cumberland, left it, and become a clerk on the railroad. Tabby has left us, Martha Brown has come in her place. We have got Keeper, got a sweet little cat and lost it, and also got a hawk. Got a wild goose which has flown away, and three tame ones, one of which has been killed. All these diversities, with many others, are things we did not expect or foresee in the July of 1837. What will the next four years bring forth? Providence only knows. But we ourselves have sustained very little alteration since that time. I have the same faults that I had then, only I have more wisdom and experience, and a little more self-possession than I then enjoyed. How will it be when we open this paper and the one Emily has written? I wonder whether the Gondalians will still be flourishing, and what will be their condition. I am now engaged in writing the fourth volume of Solala Vernon's Life.

For some time I have looked upon 25 as a sort of era in my existence. It may prove a true presentiment, or it may be only a superstitious fancy; the latter seems most likely, but time will show.

Anne Brontë.

Neither girl mentions in these notes her own or her sister's verse, inconsiderable in mass compared with their volumes of prose and probably thought of as a mere by-product of more ambitious work. It may be that the temptations of poetry account for Emily's small progress in her books. The years 1840 and 1841 swelled her epic by twenty or more poems, including several of its most important narratives: the story of Julius's assassination as told to the Queen; a picture of the Queen as a fugitive with her child; and a graphic account of the Queen's death at the hands of Douglas and Angelica, actually a drama in four acts. Three poems written between September and July, with another of later date, show that Emily had her occasional inner conflicts, though never bitter ones, when nature contended with Gondal for dominion in her heart. In the first, beginning, "Shall earth no more inspire thee," nature, the one time favorite, pleads,

> Then let my winds caress thee;
> Thy comrade let me be:
> Since naught beside can bless thee,
> Return and dwell with me.

"In summer's mellow midnight," the night wind continues its wooing, whispering softly of murmuring streams, rustling trees, and scented flowers:

> Have we not been from childhood friends?
> Have I not loved thee long?

At last in "Ay—there it is!" the same night wind, grown more passionately insistent, wins a momentary victory:

> Yes— I could swear that glorious wind
> Has swept the world aside,
> Has dashed its memory from thy mind
> Like foam-bells from the tide.

Again in "Often rebuked, yet always back returning" [2] Emily seeks in nature relief from the excitement of her own imagination:

> Today I will seek not the shadowy region:
> Its unsustaining vastness waxes drear;
> And visions rising legion after legion,
> Brings the unreal world too strangely near.
>
> .   .   .   .
>
> I'll walk where my own nature would be leading:
> It vexes me to choose another guide;
> Where the grey flocks in ferny glens are feeding
> Where the wild wind blows on the mountain side.

The seer would rest from visions.

[2] Mr. Hatfield thinks this may have been written by Charlotte after Emily's death.

Chapter XXI

PENSIONNAT HÉGER

As EMILY'S AND ANNE'S birthday notes suggest, the Brontë girls felt they had found at last an escape from their dilemma: the necessity of earning their living and the impossibility of health and happiness away from home. The solution was to be a boarding school in the Parsonage. Their father approved the scheme, and their aunt advanced the money for Charlotte and Emily to study on the Continent, since French was the subject most needed to attract pupils. They chose, because of its comparative cheapness, a school for girls in Brussels kept by Mme. Héger, wife of M. Constantin Héger, professor of Latin in the Royal Athénée and teacher of literature in his wife's school.

Thus Charlotte and Emily, at the ages of almost twenty-six and twenty-four, found themselves in the roles of schoolgirls in a foreign land. Charlotte, glad to exchange the exercise of authority for submission, was on the whole happy, taking up her studies with the avidity—to use her own figure—of a cow that has long been kept on dry hay returning to fresh grass. In M. Héger she had the first stimulating teacher of her life, and willingly put up with his irritable and choleric temper for the benefit of his instruction. In an early letter from Brussels she pictures him as "a little black being with a face that varies in expression," borrowing sometimes "the lineaments of an insane tom-cat, sometimes those of a delirious hyena," only occasionally approaching the "mild and gentlemanlike." But for Emily there was no such relaxation and expansion of spirit. She worked like a horse—again to use Charlotte's simile—out of pride and dogged determination to accomplish the purpose that brought her to a foreign country. She and M. Héger did not "draw well together at all." She probably saw through his temperamental tantrums to the nature of a commonplace schoolmaster and showed her contempt of such histrionics. He, on his part, found her stubborn, in contrast to Charlotte, and "obtuse to all reasoning where her own wishes, or her own sense of right was concerned." To him she appeared egotistical and exacting, exerting over Charlotte, always unselfish, according to M. Héger, a kind of unconscious tyranny. Yet he rated Emily's genius above Charlotte's, regretting that she was not a man to put her gifts to fitting use. She should have been a great navigator, he thought, deducing new spheres of discovery from knowledge of the old—undaunted by opposition or difficulty; or a great historian, using her strong imagination and sense of logic to present scenes and characters and opinions so powerfully as to convince her readers, whatever their previous judgments or cooler perceptions of the truth.

Out of consideration for the English sisters' mature years and foreign shyness, Mme. Héger allowed them a curtain separating their beds from the others in the dormitory and giving them a degree of privacy. Behind this curtain they found occasional escape into Angria and Gondal. Here Emily wrote the poem headed "H.A. and A.S." ("In the same place when nature wore") and drafted, August 20, "Aspin Castle," one of the pivotal poems of her Gondal epic, revised and completed at Haworth the following February.

The girls' original plan for study included only six months in this school, but their work proved so profitable and satisfactory that when the term expired in September, Mme. Héger invited them to remain another six months, offering board and lodgings, with lessons in French and German, in exchange for Charlotte's services as resident teacher of English, and Emily's as instructor in music. The new arrangement was well under way when, early in November, intelligence of Miss Branwell's sickness and death, recalled the girls to Haworth.

Miss Branwell's small fortune, less than £1,500, was by the terms of her will divided equally between the three Brontë girls and another niece, Anne Kingston. Charlotte's share of the legacy gave her the means to return to Brussels in January, leaving Emily at home to look after their father. Anne was still at Thorpe Green, where Branwell joined her as tutor in the Robinson family in January, 1843.

Charlotte's return to the Continent was ill-advised and unfortunate. Mme. Héger, though she received Charlotte with a show of kindness, drove a hard bargain in arranging her work. In addition to teaching English, Charlotte was to act as *surveillante* at all hours over the First Class, receiving in return £16 for the year, out of which she must pay 10 francs per month for lessons in German. This change in her status from an eager pupil feeding her own hungry mind, to a shy teacher struggling to impart knowledge to stupid, unruly girls of another language and country, was death to Charlotte's happiness in Brussels. She always sickened under the drudgery of teaching—at Miss Wooler's, as a private governess, and now at Pensionnat Héger. To make the situation worse, she was lonelier than she had ever been in her life. She no longer had the comfort of Emily's presence or the necessity of bearing up for her sake. She disliked and avoided her fellow teachers, and fear of intruding made her refuse Mme. Héger's invitations to share the family living room in the evenings.

In early letters she attributes her "constant sense of solitude in the midst of numbers," to the fact that she is a Protestant among Catholics, but admits that when she contrasts her life at Mme. Héger's with her previous condition as governess, she is thankful. A month later she writes, this time to Branwell, a vehement denunciation of the "120 persons who compose the daily population of this house," save only one or two who deserve something like regard. Except for the total want of companionship, she declares, she had nothing to complain of. In this same letter she refers longingly to her old dream life: "It is a curious metaphysical fact that always in the evening when I am in the great dormitory alone having no other company than a number of beds with white curtains, I always recur as fanatically as ever to the old ideas, the old faces, and the old scenes in the world below."

Charlotte and Branwell both referred to their dream world as "the infernal world" or "the world below."

Soon she reports that even M. and Mme. Héger are speaking to her but rarely. Madame, she has discovered, is cool and calculating like the other women in the house, no longer to be trusted, and Madame has begun to dislike her, though why she cannot guess unless it is because she holds herself aloof from the other teachers.

Left alone through the five weeks of summer vacation, Charlotte sought relief from the gloom of the empty school in long walks about the city. Wandering one day into the Church of Ste. Gudule, her attention was attracted to penitents at confession. As she watched, a sudden whim seized her to break her monotony of mind by making a confession herself "to see what it was like." Though conscience and her ignorance of the order of confession forced her to acknowledge that she was a Protestant, the priest received her confidence. To Emily she wrote, "I actually did confess—a real confession," and later she repeated the story as the experience of Lucy Snowe in *Villette*.

Before the middle of October her homesickness was so acute she gave Madame notice of her speedy return to England, but was deterred from carrying out this plan by the interference of Monsieur, who flew into such a passion that Charlotte gave in rather than provoke a further scene. A few days later (October 14) she wrote inside the cover of one of her school books (Russell's *General Atlas of Modern Geography*):

First Class. I am very cold—there is no fire—I wish I were at home with Papa—Branwell—Emily, Anne, and Tabby— I am tired of living among foreigners—it is a dreary life—especially as there is only one person in this house worthy of being liked—also another who seems a rosy sugar-plum but I know her to be colored chalk.

In November she concludes an account of Mme. Héger's coldness to her with the tantalizing hint: "I fancy I begin to perceive the reason of this mighty distance and reserve; it sometimes makes me laugh, and at other times nearly cry. When I am sure of it, I will tell you." Endurance breaking at last, she wrote her family to expect her home the day after New Year's, explaining that only her mind, not her body, was ill.

Branwell and Anne, both still employed by the Robinsons of Thorpe Green, were at home for the holidays when Charlotte arrived. The question of opening a school in the Parsonage was carefully considered in family conclave and put aside for several reasons: Mr. Brontë's eyesight was failing, and it would take most, if not all, of their aunt's legacy to build the additional wing needed for the school. The plan was revived later in the year, to be permanently abandoned when a carefully prepared prospectus of the proposed school failed to draw a single pupil.

Charlotte was little happier at home than she had been at Brussels; the evil spirit of depression still pursued her. Within the two years following her return to Haworth, she wrote a series of letters to M. Héger, represented by the four his son, Dr. Paul Héger, presented the British Museum in 1913, preserved, it seems, by his mother in the conviction that they were love letters proving Charlotte's unhappy infatuation for her husband. Biographers, accepting them as such, find in these letters not only the reason for Charlotte's three years of mental suffering, but the long-sought emotional experience which awoke her latent genius to the miracles of *Jane Eyre* and *Villette*. But the Héger letters are not the whole of the evidence, nor have they themselves been examined in the light of other documents.

There is reason to believe that Charlotte's literary ambition, the strongest urge of her being, received in course of this second stay at Brussels what she felt was its death blow. Several of her poems bear the tell-tale note "Copied at Bruxelles, 1843," and there is in the British Museum a group of Angrian prose manuscripts whose binding betrays their sojourn in Brussels. It is quite probable that Charlotte, who had twice submitted specimens of her work to strangers, took these stories with her for M. Héger's inspection, and it is fairly certain that he—if he saw them—frowned upon them, as he did upon other evidence of her romanticism, adjuring her to give up literary aspiration and to devote herself in single-minded attention to her teaching. Whatever the occasion of her depression in Brussels, conscience used the opening to renew its attack on her dream life, tearing and rending her to extort a recantation, while failing eyesight added its threat of blindness if she did not give up writing. The first of the Héger letters states the actual case clearly enough. After speaking of her plan for a school and the difficulties involved, Charlotte writes:

There is nothing that I fear so much as idleness, the want of occupation, inactivity, the lethargy of the faculties; when the body is idle, the spirit suffers painfully.

I should not know this lethargy if I could write. Formerly I passed whole days and weeks and months in writing . . . but now my sight is too weak to write. Were I to write much I should become blind. This weakness of sight is a terrible hindrance to me. Otherwise do you know what I should do, Monsieur? I should write a book and I should dedicate it to my literature-master—to the only master I have ever had—to you, Monsieur. . . . The career of letters is closed to me—only that of teaching is open. It does not offer the same attractions; never mind. I shall enter it and if I do not go far it will not be for want of industry. You, too, Monsieur—you wished to be a barrister—destiny or Providence made you a professor; you are happy in spite of it.

Again she refers to this terrifying threat of blindness, all the more vivid as she saw her father rapidly losing his sight from cataracts:

My father is well, but his sight is almost gone. . . . If Providence wills the same calamity to me, may He at least vouchsafe me as much patience to bear it.

While there are touches of real tragedy in Charlotte's letters to M. Héger, there are also suggestions of hysteria, as if she had unconsciously dramatized herself and lashed her emotions up to character. They carry the critical reader back to her letters to Ellen Nussey from Roe Head, when, shut off from her writing, she tried to solace herself with friend-ship and religion. Her warmest appeals to M. Héger fall short of the vehemence of her cries to Ellen, such as: "I am at this moment trembling all over with excitement after reading your note. . . . You have cheered me, my darling. . . . If you love me, *do, do, do* come on Friday; I shall watch and wait for you, and if you disappoint me, I shall weep. . . . I read your letter with dismay. . . . What shall I do without you? Why are we to be denied each other's society? . . . If I could always live with you, if your lips and mine could at the same time drink the same draught at the same pure fountain, I hope, I trust, I might one day become bet-ter. . . . I often plan the pleasant life we might live together. . . . My eyes fill with tears when I contrast the bliss of such a state . . . with the melancholy state I now live in. . . . It seems as if some fatality stood between you and me. I am not good enough for you, and you must be kept from the contamination of too intimate society. I wish I could live with you always. . . . I do think we might live and love on till *Death*." Just as Charlotte, five years before, trembled with excitement and joy receiving Ellen's letters, so she now counted M. Héger's letters the greatest felicities of her life, and as Ellen's letters were meat and drink to her, so her dear master's rare messages were "stay and prop—nourishment for half a year."

The Angrian stories, too, add their pertinent comments on the Héger letters, stories which, had they been written after her stay in Brussels, would substantiate the love theory. The third of the Héger letters, the most "pathetic" and "tragic" of the series in its longing for news from Monsieur begins:

Mr. Taylor has returned. I asked him if he had a letter for me. "No; nothing."

"Patience," said I—"his sister will be here soon."

Miss Taylor has returned. "I have nothing for you from Monsieur Héger," says she; "neither letter nor message. . . ."

I strove to restrain my tears, to utter no complaint. . . . One pays for external calm with internal struggle that is almost unbearable. Day and night I find neither rest nor peace. If I sleep I am disturbed by tormenting dreams in which I see you always grave, always incensed against me.

In other letters she writes:

You will tell me, perhaps,—"I take not the slightest interest in you Mademoiselle Charlotte. . . ." Well, Monsieur, tell me so frankly. . . . It will be less dreadful than uncertainty.

and

When day by day I await a letter, and when day by day disappointment comes . . . I lose appetite and sleep—I pine away.

Six years before Charlotte wrote practically this same letter with its kindred passages as an incident in "Passing Events." The time is the eve of the Great War. The Duke of Zamorna, in Adrianopolis, is initiating his scheme of revenge upon Percy by neglecting the Duchess in Verdopolis, leaving her for weeks without letter or message:

"Amelia, what time is it? Are the mails come in? Have any letters arrived?"

"No, my lady. . . ."

"I wish that the mail would come in. . . . How long is it since I've had a letter now, Amelia?"

"Three weeks, my lady."

"If none comes this evening what shall I do, Amelia? I shall never get time on till tomorrow. Oh, I do dread those long, weary, sleepless nights I've had lately. . . . I think I could sleep if I only had a kind letter for a talisman to press to my heart all night long. . . . Would he but write two lines to me signed with his name!"

"My lady, . . . you will hear from the East this evening. . . . Mr. Warner is in Verdopolis and will wait upon you immediately."

"I am thankful to heaven for it! Even if he brings bad news it will be a relief from suspense, and if good news this heartsickness will be removed for a moment. . . ."

Mr. Warner entered close muffled. . . . He began instantly to enter upon the business that had brought him there. . . .

"And, and—" continued the Duchess, throwing off restraint and writhing with impatience as she spoke, "have you no letter for me, Mr. Warner? Do you bring no message, no word of his welfare, no inquiry after mine?"

"My lady, I have not so much as a syllable for you, not so much as a scrap of paper. . . ."

Those who read Charlotte's letters to M. Héger as ordinary love letters find added evidence of her unhappy passion in the story of her confession in Ste. Gudule, for the sin she confessed, according to their interpretation, was, of course, her love for a married man. It seems far more likely, all things considered, that her confession, if it was anything more than "a whim," "a freak," as she herself declares, was an effort to ease her mind of a conflict far older than her acquaintance with M. Héger, and rid her conscience of the sin confessed in her Roe Head diary—idolatry, the worship of the creatures of her own imagination.

And yet, to quote a personal letter from Mr. C. W. Hatfield, "it is useless to say that the letters are not love letters. They are; but they are just as certainly not the kind of letters that a woman writes to her lover" —or the man she wishes for a lover.

Had M. Héger not been a married man, Charlotte Brontë would not have written the letters. It was because he was a married man that she allowed herself to write such letters to him. That seems paradoxical, does it not? Yet . . . I feel sure that you . . . will see the truth of it. . . . Héger was a professor of literature, absorbed in his work, an expert teacher with a dominating personality. C.B. enjoyed the domination because with it came knowledge, knowledge of the kind she most prized; and she amazed her teacher by the rapid progress she made under his tuition. There is no doubt that he was kind to her, kinder than he was to any other of his pupils, because they were slower of learning and roused his wrath. Out of this grew that love which is so much misunderstood; but which C.B. thought that Héger, being a married man, would understand and reciprocate. His knowledge, his power over her intellect, had made him her ideal—but he did not deserve to be, for he did not possess enough intelligence to understand her letters to him when she wrote from her loneliness at Haworth. Being what he was, just a teacher with a little of the coxcomb about him (for did he not boast about the letters to his friends?) it was well for C.B. that he did not answer the letters; yet if he had been the man to understand them . . . how much misery he might have saved her by replying as she desired!

At last Charlotte realized her mistake in expecting understanding friendship from M. Héger, and wrote:

> He saw my heart's woe, discovered by soul's anguish,
>   How in fever, in thirst, in atrophy it pined;
> Knew he could heal, yet looked and let it languish,—
>   To its moans spirit-deaf, to its pangs spirit-blind.
>
> He was mute as is the grave, he stood stirless as a tower;
>   At last I looked up, and saw I prayed to stone:
> I asked help of that which to help had no power,
>   I sought love where love was utterly unknown.

To swell Charlotte's woes of post-Brussels months came sharp anxiety for Branwell, incited by his vacation behavior and Anne's troubled reports of his strange and unseemly conduct in the house where both were employed. In July, 1845, when Branwell was at home for the summer holidays, the dreaded blow fell in a letter of stern dismissal from the Reverend Mr. Robinson, for Branwell, as a crowning folly, was frantically in love with his employer's wife, a woman seventeen years his senior. A distressing scene stretched itself through the following days, as the wretched brother thought only of drowning his distress in drugs and drink. No one in the house could have rest until he was sent away with an attendant for a week. This Charlotte knew in her heart was the beginning of the end, and she steeled herself for an indefinite period of disquietude and anxiety.

Emily, to whom Branwell was already "a hopeless being," retreated further into Gondal, leaving Charlotte to struggle alone in vain effort to save him. She—Emily—was still deep in the blissfully absorbing task of copying her Gondal poems from loose sheets and scraps of paper into notebooks, though without apparent order, either as to story sequence or date of composition. She was now at the height of her poetic powers, and in the present year (1845) had already added to her epic five or more poems including the masterpieces, "The Philosopher," and Augusta's two great laments for Julius: "Cold in the earth, and the deep snow piled above thee" and "Death, that struck when I was most confiding." Seeing Charlotte so cruelly torn between the warring factions within her, she wrote, October 14, 1845, her own great *credo,* the noblest apology for genius in the language, declaring her undivided allegiance to the God of Visions whom she worshiped through the Gondal creation. Addressing it as "radiant angel"—

> . . . ever-present, phantom thing—
> My slave, my comrade, and my king—

she begs it to justify her before the bar of reason for deserting "the common paths that others run":

> Speak, God of Visions, plead for me,
> And tell why I have chosen thee.

Within a week after the terrifying scene following Branwell's dismissal, Emily and Anne wrote the second extant set of birthday notes, both setting forth the state of Gondal. Anne, tired of the game, complains:

We have not yet finished our Gondal Chronicles that we began three years and a half ago. When will they be done? The Gondals are at present in a sad state. The Republicans are uppermost, but the Royalists are not quite overcome. The young sovereigns, with their brothers and sisters, are still at the Palace of Instruction. The Unique Society, above half a year ago, were wrecked on a desert island as they were returning from Gaaldine. They are still there, but we have not played at them much yet. The Gondals in general are not in first-rate playing condition. Will they improve?

Another paragraph reports:

Emily is engaged in writing the Emperor Julius's Life. She has read some of it, and I want very much to hear the rest. She is writing some poetry, too. I wonder what it is about. I have begun the third volume of *Passages in the Life of an Individual.* I wish I had finished it. . . .

On the same day Emily, more absorbed in Gondal than ever, exults:

Anne and I went on our first long journey by ourselves together, leaving home on the 30th of June, Monday, sleeping at York, returning to Keighley Tuesday evening, sleeping there and walking home on Wednesday morning. Though the weather was broken, we enjoyed ourselves very much, except during a few hours at Bradford. And during our excursion we were, Roland Macalgin, Henry Angora, Juliet Angusteena, Rosabella Esmaldan, Ella and Julian Egremont, Catharine Navarre, and Cordelia Fitzaphnold, escaping from the palace of instruction to join the Royalists who are hard driven at present by the victorious Republicans. The Gondals still flourish bright as ever. I am at present writing a work on the First Wars. Anne has been writing some articles on this, and a book by Henry Sophona. We intend sticking firm by the rascals as long as they delight us, which I am glad to say they do at present.

Chapter XXII

OLD WINE IN NEW BOTTLES

B Y WAY OF GONDAL Charlotte also found peace in return to her writing, for in the autumn of 1845, as she recounts years later, she "accidentally lighted on" a volume of manuscript verse in Emily's handwriting—one of the recently copied notebooks in microscopic hand-printing. She was not surprised, she says, at the existence of the poems, for she was aware that her sister wrote verse; nor was the heading of the notebook: "Gondal poems transcribed February 1844," which Charlotte does not quote, strange to her. She was, however, profoundly impressed by the quality of the poems, for they were not common effusions, nor at all like the poems women usually write; they were terse, vigorous, genuine, with a peculiar music—wild, melancholy, and elevating. Despite their distinctly Gondalan character, they possessed a universality of appeal that gave them, in Charlotte's opinion, claim to publication.

Her proposal was resented, she said, by reticent Emily as an unwarranted intrusion upon the inner recesses of her mind, and it cost Charlotte days of reasoning and persuading to reconcile her to the discovery. In the meanwhile Anne brought forth her poems, eager for Charlotte's approval.

After much discussion—Emily's reluctance having been overcome—the girls agreed to print a volume made up of selections from the work of all three. Charlotte's Angrian verse, the best she had done, was rejected, but Emily's twenty-one contributions were all of Gondal, and included the keystones of the Gondal epic, though carefully edited to hide their origin. Three of Anne's poems belonging to the Gondal cycle were included without change except the omission of their fantastic signatures.

Because Branwell had done nothing that the girls thought worthy of inclusion, the proposed publication was sadly withheld from his knowledge.

In order to keep the venture a secret, the girls agreed upon pseudonyms which preserved their own initials, Currer Bell, Ellis Bell, and Acton Bell, disguises dictated, Charlotte explains, by a sort of conscientious scruple at assuming names "positively masculine," though they did not like to declare themselves women. Charlotte had always written under pseudonyms "positively masculine": Captain Tree, Charles Wellesley, Marquis of Douro, and Charles Townshend; and Emily and Anne had frequently done so. Currer was an old Angrian name used in several combinations, such as Branwell's "Currer Haworth Warner."

Finding that no publisher would print the book at his own risk, the authors assumed the expense themselves, paying Messrs. Aylott & Jones of London £31.10.0 for its publication. It came out in May, 1846, under the simple title, *"Poems* by Currer, Ellis, and Acton Bell." About ten copies were distributed for review, but only two, Charlotte stated a year after publication, had been sold.

Indifference of the public to their little volume did not deter the Brontë girls from a more ambitious literary undertaking already under way, determined upon in earnest discussion as, arms entwined, they paced the living room through late hours of the evening: each was trying her skill in a novel designed to please publishers.

Charlotte chose from her Angrian abundance the old story of Edward and William Percy, adapted to an English setting in manuscripts of the transition months following her "Farewell to Angria," and now modified by her Brussels experience into *The Professor.* Emily, who had not yet taken leave of Gondal, continued the themes and, to some extent at least, the characters and incidents of her epic in the Yorkshire locale of *Wuthering Heights.* Anne, in whose imagination Gondal had never taken deep root, expanded her actual experiences as governess into *Agnes Grey.* All three retained their earlier pseudonyms: Currer Bell, Ellis Bell, and Acton Bell.

For this return to her old Angrian friends Charlotte propitiated her conscience by applying a theory of realism set forth in the Preface of *The Professor,* which, admirable and eminently right as it sounds, amounted in spirit and effect to a denial of her genius:

> I had not indeed published anything before I commenced "The Professor," but in many a crude effort, destroyed almost as soon as composed, I had got over any such taste as I might once have had for ornamented and redundant composition, and come to prefer what was plain and homely. . . .
>
> I said to myself that my hero should work his way through life as I had seen real living men work theirs . . . that he should not even marry a beautiful girl, or a lady of rank. As Adam's son, he should share Adam's doom, and drain throughout life a mixed and moderate cup of enjoyment.

Under pressure of this murderous expiation of her early romantic extravagances the story lost the convincing warmth and color which Charlotte had once breathed into Branwell's lifeless original. Refinement and grace she gave it, and strength of sinew, but the novel came from her hands drained of its lifeblood, a pale, gray corpse.

From publisher to publisher the manuscript went until six had read and refused it, giving for their rejection no better reason than its brevity —it fell somewhat short of the three-decker then in vogue. But Charlotte knew in her heart that the fault lay deeper than its length, as she acknowledges in another paragraph of this same Preface, written from the vantage point of success attending the publications of *Jane Eyre* and *Shirley.*

In the meanwhile *Wuthering Heights* and *Agnes Grey* found acceptance at the hands of Thomas Cautley Newby, Cavendish Square, London, "on terms somewhat impoverishing to the authors"—apparently they agreed to pay him £175 for 350 copies—to be brought out together, in the three volumes demanded by the reading public of the 1840's.

Through these same months Branwell, in an abandoned state of mind, was recasting an old familiar Angrian story in a local Yorkshire setting: Percy seducing his friend's wife, the familiar Harriet O'Connor story. The surviving fragment, entitled "And the Weary Are at Rest," probably all that he ever wrote, is sad and tragic evidence of the utter hopelessness of Charlotte's efforts to raise him, connecting itself immediately in the mind of the reader with his own infatuation for the wife of his late employer. There is no evidence that the manuscript was offered for publication, but in all probability it was this story that Branwell read to a group gathered in Cross Roads Inn, which one of his hearers, twenty years later, mistakenly identified as a portion of *Wuthering Heights*. His testimony, reinforced by others equally doubtful, gave rise to a persistent tradition that Branwell wrote or had a hand in Emily's masterpiece.

Despite its repeated rejections, Charlotte kept *The Professor* going to publisher after publisher. One of its returns found her, late in August, 1846, in a Manchester nursing home, awaiting the result of an operation to remove cataracts from her father's eyes. On this same day she began a new novel, to the writing of which she applied the experience gained from *The Professor*. Instead of bringing over another Angrian story rigidly intact, she selected from the length and breadth of her imaginary world characters and incidents to be woven together in a new pattern, colored by her own situation and experience in life to the semblance of reality. And released from her vow of repression by the failure of *The Professor*, she wrote in her old style, with renewed gusto and abandon, a tale as luridly romantic and as lyrically passionate as any that claimed Angria for a setting. One innovation the story shows that makes it in effect a new creation: the feminine personality of its narrator. Never before in her life had Charlotte Brontë written in the person of a woman.

By the middle of the following July, when the new book was almost done, *The Professor*, still on its round of publishing houses, reached Smith, Elder, and Company, Cornhill, London. They, too, returned the manuscript, but with a letter of two pages discussing "its merits and demerits so courteously, so considerately, in a spirit so rational, with a discrimination so enlightened, that this very refusal cheered the author better than a vulgarly expressed acceptance would have done." The encouraging missive added that a work in three volumes would meet with their careful attention.

A few weeks later, on August 24th, Charlotte dispatched for Smith, Elder's reading her newly finished manuscript: "*Jane Eyre*, a novel in three volumes, by Currer Bell." It was given first to an undermember of the staff, whose enthusiastic report provoked the skeptical amusement of his superiors. Mr. Smith Williams, a hard-headed Scotchman not given to enthusiasms, then took it up and found it so interesting that he carried it home with him and read late into the night to finish it. His curiosity thus aroused, Mr. George Smith, head of the firm, read the exciting manuscript for himself and agreed that the others had not overpraised it.

The first copies off the press were sent to literary friends of the publishers, who, one and all, returned expressions of high praise with their thanks for the book. The public received it on October 16, 1847: *"Jane Eyre, an Autobiography, By Currer Bell."* From the first it was a phenomenal success, one of the sensations of literature. The first edition was exhausted within six weeks, and a second was as eagerly bought. *Jane Eyre* was the novel of the season, and the reading public wondered who Currer Bell might be. That he was a man few doubted, though some thought the book showed the work of two hands. Charlotte had so managed the correspondence that the publishers themselves had no knowledge of the personality of the author.

In the meanwhile Newby delayed publishing *Wuthering Heights* by Ellis Bell and *Agnes Grey* by Acton Bell until December, 1847, about the time of the second edition of *Jane Eyre,* though the authors had corrected the proofs before *Jane Eyre* was finished. Moreover their corrections were disregarded and Emily and Anne were humiliated to find their printed pages marred by errors of spelling and punctuation. To make matters worse, Newby, eager to profit by the popularity of *Jane Eyre,* took care to circulate the surmise that the three Bells were one person, and the few who read *Wuthering Heights* and *Agnes Grey* dismissed them as earlier and cruder efforts of Currer Bell.

Notwithstanding these discouragements, Anne, impelled by conscience to sound a warning against sinful dissipation, began a second novel, *Wildfell Hall,* picturing under fictitious guise, Branwell's ruin with its consequent misery to himself and those who loved him. By late spring of 1848 this novel was completed and in Newby's hands. In July Smith, Elder, and Company, to whom Charlotte as Currer Bell, had promised her next work, complained that Newby was offering to an American publisher the advance sheets of a new novel by Acton Bell, affirming that to the best of his knowledge the authors of *Jane Eyre,* *Wuthering Heights,* and *Agnes Grey,* were one and the same person. In high indignation, Charlotte and Anne, on the very day they received this letter, walked after tea through a thunder storm to Keighley—four miles away—"got to Leeds and whirled up by the night train to London," where they showed themselves to the astonished Cornhill firm in proof that Currer and Acton Bell were separate and distinct persons. The promise of secrecy which they exacted was faithfully kept until the news broke from another quarter. Emily, remaining at Haworth, indifferent to the small tempest in a London publisher's office, was indignant when she learned Charlotte had included her in the revelation. Immediately upon her return to Haworth, Charlotte adjured Mr. Williams: "Permit me to caution you not to speak of my sisters when you write me. I mean, do not use the word in the plural. Ellis Bell will not endure to be alluded to under any other appellation than the *nom de plume.* I committed a grand error in betraying his identity to you and Mr. Smith. It was inadvertent—the words 'we are three sisters' escaped me before I was aware. I regretted the avowal the moment I had made it; I regret it bitterly now, for I find it is against every feeling and intention of Ellis Bell."

There is no clear record as to how deeply Emily felt the failure of *Wuthering Heights.* It is evident, however, that the novel did not turn her imagination away from Gondal, and the latest words we have from her pen are a narrative of its familiar scenes. She had probably just copied in her notebook a poem headed "Julian M. and A. G. Rochelle, October 9, 1845," when Charlotte made her momentous discovery, and it was from this poem that Emily took the eighteen baffling stanzas published in *Poems* as "The Prisoner, a Fragment," which, though a foundation stone in the traditional Emily Brontë canon, become meaningless and even misleading when taken out of their context. As originally written, the poem is an incident of the Republican Revolution in Gondal. Lord Julian, straying idly among the prison crypts of his father's castle, jesting at the plight of the prisoners, finds chained to the dungeon floor a young, frail, yellow-haired girl, with whom he had played as a child. She answers his thoughtless taunts with a philosophical courage that wins his heart. He frees her, and in secret nurses her back to health, while his haughty father and angry mother storm and threaten because he fails to answer his country's call to arms:

> Then oft with taunting smile, I heard my kindred tell
> How Julian loved his hearth and sheltering rooftree well;
> How the trumpet's voice might call, the battle-standard wave,
> But Julian had no heart to fill a patriot's grave.
>
>   .   .   .   .
>
> Another hand than mine my rightful banner held
> And gathered my renown on Freedom's crimson field;
> Yet I had no desire the glorious prize to gain—
> It needed braver nerve to face the world's disdain.
> And by the patient strength that could that world defy;
> By suffering, with calm mind, contempt and calumny;
> By never-doubting love, unswerving constancy,
> Rochelle, I earned at last an equal love from thee!

This is Emily's first explicit denunciation of war.

We have still two later poems from her pen: "No Coward Soul Is Mine, January 26, 1846," and the rough draft of another long narrative continuing her condemnation of war, dated September 14, 1846, about the time *Wuthering Heights* was finished. Its opening lines suggest that she was trying to raise her theme out of a local setting into the realm of universality:

> Why ask to know the date—the clime?
> More than mere words they cannot be;
> Men knelt to God and worshipped crime,
> And crushed the helpless, even as we,

while the narrator, refusing to give himself a name, speaks merely as one of thousands hardened and debased by fighting:

> Enthusiast in a name delighting,
> My alien sword I drew to free
> One race beneath two standards fighting,
> For loyalty and liberty.
> When kindred strive God help the weak.

The action of the poem shows this same enthusiast for liberty degen erated into a brutal pillager stripping a dying prisoner of his personal ornaments. A battle is fought, resulting in temporary victory for the Republicans. The Royalist leader, hardly more than a boy, badly wounded is taken prisoner, despite his prayers to die, and lodged in his own palace under guard of the narrator:

> We lodged him in an empty place,
> The full moon beaming on his face,
> Through shivered glass, and ruins made
> Where shell and ball the fiercest played.
> I watched his ghastly couch beside
> Regardless if he lived or died—
> Nay, muttering curses on the breast
> Whose ceaseless moans denied me rest.
>
>   .   .   .   .
>
> He heard my taunts and moaned again;
> And mocking moans did I reply,
> And asked him why he would not die.
> Was it not foul disgrace and shame
> To thus disgrace his ancient name?

At this point a messenger bursts in, reporting that the Royalists have counterattacked and are exacting heavy revenge for the slaughter of the day before, murdering whole families of the Republican leaders,

> And, comrade, thou hadst only one;
> They've ta'en thy all—thy little son.

Impulsively the narrator dropped at his captive's feet, adjuring him by his love for his own children to save the threatened boy.

> He wakened up—he almost smiled;
> "I lost last night my only child.
> Twice in my arms, twice on my knee,
> You stabbed my child and laughed at me.
>
>   .   .   .   .
>
> Yet not to thee, not even to thee,
> Would I return such misery.
> Write that they harm no infant there.
> Write that it is my latest prayer."
>
> I wrote—he signed—and thus did save
> My treasure from the gory grave;

And oh! my soul longed wildly then
To give his savior life again.

This manuscript, but a first draft, scratched and interlined almost beyond reading, with trial passages and experimental plot developments balanced one against another, yet shows the direction in which Emily's imagination was working. That she took the conception of this poem seriously is indicated by a revision begun on May 13, 1847 or 1848—the last figure of the date is not plain—whose twenty-five lines are actually the last from her pen which have survived. The literary career that began in revolt against Branwell's pointless battles ended in denunciation of war in general as senseless and debasing.

Chapter XXIII

"CRUEL DEATH!"

How ALL this literary activity in the Parsonage could be kept from Branwell, as Charlotte affirms it was, is explained by a passage in her letter to a friend (July 28, 1848), reporting her brother's condition:

Branwell is the same in conduct as ever; his constitution seems shattered. Papa and sometimes all of us have sad nights with him, he sleeps most of the day, and consequently will lie awake at night.

His strength failed steadily through the summer, yet the end came with startling suddenness on Sunday morning September 24, after but one day's confinement to his bed. The shock of his death struggle, the first his sisters had witnessed, was too much for their frail nervous systems, already strained to the breaking point. Charlotte went down immediately in a week of painful illness, from which she pulled herself to send brief notes to her few outside friends. To her publisher she wrote: "My unhappy brother never knew what his sisters had done in literature —he was not aware that they had ever published a line."

Emily, from a cold taken at her brother's funeral, passed into rapid tuberculosis. Weak and gasping for breath, she listened to Charlotte read from the October issue of the *North American Review* a notice of *Wuthering Heights* which characterized herself under the name of Ellis Bell as "a man of uncommon talents, but dogged, brutal, and morose," and smiled half in amusement, half in scorn. She died on December 19. Charlotte in the numbness of grief recounted her brief illness:

Never in all her life had she lingered over any task that lay before her, and she did not linger now. She sank rapidly. She made haste to leave us. . . .

Day by day, when I saw with what a front she met suffering, I looked on her with an anguish of wonder and love. I have seen nothing like it; but, indeed, I have never seen her parallel in anything. Stronger than a man, simpler than a child, her nature stood alone. The awful point was, that, while full of ruth for others, on herself she had no pity; the spirit was inexorable to the flesh; from the trembling hand, the unnerved limbs, the fading eyes, the same service was exacted as they had rendered in health.

By cruel coincidence the *Quarterly Review* chose the tragic month of Emily's death, to publish its denunciatory article on *Jane Eyre*. The third edition of that novel, published earlier in the same year, carried among its publishers' advertisements excerpts from more than thirty reviews expressing the spontaneous approval of the reading public. All agreed that *Jane Eyre* was fresh, original, sincere, powerful, absorbingly interesting, and moral in its tone and purpose. But the guardians of public morals, looking deeper, saw that the appeal of the book lay in its element of passion—the passion that was the very essence of Charlotte's genius. This was something new in fiction, new and dangerous. The guardians of public morals lost no time in denouncing *Jane Eyre* as "preëminently an anti-Christian composition." Its murmuring against the comforts of the rich and the privations of the poor was to them a murmuring against God's appointment, and for its proud and perpetual assertion of the rights of man, they found no authority either in God's Word or in God's Providence. Its pervading tone of ungodly discontent was at once, in their opinion, the most prominent and the most subtle evil which faced the law and the pulpit, all civilized society in fact. They did not hesitate to say that "the tone of mind and thought which has overthrown authority and violated every code, human and divine abroad, fostered Chartism and rebellion at home, is the same which has also written *Jane Eyre*."

Such condemnation by no less an authority than Charles Kingsley, who thought Currer Bell was coarse, measures in a fair degree the revolutionary force of *Jane Eyre* in the development of the English novel. Miss Sinclair's analysis is too good to pass by:

. . . For what did poor Jane do, after all? Nobody could possibly have had more respect for the ten commandments. . . . And yet Jane offended. She sinned against the unwritten code that ordains that a woman may lie until she is purple in the face, but she must not, as a piece of gratuitous information, tell a man she loves him, not, that is to say, in as many words. She [Jane] had done it.

And she was the first heroine who had. Adultery, with which we are fairly familiar, would have seemed a lesser sin. There may be extenuating circumstances for the adulteress. . . .

But when her enemies accuse Charlotte Bronte of glorifying passion they praise her unaware. Her glory is that she did glorify it. Until she came, passion between man and woman had meant animal passion. . . .

And it was this thing, cast down, defiled, dragged in the mud, and ignored because of its defilement, that Charlotte Bronte took and lifted up. She washed it clean; she bathed it in the dew of the morning; she baptised it in tears; she clothed it in light and flame; she showed it for the divine, the beautiful, the utterly pure and radiant thing it is, "the very sublime of faith, truth, and devotion." She made it, this spirit of fire and air, incarnate in the body of a woman who had no sensual charm. Because of it little Jane became the parent of Caterina and of Maggie Tulliver; and Shirley prepared the way for Meredith's large-limbed, large-brained, large-hearted women.

The *Quarterly's* review, while it drove *Jane Eyre* out of sight in certain quarters, accelerated its sales. The public continued to read, either openly or covertly, and wondered who Currer Bell might be. And Charlotte, though hurt by the reviewer's injustice, had little grief to spare for such misunderstanding.

Hardly was Emily buried when Anne fell ill. On May 28 she too died of the family scourge, at Scarborough, where Charlotte had taken her in hope that the sea air might help her. The plague now stayed its hand for a time, and upon Charlotte, as always, fell the burden of carrying on. In utter loneliness she returned to the writing of a novel interrupted by Branwell's death.

Chapter XXIV

CHARLOTTE CARRIES ON

In THIS NEW NOVEL Charlotte, still nagged by conscience, was resolved
to write directly from life, about people and places that she herself
knew. She would depict the West Yorkshire character in a story centering around the Luddite riots, which took place only a few years before
she was born and were still current tradition. To supplement information received at first hand from persons who had lived through those
troubled years, she borrowed from Leeds files of the *Mercury* for 1812,
1813, and 1814, realizing, perhaps with surprise, as she read how much
of Yorkshire and its people had gone into her own innumerable pages
of tiny hand-printing between 1833 and 1839, for Angria on its industrial
side, particularly its manufacturing province of Zamorna, was an adolescent projection of Haworth and its surroundings. Into its making she
had woven disturbances of the industrial revolution, rise of local fortunes
through manufacturing ventures, extravagances of West Yorkshire dis-
senters; local speech and customs, and many a vivid Yorkshire personality. In that unseen world always before her imagination there moved
a long procession of Yorkshire-Angrians, clear-cut, alive, and familiar
in their every feature and movement, mocking their creator's resolve to
copy from life, and challenging her to repatriate them in their native
environs.

Out of this group of familiars Charlotte chose her leading characters:
the Percy brothers modified into Robert and Louis Moore—Louis an
utter failure; Jane Moore, "the Rose of Zamorna," epitome of Angrian
womanhood, developed into Shirley Keeldar; and General Wilson

Thornton, taken years before from Mr. Taylor, father of Charlotte's school friends, Mary and Martha, now returned to his original status as Hiram Yorke. Holding fast, however, to her conscientious resolve, Charlotte brought into her pages a host of actual persons, strangers to her imagination, whose awkward, halting movements break the unity and impede the movement of the story. Miss Sinclair, ignorant of the cause, analyzes with her usual penetration the marring effect of these unassimulated elements upon the novel: "The elements are confused, somehow; the atmosphere is confusing; the northern background is drawn with a certain hardness and apathy of touch; the large outlines are obscured, delicate colors, sharpened; it is hard and yet blurred, like a bad steel engraving."

Charlotte finished the book on August 29; on October 26 it was published by Smith, Elder, and Company as *"Shirley*. A Tale. By Currer Bell"—her most outward work, and her poorest. Yet, notwithstanding its errors of taste and judgment and the scars left upon its construction by sickness and grief, it achieved the immediate success of *Jane Eyre.* Among its readers was a native of Haworth, then living in Liverpool, who recognized the Yorkshire setting and the three curates with whose misdoings the story opens. None but an old resident of the place, he argued, could have written this scene; and the village had but one citizen of literary bent, the daughter of the vicar. Thus the secret was out, and rapidly the news spread that the unspeakable Currer Bell, defier of convention, desecrator of the moral code, menace to church and state, was in reality the shy, lonely daughter of an Anglican churchman, an ardent Tory and a devoted daughter of the Church.

Popularity brought Charlotte as much pain as pleasure since it emphasized the public's neglect of her sisters. Anne, she admitted, deserved only mild recognition, but Emily's grandeur was beyond question. *Wuthering Heights,* in particular, needed but a fair hearing to be appreciated. Its failure, she knew in her heart, was due to its untimely appearance at the height of public absorption in *Jane Eyre.* The blame was not hers, however, but Newby's, who, having delayed the book for a year, encouraged the belief that Currer and Ellis Bell were one person. Charlotte knew him to be tricky in money matters also, for while her sisters had contracted for 350 copies of *Wuthering Heights* and *Agnes*

Grey, he claimed that he printed only 250 copies, yet did not return the proportionate £50. Charlotte was eager to break all connection with him.

The Palladium for September, 1850, brought her intense gratification through an anonymous article recognizing, though in mistaken terms, Emily's genius. Her pleasure was the greater when she learned that its author was Sydney Dobell. Mr. Dobell assumed that the three Bells were one person, a woman, for "every word she writes in *Jane Eyre* is female, not feminine, but female," and listed the novels by the Bells in "order of production, though not of publication," as *Wuthering Heights, Wildfell Hall, Jane Eyre,* and *Shirley,* the "works of one artist under sundry disguises." The author of *Jane Eyre,* he declared, need fear nothing in acknowledging her immature creation, *Wuthering Heights,* though it is obviously earlier in date and ruder in execution—"a youthful story written for oneself in solitude, and thrown aside until other successes recall the eyes to it in hope." There are in the book, he repeated, passages which any novelist, past or present, might be proud to own, while the "thinking out" of some of its pages, is the masterpiece of a poet, rather than the hybrid creation of the novelist.

In pathetic appreciation Charlotte, passing over his high praise of *Jane Eyre* as a book that will endure with the prose literature of our language, wrote to a member of her publishing firm: "I need not say how I felt the remarks on *Wuthering Heights;* they woke the saddest yet most grateful feelings; they are true, they are discriminating; they are full of late justice—but it is very late—alas! in one sense too late." And Smith, Elder, and Company sympathizing with her anxiety to establish the individuality of her deceased sisters in the public mind, suggested that she allow them to bring out a new edition of *Wuthering Heights* and *Agnes Grey* with a foreword or memoir by herself. She accepted the offer gratefully, and prepared a manuscript containing in addition, "Selections from Poems by Ellis and Acton Bell," with a second introductory essay drawing the now familiar picture of Emily's homesickness at Roe Head, which haunts one as powerfully as an incident from Emily's own pen. Charlotte concluded her simple memoirs, containing practically all that is known of the characters and personalities of Emily and Anne Brontë: "I may sum up all by saying that for strangers they [Ellis and Acton] were nothing, for superficial observers less than nothing; but for those who had known them all their lives in the intimacy of close relationship, they were genuinely good and truly great."

"Selections from the Poems of Ellis Bell" added seventeen pieces to the twenty-one which Emily herself published. Mr. C. W. Hatfield thinks that an eighteenth poem included in this group was written by Charlotte herself in her eagerness to interpret her sister's genius to the public. It is certainly true that in three instances, at least, she inserted in her sister's poems lines of her own which gave them a meaning wholly foreign to the author's thought. In preparing Emily's manuscript for the press Charlotte faced a delicate editorial problem: in her hands was a mass of good poetry, perhaps even great poetry, expressing profound human emotions in terms of an unreal world; raised to the realm of universality, these poems might bring posthumous fame to her neglected sister. She followed Emily's example and deleted every trace of Gondal. Time shows that she erred, for, ironically, in further obscuring the origin of Emily's poems, she invited the subjective interpretation which has contributed more than all other circumstances to the misunderstanding of her sister's character and genius. For instance, in substituting her own title, "The Wanderer from the Fold," for Emily's manuscript heading, "E.W. to A.G.A.," she transformed—so far as general interpretation goes —Lord Eldred W.'s grief for his murdered queen into Emily's lament for Branwell, and upon this interpretation rests in large measure the tradition of closeness of sympathy between the two, which in its turn is used as an argument for Branwell's hand in *Wuthering Heights*. More important still, perhaps, Charlotte added to the first twelve lines of "Julian M. to A. G. Rochelle," eight lines, apparently of her own composition to make the familiar poem called "The Visionary," one of the sublimest compositions bearing the Brontë name. From this composite, utterly different from the poem that Emily originally wrote, has come the popular conception of Emily Brontë the mystic, though its mysticism seems to be Charlotte's rather than Emily's. Such confusion equals in irony a blunder made by Miss Sinclair twenty-five years ago, when to prove Emily's superiority over Charlotte as a poet—an unquestionable fact—she misquoted as Emily's a poem now known to be Charlotte's own.

Charlotte concluded her "Selections from Ellis Bell" with "No coward soul is mine," to which she appended the note: "The following are the last lines my sister Emily ever wrote," implying that Emily was expressing her own feelings in the face of death, though the manuscript bears the date January 25, 1846, when Emily was in good health, and after this date she wrote at least one long poem and *Wuthering Heights.* "No coward soul is mine" was probably spoken by a Gondalian.

The publication of the new edition of *Wuthering Heights* and *Agnes Grey* by Smith, Elder, and Company bespeaks the happy personal relation that existed between Charlotte and her publisher. Correspondence with the several members of the firm and a generous stream of books from Cornhill were the chief diversions of her lonely life. It was natural enough that the unattached member of the group should lose his heart to the little novelist. He was James Taylor, one year Charlotte's junior, small of stature and red-haired, energetic, and determined. Charlotte in her loneliness tried to return his regard, but when he came to Haworth for his answer, on the eve of his departure upon a five years' mission to Bombay, she found in her heart only a stubborn negative. Perhaps it was his startling resemblance to Branwell, caught on this visit for the first time by her near-sighted eyes, awakening unbearable memories, that forced her to a refusal in spite of herself. It is certain that she dismissed Mr. Taylor reluctantly and that his going left a sore spot in her heart.

The modified victory which conscience won in *Shirley* in favor of the outer world and the actual turned to defeat as the cost was reckoned in terms of artistic loss. When, therefore, Charlotte began a new novel early in 1852, she returned to her inner world of imagination where she knew herself master. For the semblance of the actual which was now a part of her formula she went again to the only locale she knew intimately outside Yorkshire: Brussels and the Pensionnat Héger— *The Professor* was still unpublished. In this familiar setting, raised through emotion into the realm of inner consciousness, a group of her own begotten creatures move as freely and naturally as in their native Angria through the pages of *Villette,* published by Smith, Elder, and Company in January, 1853. And in this union of the actual with pure imagination Charlotte's genius fulfilled itself—conscience and Angria concluded lasting peace.

Chapter XXV

THE UNBORN

CHARLOTTE BRONTË, as she remarked of one of her characters, was exceedingly tenacious of a favorite idea. The Edward and William Percy story was more than a favorite idea, it was almost an obsession. Four times since her "Farewell to Angria" she had tried to give it realistic form: in "Mr. Ashworth" and "The Moores," which got no further than the opening chapters; and in *The Professor* and *Shirley*. *The Professor* was still unpublished, and in *Shirley* the brothers were so changed in their relation to each other that the major theme of the original story was lost. Hardly was *Villette* in circulation before Charlotte was again at work on the fascinating problem. In her new version she called the brothers Edward and William Ellin—a Mr. Ellin was numbered among Branwell's lowest Angrians—and emphasized the suffering of the sensitive younger boy under the brutal tyranny of the older.

Three distinct trial openings of this story have survived from the summer of 1853.[1] The first identifies itself with the series through a single paragraph:

Ellin Hall had for five ages been the home of the Ellins. In my youth it passed out of their hands. My eldest half-brother sold it. He died suddenly, leaving neither will nor direct heir; his fortune fell to me, and I purchased back the ancient homestead. That eldest half-brother of mine was a stronger man in body and a tyrant in heart. I would advert to his deeds, but they are such as we suffer Death to cancel from memory.

---

[1] In the Bonnell Collection and the Howe Library. All were printed by C. W. Hatfield in The Brontë Society Publications, 1936.

Again, Charlotte tried to tell the story through a disembodied spirit haunting Ellin Balcony:

Who am I? Was I owner of the house? No. Was I its resident tenant . . . ? No. Was I a child of the family? No. A servant? No. Ask me no more questions, for they are difficult to meet. I was there, and it was my home.

In a third start the story gets under way through the pen of an impersonal third person. Mrs. Hill, the solitary housekeeper of Ellin Balcony, was sitting one evening reading a pamphlet sermon as old as herself when there appeared at the gate a lad well dressed, but dusty and tired. He was "little Willie Ellin," he told her, whom she had nursed when he was a baby, and he had walked the fifteen miles from Golpit to escape his elder half-brother's brutality. He begged her for food and shelter.

Mrs. Hill fed him and tucked him asleep in a bedroom on the second floor. The next day Edward arrived in a gig, accompanied by a man of foreign appearance, evidently of "Hebrew origin." Pouring out threats, Edward searched the house until he came to the room where Willie had barricaded himself, and breaking the door, he had his gig whip raised over the cringing child, when Mr. Bosas, his companion in the gig, intervened.

Edward took the child back to Golpit, but so long as Mr. Bosas, to whom he owed some business obligation, remained in the house, Willie was unmolested. One day the lad was sent on an errand, and when he returned his protector was gone. That night as Willie sat in his little garret room, bare except for a stool and crib, lost in the fascination of *Robinson Crusoe,* Edward's heavy step shook the ladder-like stairs leading to this refuge. He had the gig whip in his hand, and, turning back his cuff to show a "thick wrist not soon to be wearied," he fell to work, despite the child's piteous pleading not to be thrashed alone and at night. At length

the man of bad propensities withdrew. Willie was left kneeling by his cribside, his face and hands pressed against the mattress. He had been severely flogged, and for a time felt sick, but he was not maimed or dangerously hurt —not corporeally maimed. How his heart fared is another question.

He was roused from his numb misery by the comforting words and caresses of a girl of seventeen, blooming and with features, "which if they borrowed at this moment interest of pity, gave back in return beauty distinct, undoubted, and undenied." She heard the brutal beating from her room below and came to comfort the victim.

Here the manuscript breaks off, interrupted, perhaps, by a crisis in Charlotte's own affairs.

Mr. Brontë's curate, Mr. Arthur Bell Nicholls, at whom as Mr. Macarthey Charlotte took a satirical fling in *Shirley,* had loved her in silence for several anxious years. One December evening a few weeks after the manuscript of *Villette* was dispatched to the publishers, he found courage to make his faltering declarations. Charlotte heard in utter indifference, except for her sympathy with his evident suffering, and referred his proposal to her father, who rejected it in hot anger at his curate's presumption. So violent was his agitation that Charlotte hastened to assure him that she would return Mr. Nicholls "a distinct refusal."

Mr. Brontë's continued hardness and contempt drove Mr. Nicholls to accept another curacy, serving at the same time to rouse Charlotte's interest in the abused young clergyman. Letters and visits kept his love fresh in her notice, and within a year she not only persuaded her father to invite him back to his old post, but promised to marry him.

The wedding took place on June 29, 1854. After a honeymoon in Ireland, Mr. and Mrs. Nicholls settled down to quiet Parsonage routine. Charlotte was happy in her married life, but not even her husband's absorbing and demanding love could hold her from her old world of imagination. Late in December she brought forth and read to him the beginning of a new novel.

A gentleman named Conway Fitzgibbon leaves his young daughter Emma at an expensive seminary to be given all the accomplishments the school affords. The headmistress showers the child with favors, only to find, when the time of payment arrives, that the father has disappeared. Favoritism turns to persecution from which the poor child is saved by a kind-hearted gentleman of the neighborhood, Mr. Ellin.

At this point Charlotte's writing was interrupted by illness, which sent her to bed in January. On March 31, she died of pregnancy complicated by a cold.

The sixteen pages of "Emma" is too little to show whither the novel tended, but that little savors so strongly of Percy in his bankrupt days,

Percy and his daughter, as to suggest that Charlotte had at last found realistic expression for one of the very dearest of her Angrian themes. However this may be, it is certain that the half-dozen immortals given to the world through *Jane Eyre, Shirley,* and *Villette* represent an infinite host of living beings who took their flight with Charlotte Brontë and her unborn child on that Easter eve.

Chapter XXVI

FRUITS OF THE ALMOND TREE

THE YOUNG MEN'S PLAY was ended at last. For twenty-nine years it served the Brontë genius, giving life to wooden puppets and bodies to flaming spirits, creating a vast dream world preserved in a voluminous literature. Beginning as the exaggerated make-believe of four small children at their toys, the play adapted itself in perfect understanding to all their needs through precocious childhood, wistful, imitative adolescence, and ambitious youth. It was at once the medium which caught and held in pristine freshness the impression of these formative periods and the agent of imagination in weaving them into a vivid, tangible pattern. It was the master who taught the girls—their brother was but a bungling pupil—the fluent and precise use of their native tongue and the exercise that gave them perfect coördination between thought and expression.

It assumed in course of long indulgence the nature of a religious creed, absorbing all their interests that were not purely mechanical, giving its devotees in return escape from the material world. Charlotte at twenty, in the shock of sudden realization of the place the play had taken in her life, figured it as a web of childhood spread to all encompassing proportions; a trickling spring swollen into a mighty ocean; a mustard seed grown into a forest giant; and a shriveled almond rod, quickened into miraculous life, towering to eternity. Emily at a more mature age addressed it lovingly as her slave, comrade, and king, and worshiped it as her God of Visions. Branwell, long past man's estate, chronicled its grotesque episodes with the pompous seriousness of world history. Anne alone of the four remained independent of its seducive charms. Its power over its creators made it, in the end, the instrument of destiny for meting out to each in turn the fate inherent in his own nature, crushing Branwell, wearying Anne, consuming Emily, comforting and sustaining Charlotte.

It gave to literature a noble epic and five novels esteemed among the world's greatest fiction. Of these *Jane Eyre, Villette,* and *Wuthering Heights,* so wildly and strangely romantic as to suggest a gothic inspiration and yet so original and emotionally convincing that they are interpreted by some as autobiographies, have stood for more than three score years a perennial challenge to critics.

The riddle is read, and the challenge answered when the novels are analyzed in light of Brontë *juvenilia.*

The Professor

The Professor, first written and last published of Charlotte Brontë's four novels, is an early Angrian story transferred with remarkably few changes to an English setting: the oft-repeated story of the Percy brothers, first set down in writing by Branwell in "Wool Is Rising," 1834. Edward and William, Branwell explains, were the cast-off sons of Alexander Percy, archvillain of the Angrian cycle, who, possessed of an insane antipathy against his male children, orders them put to death, each in turn, as they come into the world. His unnatural plans miscarrying, he took no notice whatsoever of his sons' existence, either through their childhood, when he was himself a bankrupt, or in later years, after he had rebuilt his fortune. They, with a foundling called Timothy Steaton (or Steighton), "the cast-off son of Percy's steward," by some unexplained dispensations of providence, survived a childhood of want and misery, a youth of low, degrading labor and even crime, to set themselves up in Verdopolis as wool-combers, and, a little later, as small manufacturers. No sooner was a profitable business established than Edward, exerting his coarse sensibilities, strong will, and superior bodily strength, made himself master and sole beneficiary of it, William and Timothy being virtually his slaves.

Edward's handsome face, athletic figure, "well-known energy and ambition," Branwell continues in his awkward, pompous style, added to a fortune rapidly acquired by clever and unscrupulous methods, opened to him the doors of politics and society. Beginning his career as a member of Parliament, he rose rapidly to the post of secretary of trade in the Angrian cabinet. Earlier, he married the proud, haughty, vivacious flirt, Maria Sneachi, Princess Royal of Sneachiesland. Toward his brother he was brutal and cruel, as well as dishonest.

Charlotte takes up the story at this point, and carries it forward in "The Spell" and Sir William Percy's diary and letters, refining its style, vivifying its characters, and motivating its action. She depicts, for instance, the crushing grief of the gentle, loving, and submissive mother as her sons were taken from her, one after the other, and she employs all her skill to show how William, Edward's superior in intelligence, taste, and refinement, grew to hate his tyrant all the more because of his enforced submission. Many and violent, she says, were the scenes between the brothers before William obtained his freedom by joining the Angrian army. About the time of his emancipation, she records, he married Cecilia, one of the famous "six Seymour girls," represented as gentle, refined, and tactful, in contrast to her showy and haughty elder sisters. With their marriage there devolved upon William and Cecilia a fortune that might with reason have incited even Edward and his royal bride to envy.

This marriage, recorded in a story of 1835, concludes Charlotte's original conception of William Percy, and for a time he drops out of her stories to reappear as Sir William Percy, an officer in the Angrian army and "an important and highly trusted government attaché." His marriage to Cecilia Seymour forgotten, he is now represented as a cynical bachelor and man of the world, albeit a secret idealist.

Following her "Farewell to Angria," Charlotte recasts the Edward and William Percy story in an English setting, calling the heroes Ashworth, a name the older Percy was wont to assume in Angrian days with the disguise of a Methodist ranter to cloak his subversive activities against the government. In the new version, Mr. Ashworth (Percy) does not attempt to destroy his sons, Edward and William, for Charlotte now had the English law in mind, but puts them out to nurse in a farmhouse on one of his estates, where they stay until they are "stout, healthy urchins, capable of toddling after the poultry, cows, and horses with the little rustics" of the place. Their father never gives them a thought, but their mother, broken-hearted at her husband's cruelty, visits them as often as she dares until her death following the birth of a daughter, whom the father receives with the order, "She must remain here and be nursed at home."

Ashworth, soon after his wife's death, became a bankrupt, and the three little children, "the eldest of whom was scarsely four years old," were looked after by their grandmother, Lady Helen (Lady Helen Percy in the Angrian version), who kept them in school until she died, when Edward was eighteen and William seventeen. From that time on the boys "were quite alone" and "went down into obscurity, dived as their father had done, but into a worse gulf than he ever visited." He never owned them, "never spoke to them; never extended to them the aid of a farthing." Their sister, when she reached the proper age, was placed in a fashionable boarding school in London, where she was maintained, after the death of her grandmother, by her father, who had built up his shattered fortune through mysterious speculation cloaked under the guise of "cattle-droving."

Here Charlotte's story goes off into the school adventures of "Miss Ashworth," introducing a half-boarder named Ellen Hall, who becomes Helen Burns in *Jane Eyre,* and no more is heard of the Ashworth brothers in this fragment. They reappear, however, as John Henry and William Moore of a later undated manuscript fragment which links *The Professor* to *Shirley* through the names Moore, Wynne, and De Walden.

The Professor follows the earliest and simplest version of the Percy story, modified only for realistic effect. Edward and William Crimsworth are the sons of a bankrupt father, a man of "an unscrupulous race," who died when William was an infant. Their mother soon followed him, leaving the two children to the care of relatives, who renounced their obligations at the earliest possible moment. Edward, ten years William's senior, enters trade and by selfish astuteness, ambitious energy, and a convenient marriage to the daughter of a rich millowner makes himself master of the mill and business which had once belonged to his father.

William, kept in school by a grudging guardian until he is old enough to decide upon a career, is offered a church living by an Uncle Tynedale if he will take orders, and an Uncle Seacombe whispers that William may have one of his six daughters for a wife. Though William has no taste for trade, he prefers life in a mill office to the church and a home shared with one of his Seacombe cousins, so he appeals to his brother, asking for work by which he can support himself. A position is given him, but it proves such "nauseous slavery" that after three months, the brothers part in violence.

William Crimsworth, the hero of *The Professor,* introducing himself and his situation in life, addresses a long letter to a friend Charles—identified at once as William Percy's old Angrian companion, Charles Townshend—recounting his life since they parted. Charlotte's vivid realization of these two intertwined Angrian personalities betrays her in this letter into a digression reviewing their strange relationship, which has no part in the revised story:

You were a sarcastic, observant, shrewd, cold-blooded creation; my own portrait I will not attempt to draw. . . . What animal magnetism drew thee and me together I know not; certainly I never experienced anything of the Pylades and Orestes sentiment for you, and I have reason to believe that you, on your part, were equally free from all romantic regard for me. Still, out of school hours, we walked and talked continually together; when the theme of conversation was our companions or our masters we understood each other, and when I recurred to some sentiment of affection, some vague love of an excellent or beautiful object . . . your sardonic coldness did not move me. I felt myself superior to that check *then* as I do *now*.

The last sentence of this paragraph echoes one of William Percy's letters to Charles Townshend: "Townshend, you'll never dare twit me about what I've written above—but if you do, I've another answer ready. How do you know whether the sentimentality is in jest or earnest? Ain't it very probable that I may be bamming you by doing a bit in the soft line?"

Again, William Percy-Ashworth cherished in his heart a vague half-memory, half-dream of his beautiful, gentle, Christian mother:

Her aspect was benign; her voice was low and peaceful, her deportment very full of the grace of kindness. . . . She looked kindly at you with her dark eyes, and spoke kindly to you with her sweet voice.

And William Crimsworth after seeing in his brother's house a portrait of his mother, writes:

The face, I remembered, had pleased me as a boy, but *then* I did not understand it; *now* I know how rare that class of face is in the world, and I appreciate keenly its thoughtful, yet gentle expression. The serious grey eyes possessed for me a strong charm, as did certain lines in the features indicative of most true and tender feeling. I was sorry it was only a picture.

Charlotte's Edward Crimsworth as he greets his brother, upon his arrival, is exactly the figure Branwell introduces as Edward Percy in the mill office in Verdopolis. "I saw," wrote William Crimsworth, "a fine looking and powerful man, light-complexioned, well-made, and of athletic proportions; the first glance made me aware of an air of promptitude and sharpness, shown as well in his movements as in his port, his eye, and the general expression of his face. He greeted me with brevity, and in the moment of shaking hands, scanned me from head to foot."

Branwell, it will be remembered, wrote of Edward Percy:

Although the young man is young and slender . . . his tall frame and finely proportioned figure promise great bodily strength and activity. . . . The light complexion and restless mouth all proclaim him a genuine Percy. A haughty arrogance in the eye, an aspect of active apprehension in business, and an appearance of incessant employment, vigor of thought, inflexible determination, and an abominable disposition give by turn an animated or repulsive aspect to the well-chiselled countenance of Edward Percy, Esqr.

William Crimsworth's characterization of his brother's middle-class wife is a subdued, realistic version of Edward Percy's bride, Maria Sneachi, though expressed in harsher terms than adolescent Branwell or Charlotte would have used for an Angrian "princess of the blood":

I sought her eye, desirous to read there the intelligence which I could not discern in her face or hear in her conversation; it was merry, rather small; by turns I saw vivacity, vanity, coquetry, look out through its irid, but I watched in vain for a glimpse of soul.

Vivacity, vanity, coquetry are indices to the character of both Maria Percy and Maria Crimsworth; and, Maria Percy or Maria Crimsworth, Edward's wife, in his eyes, is a beautiful possession, a symbol of his success, to be bent in private to his will.

The landscape that opens before William Crimsworth the morning after his arrival at Crimsworth Hall is the same that stretched before Charles Townshend and William Percy as they walked out from Zamorna. William Crimsworth writes:

The autumn sun, rising over the ——shire hills, disclosed a pleasant country; woods brown and mellow varied the fields from which the harvest had
been lately carried; a river, gliding between the woods, caught on its surface
the somewhat cold gleam of the October sun and sky; at frequent intervals
along the banks of the river, tall, cylindrical chimneys, almost like slender,
round towers, indicated the factories which the trees half concealed; here and
there mansions, similar to Crimsworth Hall, occupied agreeable sites on the
hillside; the country wore, on the whole, a cheerful, active, fertile look. . . .
At a distance of five miles, a valley, opening between the low hills, held in its
cups the great town of X——. A dense, permanent vapour brooded over this
locality—there lay Edward's "Concern". . . .

X—— was all stir and bustle when we entered it; we left the clean streets
where there were dwelling houses and shops, churches, and public buildings;
we left all those, and turned down to a region of mills and warehouses; thence
we passed through two massive gates into a great paved yard, and we were
in Bigben Close, and the mill was before us, vomiting soot from its long
chimney, and quivering through its thick walls with the commotion of its
iron bowels.

Years before Charles Townshend wrote:

When we came out the atmosphere was quite clear. We left the west end
and approached the bridge and river, whose banks were piled with enormous
manufactories and bristled with mill chimneys, tall, stately, and steep as slender towers. We breathed a denser air. Columns of smoke as black as soot rose
thick and fetid from the chimneys of two vast erections—Edward Percy's, I
believe, and Mr. Sydenham's—and slowly spreading, darkened the sky above
all Zamorna.

"That's Edward's tobacco pipe," said Sir William, looking up, as we passed
close under his brother's mill chimney, whose cylindrical pillar rose three
hundred feet in the air.

Having crossed the bridge, we turned into the noble road which leads
down to Hartford, and now the full splendor of the June morning began to
disclose itself around us.

I saw before us the valley of the Olympian opening broad and free. The
road with gentle descent wound white as milk down the rich pastures and
waving woods of the vale. My heart expanded as I looked at the path we
were to tread, edging the foot of the gentle hills whose long sweep subsided
to the level on the banks of the river—the glorious river, brightly flowing,
green as Eden.

The office of Crimsworth mill in Bigben Close, too, is a condensed and
simplified sketch of the elaborate, loosely detailed picture of Edward
Percy's mill office crudely painted by Branwell in "Wool Is Rising":

We entered . . . a place for business, with a bare, planked floor, a safe, two high desks and stools, and some chairs. A person was seated at one of the desks, who took off his square cap when Mr. Crimsworth entered, and in an instant was again absorbed in his occupation of writing or calculating—I know not which.

This person, Timothy Steighton, William Crimsworth continues, is "a man of about thirty-five, with a face at once sly and heavy," a "religious man" and "a joined Methodist," which "did not (be it understood) prevent him from being at the same time an ingrained rascal," Edward's henchman and spy upon his brother. Not a feature of his face, a line of his figure, an odor of his body, or a quality of his character has changed since Branwell introduced him in Edward Percy's mill office in Verdopolis, as Timothy Steaton, "a low, broad-backed fellow, with a not very scrupulous brown coat, rather greasy trousers, and not particularly refulgent shoes," a figure of "squat industry" (when Edward was near), "old in meanness, treachery, and hypocrisy," a ranting, praying, scripture-quoting Methodist, Edward Percy's spy upon his brother and his agent in all dubious or illicit transactions. In "The Moores," Charlotte characterizes this same Tim as "a joined Methodist and an eminent class-leader," a consummate hypocrite, and makes Moore's wife exclaim of him: "Your bookkeeper—dirty, greasy, ugly being! I always use my vinaigrette when he comes near me. He smells so of musty wood and rancid oil."

At the end of his first quarter's service with his brother, William Crimsworth summarizes the unhappy period thus:

I should have endured in silence the rust and cramp of my best faculties; I should not have whispered, even inwardly, that I longed for liberty; I should have pent in every sigh by which my heart might have ventured to intimate its distress under the closeness, smoke, monotony, and joyless tumult of Bigben Close. . . . But this was not all; the antipathy which had sprung up between myself and my employer striking deeper root and spreading denser shade daily, excluded me from every glimpse of the sunshine of life; and I began to feel like a plant growing in humid darkness out of the slimy walls of a well.

Antipathy is the only word which can express the feeling Edward Crimsworth had for me—a feeling, in a great measure, involuntary, and which was liable to be excited by every, the most trifling movement, look, or word of mine.

And having broken with his brother and taken leave of the mill for-ever, he exults in his freedom:

A load was lifted off my heart; I felt light and liberated. I had got away from Bigben Close. . . . Circumstances had freed me. Life was again open to me; no longer was its horizon limited by the high, black wall surrounding Crimsworth's mill.

Nine years earlier, William Percy had expressed a similar exultation at his emancipation from a similar slavery:

I knew nothing of this glorious hope six years ago. I thought only of gain-ing reckless freedom where I might live without the crushing insolence of tyranny. I thought of enlisting as a private soldier and hardly had a wish to rise above the ranks.

When Edward and I were in penury, kept chained together by want, and abhorring each other for the very compulsion of our union, I used to endure worse torments than those of Hell. Edward overwhelmed me by his strength and bulk. He used his power coarsely, for he had a coarse mind, and scenes have taken place between us which remembrance to this day, when it rushes upon my mind, pierces every nerve with a thrill of bitter pain no words can express.

I always affected indifference to his savage, hard, calculating barbarity, and I always will affect indifference to it to my dying day.

Yorke Hunsden of *The Professor,* manufacturer and mill owner of X——, and self-appointed mentor to William Crimsworth, is Sir Wil-liam Percy, officer and gentleman, as opposed to William Percy, clerk, who is William Crimsworth, "the Professor," with a dash of the omni-present, all-knowing, impersonal Charles Townshend thrown in. Di-rectly from Sir William comes Hunsden's cynical attitude, sarcastic speech, acrid tongue, and inner secret idealism, together with such less tangible qualities as are suggested by the phrases: "dash of something Gallic," "searching glance," "shrewd bantering glance of the eyes," "bitter and haughty taunts," "contrast between his inward and outward man," "his soul had more of will and ambition than his body had of fibre and muscle," "he had learnt somewhere the art of setting himself quite at his ease," and "sensitive himself, selfishly relentless toward the sensitive-ness of others." Hunsden explains his antagonism against Edward Crimsworth by saying, "The Hunsdens are all unrivaled at tracking a rascal. . . . We scent a scoundrel a mile off," echoing Sir William's characterization of himself when he was tracking Henry Hastings. And Hunsden showing his friends a miniature of the woman he had once secretly loved, retells Sir William's old passion for Mina Laury, Zamorna's mistress:

"And she was somebody you would have liked to marry—but could not?"
"I should certainly have liked to marry her, and that I *have* not done so is a proof that I *could* not."
He repossessed himself of the miniature . . . and put it away.
"What do *you* think of it?" he asked of my wife, as he buttoned his coat over it.
"I am sure that Lucia once wore chains and broke them," was the strange answer. . . . "social chains of some sort. The face is that of one who has made an effort, and a successful and triumphant effort, to wrest some vigorous and valued faculty from insupportable constraint; and when Lucia's faculty got free, I am certain it spread wide pinions and carried her higher than—" she hesitated.
"Than what?" demanded Hunsden.
"Than *'les convenances'* permitted you to follow. . . . You never seriously thought of marrying her; you admired her originality, her fearlessness, her energy of body and mind; you delighted in her talent whatever that was, whether song, dance, or dramatic representation; you worshipped her beauty, which was the sort after your own heart; but I am sure she filled a sphere from whence you would never have thought of taking a wife."
"Ingenious," remarked Hunsden; "whether true or not is another question."

Compare this with Sir William's rhapsody over Mina Laury, Zamorna's famous mistress:

She indeed added fine symmetry of form and transcendent beauty of feature to the interest of a noble spirit and disastrous destiny. . . . Imagination had to struggle through no dull intervening obstacle to show its light divine. That face offered a clear medium; her eyes were large with dark orbs and long romantic lashes. Sorrow in them was doubly wild—they flashed frenzy when the tears gushed into them—and joy, hope, love looked in their expressive smile, so soft and touching. She never smiled on me, however. . . . It is enough for me to have seen her once, and after that to carry the vision of her pale, inspired face to my deathbed. . . . I'll never marry, but spend my life finding out resemblances to the single shape I glorify, and when I am very lovesick, I'll remember my idol is altogether terrestrial, and so far from perfect that the other day a modest young lady in turning over a volume of portraits . . . chanced to come to hers and perceived at the same moment that my eye had caught the name— Heavens! but it told tales.

William Crimsworth, having discharged himself from his brother's office, accepted Hunsden's suggestion that he seek his fortune in Brussels. There he found employment as a teacher of English in a school for boys kept by M. Pelet, supplementing a fairly good salary by giving lessons in English in an adjoining school for girls. He was on the point of falling in love with the young proprietress of this school, Mademoiselle Reuter, when he discovered her falseness. Whereupon he turned his attention to Mademoiselle Frances Henri, a young girl of English extraction who taught sewing in the school and visited his classes in an effort to fit herself for a higher position. His attentions were attracted to her by her original and lively treatment of a trite assignment: the story of Alfred the Great in the peasant's hut. There is in the Bonnell collection a manuscript of the same exercise done in verse, probably discarded for the prose essay used in the novel.

Despite its Belgian setting, the second half of *The Professor* holds an occasional reminder of Angria. Mademoiselle Reuter's name, for instance, Zoraïde, at which Charlotte pokes a bit of fun: "Continental nations do allow themselves vagaries in the choice of names, such as we sober English never run into," is carried over from Zorayde, the heroine of "A Leaf from an Unopened Volume," Charlotte's wildest Angrian romance.

The Professor was not published in Charlotte's lifetime, and the story of the Percy brothers continued its struggle for satisfying expression in one form after another as long as she lived, appearing last in the fragment "Willie Ellin," which post-dates *Villette*. Through the long series, written over a period of twenty years, recur many small details, like identifying thumbprints of the several characters, such as Edward Percy's gig whip, indicating how sharply minute details were etched upon Charlotte's inner vision. Branwell in "Wool Is Rising" relates that Edward Percy's first extravagances on making his fortune were his own portrait painted by De Lisle and "a first-rate blooded horse." The portrait early drops out of the story, but the blooded horse and the gig it draws pass with Edward's personality from name to name, while the gig whip becomes a sort of coat-of-arms or sign-manual. Edward Percy flourishes it over the groveling, praying Steaton and threatens William with it in the mill office of Verdopolis. Again he snaps it viciously from his gig on his farewell meeting with his brother in Zamorna Road. Edward Crimsworth, likewise, threatens his brother with it in one of his mill-office rages. Edward Ellin carries it in his hand when he overtakes little runaway Willie, and, though prevented from using it at that moment, he brings it into full play on the terrified child a few nights later in his attic room of Golpit.

Notwithstanding its carrying over of old Angrian characters and scenes, *The Professor* stands by itself, as widely separated from its prototype as from the novels which followed it. In its preface, written soon after the success of *Shirley,* when Smith, Elder, and Company were planning to bring out the story they once rejected, Charlotte half defends, half condemns her first prose offering to the public, written, she confesses, under a self-denying ordinance imposed by conscience in expiation of youthful extravagances. The result of these principles, so admirable in theory, brought, she admits, when applied to the old story of the Percy brothers, more surprise than pleasure. The novel reached the publisher's desk finished in form, and better constructed than any of her later books; delicate and firm in drawing; virtuous in its extreme sobriety, but pulseless, a cold, colorless, lifeless exercise. The publishers refuse it, and Charlotte, seeing her mistake, turned to the writing of a new novel.

Jane Eyre

Jane Eyre in several of its essential features is older than the Percy story which is the basis of *The Professor.* The Reed family (with whose misdoings the novel opens), Rochester, and Rochester's mad wife, together with the call and answer between Rochester and Jane, come from the days of wooden soldiers, appearing in recognizable form in the tiny booklets antedating Charlotte's departure for Roe Head in January, 1831, three months before she was fifteen. The novel in its separate essential parts was complete before she bade farewell to Angria in 1839 or 1840, but as a plot entity it is a product of the year between late summer 1846 and 1847.

Captain Dunally (so runs the story) of "The Silver Cup," published in "Blackwood's Young Men's Magazine" for October, 1829, was a man of great wealth, "the owner of a beautiful country seat about 10 miles from the Glass Town. . . . his wife a comely lady in the 30th year of her age was a person of great management and discretion given to the use of her tongue upon occasion they had 3 children the eldest of whom was 12 the second 10 and the youngest 2 years of age they went by the separate names of Augusta Cecilia Henry Fearnothing (the name of a maternal uncle of no great character among the more sober part of mankind . . .) and Gina Rosaline . . . Augusta was given to being rather mystical among the others Henry was very wick-will [sic] boy and Gina was a pet." One afternoon as Lady Dunally was seated in her parlor reading aloud a most beautiful and affecting novel to Augusta— "Augusta was working and Gina feeding on a piece of cake which her mother had given her to keep her quiet"—Captain Dunally entered with a silver cup which he had purchased from an unknown person, without consulting his wife, at the fabulous price of 100 guineas. The omission so angered this lady of "management and discretion" that she flew into a furious passion. In one of the frequent quarrels that followed Lady Dunally expressed her irritation so hotly her husband suggested she was speaking "an untruth," then, as she waxed more vehement, he declared she was "telling lies."

About a week later, Captain Dunally came home in great dejection, announcing that Lady Dunally's brother, "Sergeant William Fearnothing Danvers, was to be hung for murder." All the family were "in a state of the utmost distress with the exception of Henry who appeared to be quite indifferent. He went out of the house after lunch and did not return until evening," giving as an excuse that he had been spending the evening with a schoolfellow. The next morning Lady Isabelle Danvers called to inform her sister-in-law that she had gravely offended against all the customs and rules of Glass Town society by allowing her son to go to see his uncle hanged, and that its leaders would henceforth give up all intercourse with her.

As soon as the caller was gone, "Lady Dunally called Henry to her and, giving him a spoonful of tell-truth salts," learned the shameful facts. At that moment his father came in, and hearing his son's confession, gave him "a hearty beating for his unfeelingness." Discord and confusion continued in the Dunally family until it was discovered that the disturbing influence emanated from the silver cup, which was thereupon dissolved with "odours." In a short time the "fashionables of Glass Town society" become convinced of Lady Dunally's innocence of any intention to violate their customs; a precious glass ship which Gina had wantonly beaten to pieces was mended by invisible hands; "Gina was no longer a pet; Augusta was no longer mystical and ever after they lived as comfortably and happy as could be."

A comparison of individual members emphasizes the basic likeness of the Dunally and Reed families.

Lady Dunally was a comely woman of thirty, "a person of great management and discretion," weakly indulgent to her children, who defied her, violent in temper when angered, and quite capable of lying when it suited her purpose. Mrs. Reed "might be . . . six or seven and thirty . . . ; she was an exact, clever manager, her household and tenantry were thoroughly under her control; her children, only, at times defied her authority, and laughed it to scorn; she dressed well, and had a presence and port calculated to set off handsome attire." She was violent and cruel to Jane, and lied about the child's character to the Rev. Mr. Brocklehurst. And when Jane's rich uncle came to claim her, she told him that Jane was dead.

The picture of Lady Dunally in her parlor, reading to Augusta, who busied herself with sewing while Gina was kept quiet by a bribe, is developed by a mature hand into the opening scene of *Jane Eyre:* "The said Eliza, John, and Georgiana were now clustered round their mama in the drawing-room: she lay reclined on a sofa by the fireside, and with her darlings about her (for the time neither quarreling nor crying) looked perfectly happy."

Augusta Dunally, "given to being rather mystical among the others," sewing while her mother read to her, becomes Eliza Reed, always busy at her own little work, affecting an air of mysterious superiority to her brother and sister, carefully gathering and saving her money while they waste theirs, and, in her grown-up years, fanatically ritualistic. Henry Fearnothing Dunally, named for his uncle, and much like him, is an equally clear forecast of John Reed. Henry is indifferent to his mother's feelings and enjoys seeing her brother hanged, thus bringing distress and disgrace upon his family. John Reed is heavy of body and dull of mind, with "not much affection for his mother and sisters," cruel to helpless things. In the end his selfish dissipation brings his mother in sorrow to the grave. Mrs. Reed, in her last delirium, declares, "John is like me and my brothers—he is quite a Gibson." Gina Dunally, "a pet" and her mother's favorite, is easily elaborated into Mrs. Reed's darling Georgiana, fair as waxwork, whose pink cheeks, languishing blue eyes, and golden curls purchased indemnity for every fault, though she had "a spoiled temper, a very acrid spite, and a captious and insolent carriage."

The eighteen years between "The Silver Cup" and *Jane Eyre* show but one intermediate step in the evolution of the Dunallys into the Reeds: Eliza and Georgiana Seymour, Zamorna's cousins—"Tall haughty blonds, proud of their beauty, proud of their first-rate accomplishments . . . proud of everything." Georgiana Seymour, at the end of a somewhat varied career, was listed among the ladies of unenviable reputation in Verdopolis, being at one time the mistress of the Earl of Northangerland. From this period of her prototype's life comes Georgiana Reed's questionable social triumph in London, her frustrated elopement with a dissipated nobleman, and her marriage to "a wealthy, worn-out man of fortune."

Though Captain Dunally does not appear in the flesh in *Jane Eyre,* he is present in effect in the reminiscent picture of Mr. Reed, who died before the story opens, a person of finer nature and higher moral qualities than his wife, while, to complete the parallel of the two groups, the figurative equivalent of the Captain Dunally's silver cup as a cause of family discord operates in the person of Jane Eyre, his orphan niece, whom he had brought into his home against his wife's wishes. Jane, relating how her uncle on his deathbed charges Mrs. Reed with her care, concludes, "I was discord in Gateshead Hall."

Edward Fairfax Rochester, typical Byronic figure that he is, has yet a long and roundabout derivation, written in the history of Angria's superhero, Arthur Augustus Adrian Wellesley, Duke of Zamorna and Emperor of Angria. From this fantastic composite of the Duke of Wellington, Byron, and an Eastern voluptuary, Charlotte at thirty isolated the familiar elements which she at thirteen had transferred from Childe

Harold to the young Marquis of Douro, recombining them in their original pattern to make the hero of her first successful novel. Along with the general characteristics of the Byronic hero she took also traits of Zamorna's individual personality which indicate that she still saw "the god-like Majesty of Angria" under the unheroic mould and less handsome features of an English squire. For instance, Rochester, disguised as a gypsy fortuneteller, testing Blanche Ingram's love for himself and talking strange nonsense to Jane, is re-acting Zamorna's escapade when, disguised as Major Howard, he betrayed a group of his female friends and cousins into speeches which embarrassed them greatly when the trick was discovered. Rochester's impatient retort to Jane: "Station! Station!—Your station is in my heart," repeats Zamorna's answer to a child he held in his arms who asked where his wife lived: "She has no home until I come back—her home is just where you are at this moment; she would be happy in no other." And Jane on another occasion said to Rochester, "Wherever you are is my home—my only home."

Rochester's mad wife, a much more interesting and significant evolution than her husband, takes her being from Lady Zenobia Ellrington, one of the principals in Charlotte's first love story, written in 1830, when the author was fourteen. Zenobia is introduced in this story as a "lady apparently about twenty-five or twenty-six years of age . . . the most learned and noted woman in Glass Town," a bluestocking of deepest dye, a Verdopolitan de Staël. "In figure she was very tall, and both it and her face were of a perfectly Roman cast. Her features were regularly and finely formed, her full and brilliant eyes jetty black, as were the luxuriant tresses of her richly-curled hair."

The Marquis of Douro, meeting this paragon at a party, was impressed with her charms. "Her dark, glowing complexion was set off by a robe of crimson velvet trimmed with ermine, and a nodding plume of black ostrich feathers added to the imposing dignity of her appearance." Ambitious to please so distinguished a person as the young Marquis of Douro, Zenobia exerted her "conversational talent" to the utmost, entertaining him "with a discourse of the most lively eloquence." It was her singing of one of his own lyrics, however, that drew his heart to her. How far he might have gone in his interest, can only be guessed, had not the apparition of his sweetheart, Marian Hume, speaking his name, re-called his wandering fancy.

Other stories show the dignified, learned Zenobia in the madness of unrequited love for the Marquis, when she would have killed his fiancée with a knife had he not appeared to save her:

Her head was bare. Her tall person was enveloped in the tattered remains of a dark velvet mantle. Her dishevelled hair hung in wild elf-locks over her face, neck, and shoulders, almost concealing her features, which were emaci-ated and pale as death.

In a dramatized version of the story, she seizes Marian, knife in hand, and exclaims with a violent gesture:

> Wretch I could kill thee!
> . . . Where dids't thou weave the net
> Whose cunning meshes have entangled round
> The mightiest heart that e'er in mortal breast
> Did beat responsive unto human feeling?

Other stories carry the picture of Zenobia through the Angrian cycle, amplifying and varying it from time to time. At her best she is represented as a noble woman of strong mind and lofty thought. On the other hand, she is given to fits of rage in which she shrieks like a wild beast and falls upon her victim hand and foot. On one occasion she kicked Lord Charles down the stairs. Always she is depicted as tall of stature and strong of body. Lord Charles once declared that she could spar on equal terms with her husband, "one of the best boxers on record," or any other man in Verdopolis. In the later stories it is stated that she is a creole of Latin blood, the daughter of an evil and infamous mother, Paulina Louisiada Ellrington.

Rochester's story of his courtship of and marriage to Bertha Mason, as he told it to Jane Eyre, emphasizes her direct derivation from Zenobia Ellrington:

My father . . . told me Miss Mason was the boast of Spanish Town for her beauty [*Zenobia was "the most . . . noted woman of Glass Town" for her beauty and learning*]; and this was no lie. I found her a fine woman . . . tall, dark and majestic [*tall, dark, and majestic are the adjectives commonly used singly or together to describe Zenobia*]. Her family . . . showed her to me in parties, splendidly dressed [*Zenobia was habitually dressed in flowing velvet robes and plumes*]. . . . She flattered me, and lavishly displayed for my pleasure her charms and accomplishments [*Zenobia "entertained the Marquis of Douro with a discourse of the most lively eloquence. . . . She exerted herself to the utmost*]. . . . I was dazzled, stimulated: my senses were excited; and being ignorant, raw, and inexperienced, I thought I loved her. . . . A marriage was achieved almost before I knew where I was . . . —gross, grovelling, mole-eyed blockhead that I was! [*Just so was the Marquis of Douro dazzled by "the majestic charms" of Zenobia, and was in a fair way to fall a victim to them when he was saved by the mysterious call of Marian's spirit*]. Bertha Mason,—the true daughter of an infamous mother,—dragged me through all the hideous and degrading agonies which must attend a man bound to a wife at once intemperate and unchaste [*Infamous is too mild a word to designate Zenobia's mother*]. . . . I knew that while she lived I could never be the husband of another and better wife; and, though five years my senior (her family and her father had lied to me even in the particular of her age), she was likely to live as long as I [*Zenobia was "twenty-five or twenty-six" when she fell in love with Douro, who was then but nineteen*]. . . .

My ears were filled with the curses the maniac still shrieked out . . . the thin partitions of the West-India house opposing but slight obstruction to her wolfish cries [*Zenobia never gave way to profanity, but she frequently lashed out with adjectives which had the malevolent force of profanity, and she frequently emitted "yells of ungovernable rage"*].

Zenobia's skill in sparring with her husband becomes in *Jane Eyre* the strength of the maniac Bertha Mason struggling with Rochester: "She was a big woman, in stature almost equalling her husband. . . . She showed virile force in the contest—more than once she almost throttled him, athletic as he was."

But Zenobia Ellrington accounts for Bertha Mason Rochester only in part. The rest of the picture is found in "The Green Dwarf," written in 1833, an adaptation of Scott's *Ivanhoe* to the Glass Town setting. In this story the heroine is abducted by the villain on the eve of her marriage to his rival and taken to a ruined castle, where she is left in care of an old hag named Bertha, described as "an old woman bent double . . . her countenance all wrinkled and shriveled . . . while her small red eyes gleamed with fiend-like malignity. In one hand she held a huge bunch of rusty keys, and in the other a dimly glimmering torch."

These two combined, Zenobia Ellrington, shorn of her romantic aspect and given over to her evil nature, and Bertha, of "The Green

Dwarf," gave Charlotte the red-eyed maniac in *Jane Eyre,* creeping along the dark passages of Thornfield on her midnight errand of mischief, in one hand the keys which she had cunningly taken from the drunken Grace Pool, and in the other a flickering candle, the terrifying vision that bent over Jane's bed the night before her projected marriage to Rochester:

"A woman tall and large, with thick and dark hair hanging long down her back . . . visage and features . . . fearful and ghostly. . . . It was a discoloured face—it was a savage face. I wish I could forget the roll of the red eyes and the fearful blackened inflation of the lineaments . . . This face was purple; the lips were swelled and dark, the brow furrowed; the black eyebrows widely raised over the blood-shot eyes. Shall I tell you of what it reminded me? Of the foul German spectre—the Vampire."

Bertha of "The Green Dwarf," the hag of a deserted castle—uncivil in her speech and unserviceable in spirit to the beautiful young girl placed under her care by a licentious kidnapper until she should consent to marry him—was, in her turn, Charlotte's youthful adaptation from *Ivanhoe* of the Saxon Ulrica of Front-de-Bœuf's castle, gruff and rude to the beautiful Rebecca, who was delivered to her by De Bracy to be held until she should become his wife. Ulrica, howling her song of revenge from a tower of the blazing castle, was a picture that long remained in Charlotte's mind to reappear in her own novel as Bertha Mason Rochester on the blazing roof of Thornfield.

The experiment that Charlotte Brontë set for herself in *Jane Eyre*—bringing together in one story a group of major Angrians in new interplay—raised many nice problems of proportion and emphasis. Her success in reducing stars to minor roles, even to foils for other stars, is demonstrated in Rochester's ward Adèle and Adèle's mother, Céline Varens, his former mistress. These two, who in Angrian days enjoyed the monopoly of one entire novel and numerous pages in other stories, here serve as mere plot agents, yet without the slightest change in nature. Adèle, flitting familiarly about through most of the action, is Zamorna's ward, Caroline Vernon, and her mother, Céline Varens, seen in but one brief retrospective glance, is Louisa Danci or Louisa Vernon—she changed her name with each new love intrigue—onetime wife of Zamorna's uncle, the Marquis of Wellesley, and Percy's mistress. Recognition is made sure by her profession (opera dancing), her faithless soul, her hysterical temper, and her very small feet. The only change in the picture is one of relationship. Louisa never succeeded, even after years of effort, in entangling Zamorna, while Céline brought Rochester under her sway for a time.

Helen Burns, the supposed portrait of Charlotte's sister Maria Brontë, who died of tuberculosis contracted in the Clergy Daughters' School at Cowan Bridge, has no antecedent in the Angrian stories, but her prototype appears in the transition fragment of "The Ashworths" as Ellen Hall, the drudge of Miss Turner's fashionable school:

"Where do you intend to spend the holiday, Miss Hall?" she [Miss Ashworth] asked, after having watched in silence till her trunk was again closed up.

"I always spend it here in London," replied the half-boarder.

"Probably you have no parents then?"

"No, m'am."

"But you have sisters or brothers?"

"I have one brother who is a surgeon on board an East India vessel."

"Older than you, of course?"

"Yes, he is three-and-twenty. I am only fifteen."

"Have you any other relations?"

"I believe I have an uncle and aunt somewhere in England; but they are rich people and, of course, think little about me."

The last part of the sentence was said not sadly, but rather in a cheerful, matter-of-fact way, and with a glance upward at Miss Ashworth, accompanied by a smile.

It was the first time the half-boarder had looked up, and it was now seen that she had a face of not unpleasing cast, though somewhat thin and careworn for her age.

Miss Ashworth returned the smile. In a gentle tone she continued the conversation.

"Where did you live before you came to Miss Turner's, Miss Hall?"

"I lived a considerable distance from London, on the borders of Lancashire," was the reply, and the speaker again bent busily over her boxes.

"Do you feel particularly unhappy here?" again inquired Miss Ashworth.

"Oh, no. We've good times and bad times, and all times get over. I shall be sorry, however, Miss Ashworth, when you are gone." . . .

"You are almost old enough to leave Miss Turner's," continued Miss Ashworth after a pause.

"I am to leave here, when Miss Turner can get me a situation as a companion or nursery-governess."

"Nursery-governess! You might be better than that."

"Miss Turner says I have not capacity for anything higher."

"On what grounds does she rest that opinion?"

"You know, I never say the lessons correctly that she gives me."

"In the name of common sense, how can she expect it when the moment she has given you two pages of history to study or three pages of French prose to learn by heart, she sends you into the laundry to clear-starch a basketful of lace and muslin."

The brief inscription, "Resurgam," on Helen Burns's tomb earlier marked the Angrian grave of Rosamond Wellesley, Zamorna's cousin who loved him "not wisely, but too well."

The principal plot incidents of *Jane Eyre* are: Jane's fright in the Red Room of Mrs. Reed's home; Rochester's testing of Jane's love in the garden of Thornfield; Jane's temptation on the night following the frustration of her marriage to Rochester; and the call and answer between Rochester and Jane. The first has its parallel in Lord Charles's several ghostly adventures recorded in the "Young Men's Magazine." The second comes from Charlotte's first love story (1830). The other two belong to her later Angrian period.

Rochester's testing of Jane's love in the garden, for instance, was rehearsed in Zamorna's jealous trial of Mina Laury, following his discovery that Lord Hartford was in love with her, a scene dated January 17, 1838:

"Come here," he [Zamorna] said, drawing a chair close to his side.

Mina never hesitated, never delayed through bashfulness or any other feeling to comply with his orders.

"Now," he continued, leaning his head toward hers and placing his hand on her shoulder, "are you happy, Mina? Do you want anything?"

"Nothing, my Lord." . . . The lamps burned as if they were listening. The fire sent up no flickering flame, but diffused a broad, still, glowing light over all the room. Zamorna touched her; his form and features filled her eye; his voice her ear; his presence her whole heart; she was soothed to perfect happiness.

"My Fidelity!" pursued that musical voice, "if thou hast any favours to ask, now is the time. I'm all concession: as yielding as a lady's glove. Come, Mina, what is thy petition?"

"Nothing," again murmured Miss Laury. . . . "Oh, my Lord, nothing! What can I want?"

"But . . . what if I have devised something worthy of your acceptance? Look up now and listen to me. . . . I say, love," pursued the individual, drawing her a little closer to him, "I will give you as a reward a husband. . . . And that husband shall be a nobleman; and that nobleman is called Lord Hartford! Now, stand up and let me look at you."

He opened his arms and Miss Laury sprang erect like a loosened bow.

"Your Grace is anticipated," she said, "that offer had been made me before. Lord Hartford did it himself three days ago."

"What did you say? Speak the truth. . . ."

"What did I say? I don't know; it little signifies; . . . I cannot bear this: I feel sick."

With a deep, short sob, she turned white, and fell close by the Duke, her head against his foot. . . .

While he gazed she began to recover.

She rose feebly and with effort. The Duke stretched out his hand to assist her.

"Mina," he said, "are you collected enough to hear me?"

"Yes, my Lord."

"Then listen. I would much sooner give half, aye, the whole of my estates to Lord Hartford, than yourself! What I said just now was only to try you. . . . Would . . . I resign the possession of my first love to any hand but my own? I would far rather see her in her coffin. . . . I know you adore me now, Mina."

Rochester's torturing of Jane, while following step by step the pattern set by Zamorna, was slower, more refined, more excruciating, because Jane's resistance was stronger than Mina's, and Charlotte had learned something of suffering in the years between. For an endless period, it seemed to Jane, the inquisition ground on until she found relief, not in unconsciousness, but in confession of her love.

Just as plainly Jane's dramatic temptation to go with Rochester to the Continent is a development of Sir William Percy's proposal to Elizabeth Hastings. Jane's intensified suffering here is accounted for, not only by Charlotte's increased power of portraying emotion, but by the fact that Jane was combating, not Sir William Percy, but Zamorna (in person of Rochester), who had never before been resisted by any woman. Sir William's proposal is direct and crude:

"Now Elizabeth," continued Sir William, "listen to the last question I have to put and don't be afraid of me. . . . You said just now that all men of rank were scoundrels; I am a man of rank, will you be my mistress?"

"No."

"You said you adored me."

"I do, intensely, but I'll never be your mistress. I could not without incurring the miseries of self-hatred."

"That is to say . . . that you are afraid of the scorn of the world."

"I am. The scorn of the world is a horrible thing. . . ."

"You would risk nothing for me then. . . . You would find no compensation for the loss of the world's favour in my perfect love and trusting confidence. . . . It is no pleasure to you to talk to me, to sit by my side as you do now, to allow your hand to rest in mine?"

The tears came into Miss Hastings' eyes. "I dare not answer you . . . because I know I should say something frantic. I could no more help loving you than that moon can help shining. If I might live with you as your servant, I should be happy, but as your mistress, it is quite impossible."

"Elizabeth . . . your eyes betray you . . . they confess not only that you love me, but that you cannot live without me. Yield to your nature and let me claim you this moment as my own."

Miss Hastings was silent, but she was not going to yield. Only the hard conflict of passionate love with feeling that shrank horror-struck from the remotest shadow of infamy compelled her for a moment to silent agony. Sir William thought his point was really gained.

"One word," said he, "will be sufficient, one smile, or whisper. You tremble, rest on my shoulder, turn your face to the moonlight, and give me a single look. . . ."

She slipped from his hold like an apparition. "If I stay another moment, God knows what I shall say or do."

The moral aspect of love and passion had long had a definite interest for Charlotte, evidence of which early showed itself in Mina Laury, who while yet no more than a child fell under the fascination of a personality she could not resist. Pure in her love, and high-minded and noble in her nature, she counted the respect of the world well lost for the privilege of serving, with little reward, the man she loved and acknowledged as master. In "Caroline Vernon," Charlotte plays with another aspect of the same subject. An illegitimate child of two utterly immoral persons, inheriting dangerous propensities from both, left without training and protection, seemed coldly predestined to the tragedy that overtook her. But in *Jane Eyre,* Adèle, the same child, given Christian training and the proper protection in her formative years, was brought safely through to a useful and happy life— "As she grew up, a sound English education corrected in a great measure her French defects; and when she left school, I found in her a pleasing and obliging companion, docile, good-tempered, and well-principled."

Elizabeth Hastings of Angria was Charlotte's first heroine to resist and overcome temptation. She was saved by her respect for public opinion and her terror of failing the few persons who knew and trusted her. But never was temptation faced in its full severity until Jane Eyre, hardly older than Mina Laury, under the fascination of the same personality, unprotected by the restraint of family and friends, met it in all the insidious strength that Charlotte's fertile imagination could realize, and triumphed on the basis of ultimate and eternal principles. Charlotte's genius had been working toward that scene for more than fifteen years.

The call and answer between Rochester and Jane Eyre is an amplification of a similar incident between the Marquis of Douro and Marian Hume. The young Marquis, in danger of forgetting his faithful sweetheart in the charms of a lower nature, was recalled by the voice and apparition of his true love. "He made a memorandum of the day and hour, namely, the 18th of June, 1815, at 12 o'clock midnight." A few weeks later, he read on Marian's tomb:

She died 18th of June 1815 at 12 o'clock midnight.

Jane, convinced that she will never see Rochester again, exhausted physically and spiritually from her struggle against St. John Rivers's insistence that she marry him as a duty and go with him on a mission to India, is saved by the voice of her "dear master" coming to her out of space.

All the house was still. . . . The one candle was dying out: the room was full of moonlight. My heart beat fast and thick; I heard its throb. Suddenly it stood still to an inexpressible feeling that thrilled it through, and passed at once to my head and extremities. The feeling was not like an electric shock; but it was quite as sharp, as strange, as startling. . . . I saw nothing: but I heard a voice somewhere cry—

"Jane! Jane! Jane!" nothing more. . . . It did not seem in the room—nor in the house—nor in the garden: it did not come out of the air—nor from under the earth—nor from overhead. I had heard it—where, or whence, for ever impossible to know! And it was the voice of a human being—a known, loved, well-remembered voice—that of Edward Fairfax Rochester; and it spoke in pain and woe wildly, eerily, urgently.

"I am coming!" I cried. "Wait for me! Oh, I will come!" I flew to the door . . . I ran out into the garden. . . . "Where are you?" I exclaimed.

Obeying the summons as fast as the means of traveling permitted, Jane finds Rochester sightless and in agony of spirit. Before she can tell him the cause of her coming, he relates the story to her:

"I longed for thee, Jane! Oh, I longed for thee both with the soul and flesh! . . . The alpha and omega of my heart's wishes broke involuntarily from my lips, in the words—'Jane! Jane! Jane!' "

"Did you speak those words aloud?"

"I did, Jane. If any listener had heard me, he would have thought me mad. I pronounced them with such frantic energy."

"And it was last Monday night: somewhere near midnight?"

"Yes; but the time is no consequence: what followed is the strange point. . . . As I exclaimed, 'Jane! Jane! Jane!' a voice—I cannot tell whence the voice came, but I knew whose voice it was—replied, 'I am coming: wait for me,' and a moment after, went whispering on the wind, the words—'Where are you?' "

Reader, it was on Monday night—near midnight—that I too had received the mysterious summons: those were the very words by which I replied to it.

Yet many small touches *Jane Eyre* does have, justifying a literal interpretation of its subtitle, *An Autobiography.* For instance, Jane at Lowood, finding Helen Burns reading Johnson's *Rasselas,* pronounced it dull to her "trifling taste," for she found in it "nothing about fairies, nothing about genii," beings that absorbed Charlotte's own childhood fancy and filled her early pages. And Jane, in her last days at this same school, complained quite in tone of Charlotte at Roe Head, interrupted in her Angrian dream, "I was not free to resume the interrupted chain of my reflections till bedtime: even then a teacher who occupied the same room with me kept me from the subject to which I longed to recur, by prolonged effusion of small talk. . . . Miss Gryce snored at last . . . I was disembarrassed of interruption; my half-effaced thought instantly revived." And Charlotte was certainly thinking of her Angrian escape when she had Jane write: "Then my sole relief was to walk along the corridor of the third story . . . and allow my mind's eye to dwell on whatever bright vision rose before it . . . best of all to open

my inward ear to a tale that was never ended,—a tale that my imagination created and narrated continuously, quickened with all the incident,
life, fire and feeling that I desired and had not in actual existence."

Shirley

Shirley, the poorest of Charlotte Brontë's novels, represents a com-
promise between conscience urging her toward outward realism, and
her inner visions crying out for expression. And, though it is cumbered
and weighted down by too much that is taken directly from observation
and the *Leeds Mercury*, its leading characters save it from actual failure:
the Moore brothers, Shirley Keeldar, and Hiram Yorke, all true children of imagination, Angrians in spirit and origin. Robert Moore spoke
for the group when he said, "I am learning to be a naturalized Englishman; my foreign habits are leaving me one by one." Yet in a certain
respect the Moores are unique, for of all Charlotte's naturalized Angrians
they are the only ones to suffer essential change of nature in the process. Basically they are Edward and William Percy, the one elevated, the
other dulled by interchange of qualities. Robert Moore is Edward Percy
with his coarseness refined and his spirit enlivened by a liberal dash of Sir
William Percy (always to be distinguished from William Percy, clerk).
From Edward he takes his handsome face and athletic body, his ambition, energy, and business acumen, his devotion to his own interest and
his ruthlessness toward others, and his experience with mills, strikes,
and riots—Edward Percy had faced many an Angrian mob. From Sir
William he inherits his refined tastes, his quick wit, his capacity for
dreaming, and the element of kindness in his nature—all those qualities
that made Caroline Helstone love him. From Sir William, too, comes
his tenacity and his energy in tracking lawbreakers. Shirley tells him,
"I cannot understand why Nature did not give you a bull-dog's head,
for you have all of a bull-dog's tenacity!" Charles Townshend declared that Sir William never gave up an idea that had once taken hold
of his mind, whether it was a matter of principle or merely a whim of
his fancy. The author observes, that only half of Moore's activity and
resolution had been seen in his defense of the mill. He showed the other
half (and a terrible half it was) "in the indefatigable, the relentless assiduity with which he pursued the leaders of the riot. . . . These persons

Moore hunted like any sleuth-hound [just so Sir William had hunted Hastings and his confederates]; and well he liked the occupation . . . he liked it better than making cloth." Robert himself analyzes his dual nature for Caroline: "I find in myself two natures, one for the world and business, and one for home and leisure. Gérard Moore is a hard dog brought up to mill and market: the person you call your cousin Robert is sometimes a dreamer, who lives elsewhere than in cloth hall and counting house." In the first aspect he is Edward Percy, in the second, Sir William.

Another trace of Sir William in Robert Moore is his attitude toward Shirley Keeldar, which is precisely that of Sir William toward her Angrian prototype, Jane Moore. At times he expressed high admiration and hinted that he should like to marry her, again he spoke slightingly of her, with a touch of bitterness that indicated the grapes hung too high for his reach. Once when Charles Townshend asked Sir William if he were smitten with Jane, he answered peevishly: "Not I; there is no mind there, and very little heart. If I ever marry, rest satisfied my choice will not fall upon the Rose of Zamorna." Just so Robert Moore speaks of Shirley Keeldar to Caroline: "I esteem her; I admire her; and yet my impressions concerning her are harsh—perhaps uncharitable. I believe, for instance, that she is incapable of love . . . that she will never marry; I imagine her jealous of compromising her pride, or relinquishing her power, of sharing her property. I acknowledge her charms and feel none of them."

Louis Moore, on the other hand, is, fundamentally, William Percy, clerk, also enlivened by a few characteristics of his later self, Sir William. For instance, Louis's irritating, tantalizing slowness that gave him the victory over Mr. Simpson, comes directly from Sir William, whose most effective weapon it was in diplomacy, employed with particular malice against Lord Hartford. Louis Moore boasts, "I never was in a hurry in my whole life," and gives thanks that he is blessed with the power to conceal "inward ebullition with outward calm," quite after the manner of Sir William, whose calm face alone told his intimates that he was burning with venom against his enemies or seething with conflicting emotions.

Again, just as Louis Moore's reserve occasionally broke under the charm of Shirley's sweetest mood, so William Percy's pride relaxed and his spirits expanded in the presence of Cecilia Seymour. Compare Louis in Shirley's company with William Percy in Cecilia's presence:

Louis . . . did not laugh much, but he uttered in the quietest tones the wittiest things. Gravely spoken sentences, marked by unexpected turns and a quiet fresh flavour and piquancy fell easily from his lips. He proved himself to be excellent company. . . . Nobody there seemed a bore—a check—a chill to him.

In the midst of my cousins Seymour, I saw William Percy. . . . His handsome face filled with spirit and intellect as he conversed. . . . But it was only in answer to the low, yet cheerful voice of Cecilia that he kindled to the full extent of his powers. . . . I never heard him speak so much before, and I never heard anyone speak more animatedly and well. His talents and acquirements are little known because he is seldom seen except in the company of Edward.

Shirley Keeldar, the orphan heiress of the first family of the Yorkshire neighborhood in which her estate lies, passes across the pages of this novel a tall, lithe girl, proud and graceful in her carriage, beautiful of features and brilliant in dress, rich, gifted, youthful, and lovely, the personification of exuberant life and perfect health. With her clear, glowing skin, sparkling eyes, red lips, and glossy curls resting on a snowy white neck, she is a joy to the eye. If one thinks of her in terms of flowers, it is to liken her to a rose rather than a lily. But real and vital as she is, she appears at times unearthly and ethereal, a thing of fire and air. Her countenance is in rapid succession careless and pensive, musing and mirthful, serious and mocking. Her features are distinguished, mobile, and speaking, but their changes are not to be understood nor their language interpreted all at once. When she is quiescent, wistfulness and carelessness are the wonted cast of her looks and character of her bearing. When she is animated, the carelessness quite vanishes, the wistfulness blends with a genial gaiety, seasoning the laugh, the smile, the glance, with a unique flavor of sentiment, so that mirth from her never resembles the crackling of thorns under a pot.

Usually she is a wild, laughing thing, whose brilliant smile and cheery presence keeps the dark old manor house bright. Then she is all good nature and chatter and gay repartee. She has a clear, sweet voice, which she delights to use in singing. When she is neither talking nor laughing, the fact is a matter of comment. But she can be very proud and haughty and may even show a fiery temper. Dark days and twilight make her pensive, and she is more likely to seek company and gaiety at such times than to muse in solitude. She is proud, impetuous, self-willed, and impatient of restraint, but she is generous, magnanimous, and hospitable. Though indolent at times, she can be energetic when the welfare of others is involved. She is no angel, but she is beloved of everybody and courted of all men.

All this was originally written of "Jane Moore, the beautiful Angrian, the Rose of Zamorna," who first appeared as "one of the transcendently fair and inaccessibly sacred beings" who thronged Charlotte's vision in her Roe Head days, "not like airy phantoms, but as noblemen and ladies of flesh and blood," as clearly realized "as Anne's quiet image sitting at her lessons on the opposite side of the table"—Jane Moore, the epitome of Angrian (Yorkshire) womanhood as contrasted with the super-refined, highly romantic Senegambian (Irish) women, typified by Mary Percy and Mina Laury.

Jane was the daughter of George Moore, sometimes spoken of as a barrister, sometimes as a "merchantileman, whose fortune was made on the night that Angria was declared a kingdom." In the earliest sketch of her it was said that she was no petted only child, but neither brother nor sister ever appeared, and in the later stories she is represented as her father's sole heiress and the mistress of his various houses.

Her picture, summarized from the few fragments that have survived, agrees in almost every detail with Shirley's. Jane, like Shirley, was "tall, well and roundly formed" with white neck and shoulders as a gleaming background for profuse curls as fine as silk and pearls which were her favorite ornament, as they are Shirley's. The sweetness of her features was inexpressible. She had a beautiful little mouth, an oval chin, fine, animated eyes, which looked out upon the world with a frank, cheerful expression, and fair, blooming skin. The movements of her figure were unstudied, prompt, and natural, in contrast to "the inceding grace" of Western women. Her voice was sweet and clear, possessing a charm of its own, again in contrast to the "rich, low, subdued melody that flows from the lips of Senegambia's daughters." The quick glance of her eye indicated a warm, excitable temperament, mingling good nature and pride, high spirit, and kindheartedness. Her laugh, always ready, was a sound of pure delight. She had a "grand show-off voice," and she enjoyed singing for the pleasure and admiration of her friends.

Shirley, though an only child, is not spoiled by the attention she receives from young and old, male and female, but she does enjoy it, and she enjoys the romance and glamour which her position as Lady Bountiful gives her, and she is her most brilliant self when the center of an admiring company. Twilight and solitude subdue, but do not crush her spirits. Caroline, once surprising tears in her eyes, asked, "Shirley, why do you cry?" She retorted, "Because it pleases me mightily to cry . . . my heart is both sad and glad. . . . I only weep tears of delight and soon wipe them away." In comparison we have this portrait of Jane Moore, written in Charlotte's Roe Head days:

> If Jane does anything well, she likes eminently to be told so. She delights in society; not for worlds would she live alone. . . . Once or twice she has by some chance found herself alone in the evening about dusk in the large parlour at Kirkham-wood, and she has gone to the window and looked out at the garden . . . and as Jane looked out, some unaccustomed feeling did seem to swell in her heart, but if you asked her why her eyes glistened so, she would not have answered, "The moonlight is so lovely," but "Angria is such a glorious land!"

Such is not Jane Moore's element. The inspiration of twilight, solitude, melancholy musing is alien to her nature. Step into this great assembly room full of Angrian grandees. A public ball is given in celebration of the third anniversary of Independence. What lights! What flashing of jewels and waving of scarlet scarfs! What a tumultuous swell of melody! . . . Angria's glorious song of victory, "Sound the loud Timbrel." . . . Jane Moore, that feeling will not last, it will die away into silence; that expression, too will leave your eye, that flush your cheek, and you will look round and greet with a careless laugh the first word of flattery uttered by that dandy at your elbow. Your spirit can take a high tone, it can respond to an heroic call. You are not all selfish vanity, all empty show—you are a handsome, generous, clever, flashing, proud, overbearing woman.

Jane Moore had, besides her "frank cheerful countenance," unstudied natural grace of movement, and "rather abrupt, but sweet clear utterances"—other characteristics of a typical Angrian woman:

> There must be wealth and estates and a noble mansion and servants and

carriages and all other means and appliances that a dashing beauty can be supposed to require to set her off. I am afraid that Jane Moore, notwithstanding her natural quickness and high education, had none of the deep refined romance of the West. I am afraid that she scarcely knows what it means. She is as matter of fact as any manufacturer of Edwardston and likes as well to receive her pennyworth for her penny. With undisguised frankness she acknowledges that this world would be nothing without a flash and glitter now and then.

It was in correction of these implied faults in Jane, that Charlotte wrote of Shirley: "Shirley's head ran on other things than money and position. She was glad to be independent as to property: by fits she was even exalted at the notion of being a lady of the manor and having tenants and an estate . . . but her exultation, being quite undisguised, was singularly inoffensive; and, for her serious thoughts, they tended elsewhere." And Louis Moore says: "I have called her careless: it is remarkable that her carelessness never compromises her refinement; indeed, through this very loophole of character, the reality, depth, genuineness of that refinement may be ascertained."

Jane Moore, like all Angrian women, was ultra-patriotic—just so Shirley. As Jane exclaims, "Angria is such a glorious land!" Shirley rejoins, "Our England is a bonny island, and Yorkshire is one of her bonniest nooks," and when the curate Donne speaks slightingly of her country, she turns him out of her garden, saying, "How dare the lisping cockney revile Yorkshire!"

One night, Louis Moore, alone at Fieldhead, wanders into a room where the spirit of Shirley lingers, warm and comforting. Here he spends the evening, pouring out his heart to his diary after the habit of his prototype Sir William. Stopping before Shirley's worktable, with writing desk open upon it, he muses on the charm of its owner's carelessness, and the pleasure of appropriating her mislaid possessions so that she has to come to him for them. He pictures Shirley, as he saw her a few nights before, dressed for a concert: "I could call her nothing in my own mind save 'stainless virgin.' To my perception, a delicate splendour robed her, and the modesty of girlhood was her halo."

This confession reminds one of the time that Charles Townshend and Sir William Percy followed Jane Moore to Kirkham Lodge in the disguise of Gardener and Clarke, clients of her father. The pranksters were shown into Jane's drawing room with its worktable strewn with her possessions, and Sir William was about to prig something from it for a souvenir when Jane appeared in the doorway. To his startled gaze she "seemed to be haloed. There was something so radiant in her whole appearance . . . just a girl in white."

The Rev. Mr. Helstone early in Shirley's residence in Fieldhead dubbed her Captain Keeldar and charged Mrs. Pryor to "take care of this future magistrate, this church warden in perspective, this captain of yeomanry, this young squire of Briarfield," and thereafter he took great pleasure in addressing her as Captain Keeldar and assigning duties to her in keeping with the title. Robert Moore took up the sobriquet and used it frequently in addressing her. Shirley was pleased with the joke and kept it going, once saying to Helstone, "You must regard me as Captain Keeldar today. This is to be quite a gentleman's affair —yours and mine entirely, Doctor."

But the joke is older than Helstone. It originated in Jane Moore's bantering with Lord Hartford, when she dubbed herself "Captain Arthur Fitz-Arthur, Commander of the *Formidable*."

Another stamp of Jane Moore on Shirley Keeldar is her friendship with Hiram Yorke, for Yorke is General Thornton of the Angrian stories, with whom Jane Moore was a great favorite.

But Jane Moore, the Angrian, does not account for Shirley's great glowing, throbbing, prophetic soul which makes the book live in spite of its loose construction and frequent false drawing. She does not embody—to quote Miss Sinclair—the Shirley who saw nature at evening worship, kneeling, a woman-Titan speaking face to face with God, nor the Shirley that Louis Moore describes as "sister of the spotted, bright, quick, fiery leopard"; "Pantheress!—beautiful forest-born!—wily, tameless, peerless nature!" gnawing her chains and pining after virgin freedom, nor yet the Shirley that Caroline Helstone shows to the skeptical Robert Moore as a woman with a heart like "a shrine,—for it was holy; like snow,—for it was pure; like flame,—for it was warm; like death,—for it was strong." Yet the greater Shirley was potential in Jane Moore—she may even have been developed in Charlotte's imagination, for our picture of Jane, with the exception of one fragment, comes through Sir

William, who, be it remembered, had been snubbed by Jane, and was unfair in his judgment of her.

There is no reason whatsoever for believing that Emily Brontë inspired or colored the character of Jane Moore, though Mrs. Gaskell states, apparently on Charlotte's authority, that Shirley Keeldar represented Emily Brontë as she might have been, had she known health and prosperity. The explanation probably lies in the fact that there is a distinct cleavage in the book corresponding to its interruption by the sickness and death of Emily and Anne. It is in the later chapters, written in grief and loneliness, that the greater Shirley is developed. Perhaps the spirit of Emily breathed itself into these last chapters, and gave life "to the unwilling mass of this vast novel."

Hiram Yorke has often been pronounced Charlotte's most faithfully drawn portrait from life, the original being Mr. Taylor, the father of Charlotte's friends, Mary and Martha. He is also Charlotte's least changed Angrian. Emerging from the Young Men's Play as Wilson Thornton, his Yorkshire character and Doric speech fixed upon him forever, he was one of her most familiar figures—an able general in Zamorna's army, Lord Charles's guardian, and Jane Moore's good friend. His most marked characteristics were the tenacity with which he clung to his native speech and customs, though he could lay both aside and appear the polished gentleman of taste that he was; his unswerving moral rectitude; and a certain impatience of temper and frankness of speech amounting at times to rudeness, which did not, however, hide his kind heart. In one of Charlotte's transition fragments he was called Mr. De Capel and given a daughter and several sons, but Mrs. Yorke and her offspring as they appear in *Shirley* are new characters, apparently taken directly from the Taylors, mother and children.

Shirley's suitor, Sir Philip Nunnely, in his character of poet recalls Young Soult, who was Branwell, and one suspects a subtle hint of family history in Shirley's wish that Sir Philip's rhymes "had possessed more accuracy," and her suggestion that if he did not know the difference between rhyme and poetry, she did. If Charlotte had Emily in mind as she drew Shirley Keelder, she must have recalled her sister's suffering under Branwell's crude rhymes.

Villette

Villette by its very success brought distress upon Charlotte Brontë and crystallized for decades to come a complete misunderstanding of her art, confirming, as it apparently did, local gossip and critical surmise. The public, ignorant of all that came before *Jane Eyre* and unable to see how a novel of such fire and passion could come from the pen of an inexperienced Yorkshire girl, premised a great emotional upheaval in her own life, an unhappy love affair which awakened latent genius to expression. Such an experience, they argued, could belong to only one period of her life, the two years on the Continent. *Villette* seemed to change surmise to certainty, for it portrays the love of Lucy Snowe, an English girl teaching in a Belgian school—Villette was at once identified as Brussels —for Paul Emanuel, teacher of literature in the same school and kinsman of the proprietress. Lucy Snowe, the public assumed, was Charlotte Brontë, and Paul Emanuel, M. Héger; therefore Charlotte was in love with M. Héger. *Villette* was read as a personal confession; the most flaming autobiography in the language, it has been called.

Charlotte made no defense; she could not without exposing her long inner life of imagination. The only voice of authority to be raised against the assumption that Paul Emanuel was taken from M. Héger was Miss Sinclair, who discredited the evidence on the basis of artistic principle, declaring that "no supreme work of art was ever 'taken.' It was begotten, born and grown, the off-spring of a faithful love between the soul of the artist and reality." Paul Emanuel, she emphasizes, is a supreme work of art, and, therefore, cannot have been taken from anybody. Stories which Miss Sinclair never saw prove the correctness of her judgment, showing that Paul Emanuel was the growth of more than half of Charlotte's lifetime, to which Constantin Héger could have contributed at most no more than the perfect outward semblance for a personality, alive and active in Charlotte's imagination ten years before she met M. Héger and twenty years before she wrote *Villette*.

These same documents show also the origin of John Graham Bretton, Paulina Mary Home, and her father, the Count de Bassompierre, together with several of the minor characters and pivotal plot incidents of the story.

Lucy Snowe, the narrator in *Villette,* a privileged guest in the home of her godmother, Mrs. Bretton, devotes her opening chapters to a diminutive miss of six years left with Mrs. Bretton while her widowed father, "a man of science," seeks to build up his health on the Continent. This child, Paulina Mary Home, or little Polly, heartbroken at the separation, finds comfort in devoting herself to her hostess's son, John Graham Bretton, a great, happy, careless, teasing boy of sixteen.

A sudden change in Lucy's fortune separates her from her friends, taking her, in course of a few years, to Villette on the Continent and the school of Madame Beck, where she finds employment as a teacher. A period of loneliness and misery, following the general outline of Charlotte's second term of service with Madame Héger, culminates in the heroine's collapse in the street. She is found by an English doctor and carried to the home of his mother. Recognitions follow, restoring Lucy to her godmother, Mrs. Bretton. Dr. John, as Graham Bretton is now called, shows the lonely girl such kindness as to bind her heart to him forever, but before he reaches the point of avowal, another accident reunites the Bretton group with Mr. Home, now Count de Bassompierre, and his daughter, matured into a *petite* lady of grave dignity. Proximity turns the old attachment into love, and Dr. John and Paulina Mary are married.

From this new hurt Lucy finds comfort in the erratic kindness of Paul Emanuel, a kinsman of Madame Beck and teacher of literature in her school. Madame, perceiving the dawning of deeper sentiment between the two, uses all her "Jesuit" cunning to separate them, at last inducing M. Paul to undertake a two years' journey to an island in the South Seas in behalf of family business. Before he leaves, however, he takes Lucy to a house which he has equipped as a school, bidding her work and wait for his return. As the period allowed for his absence draws to a close and his vessel should be nearing port, a mighty storm arises, raging for days, until all hope for his ship is abandoned.

Lucy Snowe is two distinct personalities under one name. Introduced as a mere impersonal narrator, she suddenly develops a turn of character that raises her to the role of heroine. The first Lucy Snowe, cold and disagreeable, "the detestable Lucy," Miss Sinclair calls her, etching with consummate skill the portrait of little Polly, is Lord Charles Wellesley or Charles Townshend, an impersonal, cynical, scoffing creature, employed for like purposes in the Angrian stories. The second, a highly impassioned Lucy telling her own story, follows very closely the pattern of Charlotte's latest Angrian heroine, Elizabeth Hastings. The strain of Lord Charles, or Townshend, in the first Lucy's inheritance, more quickly recognized than pointed out, betrays itself in one characteristic passage: her cryptic statement of a sudden and mysterious change in her fortune, which recalls Lord Charles's equally cryptic explanation of his break with family and station in life. "It will be conjectured," says Lucy, "that I was, of course, glad to return to the bosom of my kindred. Well! the amiable conjecture does no harm, and may therefore be safely left uncontradicted. . . . There remained no possibility of dependence on others; to myself alone could I look." Reminders of Elizabeth Hastings run through Lucy's relation to Paul Emanuel.

From the establishment of Angria as a kingdom to the end of its cycle, its home secretary was Warner Howard Warner. He was first depicted as a small, dark man, somewhat feminine in appearance, with a womanish voice which suggested to his detractors the epithet "hermaphrodite." This suggestion was soon past and forgotten, and Warner became, in Charlotte's stories, a little dynamic man of unbounded energy and industry, demanding of others the devotion that he himself freely gave. He was fussy, interfering, dominating, overbearing, and tyrannical in his manners, though unselfishly expending himself and his abilities for his king, his country, and his family. He was nervous, irritable, and hasty, at times venomous in his speech, given to raging tirades when provoked. If he were met with an apology, he was likely to become gentle, and he was childlike in his readiness to forgive personal injury. He railed peevishly at Sir William Percy for being later than was expected in answering the government's summons to service, but he was all kindness and solicitude when he found that Sir William had "travelled express" all day, and urged the hospitality of his home for refreshment and rest. He loved flattery and deference, but he never accorded them to others; on the contrary, he habitually kept his associates well informed of their faults and shortcomings, but his strictures were always for the fortunate and arrogant. When Hartford was high in royal favor, Warner labored in season and out to discredit him in his monarch's eyes, but when he fell a victim to the king's injustice, Warner braved the taunts and threats of the entire cabinet to speak for him, rebuking the monarch fearlessly for ingratitude. Northangerland in power was the object of Warner's unrelenting hatred, but for Northangerland in misfortune he had only sympathy.

Warner possessed a quick, sensitive pride, closely joined to jealousy, which made him childishly alert for personal slights or offense against his importance as home secretary. Yet he could forget himself in service to his king. Given to tormenting others, he was an easy and delightful victim to the baiting of his associates, rising to gratifying heights of rage. He was inordinately ambitious for himself and his family— "All people have their faults. . . . Mr. Warner, for instance," said Lord Charles, "is not as lewd as some, but what he wants in looseness of morals, he atones for by preposterous ambition." He ruled the clan of Warners, Howards, and Agars with a strong hand but served their interests at great personal cost. For his brothers and cousins he seized every important post upon which he could lay his grasping fingers, but the kinsman who failed to measure up to the trust was removed as arbitrarily as he was appointed.

Warner was a religious little man, too, in his way, ever on the alert for the welfare of his sovereign's soul, as well as for his temporal interest, frequently playing the rebuking Nathan, and quoting scripture with disconcerting aptness of application. He possessed the gift of "second sight," which gave him a more than natural understanding of character. Nothing so offended him as skepticism of this gift, which he had proven on numerous occasions.

Despite his small stature, he was fearless, speaking his mind to the king even in that monarch's blackest moods, inspired as often by petty irritation as by sublime principle. When Zamorna's defeated army was scattered among the Angrian hills, the king a captive in exile, and the king's son a victim of the enemy's barbarity, it was Warner who, hazarding all his family's fortunes, gathered his clan, rescued the body of the tortured, murdered prince, and gave it loving burial.

Warner had been a great favorite of the young prince in his happy days, his chief attraction for the child being his interesting and eloquent conversation—eloquence was one of Warner's greatest gifts. "Now talk, sir," the little prince said to Warner on one occasion, "and I'll learn words from you," and all the evening he continued "stationary and silent, utterly absorbed in listening to his fervent, irritable, and eloquent oracle."

In short, Warner was Paul Emanuel in a larger and more heroic world than that dominated by the little professor of rhetoric in *Villette*.

If further evidence is needed to confirm spontaneous recognition, it is necessary only to list side by side descriptive phrases used in building up each character. Charlotte characterizes Warner as follows: "little man," "pale, provoking, undersized man," "busy, interfering little fellow," "slight figure in black," "imperious, all-controlling little Bonaparte," "Warner is disposed to assume a very dictatorial tone tonight," "he did not seem vexed; he can be imperturbable when he likes," "vigilant eye," "getting irritated," "Mr. Warner was now fully excited. He turned like a wild cat on Lord A.," "he has a tongue that would outring a woman's," "usual querulous tone," "well-known silver voice," "imperious but still dulcet tone," "severe and ambitious eye," "Mr. Warner . . . was in a ruinous temper," "the little man's cursedly peevish today," "he went off with a twang." [Zamorna accuses:] "O Howard, but you're jealous—jealous! . . . You also love to control," [Warner replies:] "Your Grace is privileged to insult me with impunity. . . . Then all my labors in your Majesty's cause turn on the point of jealousy, do they? And from that motive I am wearing out life and health— sacrificing time and happiness in the service of a sovereign who rewards me with taunts," [Warner speaking of Northangerland who has sneered at his gift of second sight:] "Vile skeptic! that he should dare to doubt what I have now three times proved, even in my short span of life."

Branwell speaks of Warner as "ardent and eloquent," "fretting himself to fritters." He enlarges upon his "surpassing ability, unwearied activity, and intense ambition," and his character "unstained in honor and veracity." Warner, he declares, is "quicksilver and can never remain long in one stay."

Of these same phrases and sentences Lucy Snowe builds her famous portrait of Paul Emanuel: "Fiery little man," "most irritable nature," "choleric and arbitrary," "vivacious, kind, sociable," "crisis of irritability was covering his human visage with the mask of an intelligent tiger,"

"able, fiery, and grasping little man," "strong relish for public representation," "spite and jealousy melted out of his face," "a religious little
man in his way," "so energetic, so intent, above all, so absolute," "his
love of display and authority," "not tall, but active and alive with energy
and movement of three tall men," "deep, intense, keenness of eye," "M.
Emanuel was never resonable," "little wicked, venomous man, little
monster of malice," "strange, evanescent anger," "all-willing to forget
and forgive," "jealous side-long look," "vigilant, piercing and often
malicious eyes," "dear little man, a stainless hero," "stern, dogmatic,
hasty, imperious," "magnificent-minded, grand-hearted, dear, faulty
man," "In love of power, in an eager grasp after supremacy, M. Emanuel
was like Bonaparte," "He would always have his own way," "I liked to
see M. Emanuel jealous, it lit up his nature," [M. Paul to Lucy:] "I know
you! I know you! Other people in this house see you pass, and think
that a colorless shadow has gone by. As for me, I scrutinized your face
once, and it sufficed," "A more despotic little man than M. Paul never
filled a professor's chair," "He had penetrated my thoughts," "He
thought to provoke a warm reply, vex the passionate to expression,"
"The ironic, the sarcastic, the disdainful, the passionately exultant, I had
hundreds of times seen him express," "Never was a better little man
in some respects than M. Paul," "When overwrought, he became acutely
irritable, and besides, his veins were dark with livid belladonna tincture,
the essence of jealousy," "He had a good voice, remarkable for compass,
modulation, and matchless expression," "He was a man it made happy
to see others happy. . . . At worst it was only his nerves that were irritable, not his temper that was radically bad," "His friendship was not
a doubtful, wavering benefit," "He was born honest, not false."

Even if Warner were all of the story, there would be little left in Paul
Emanuel to credit to M. Héger, but he is not all. The little that cannot
be traced to him comes directly from the odd blending of Sir William
Percy with Charles Townshend in the last years of the Angrian cycle.
There was nothing in Warner to account for "the ubiquitous, the inevitable M. Paul," privileged to frequent private and forbidden retreats,
whose connections and varied interests took him 'everywhere. And,
though Warner was as full of curiosity as an old woman, there was nothing in him of the prying M. Paul, the spy that appeared suddenly at

classroom doors, watched Lucy when she thought herself alone, and looked down from neighboring windows upon schoolgirls at play and teachers at their walks; and there was nothing in Warner that delighted in dropping rankling words in comet-like passages. M. Paul's ubiquity comes from Charles Townshend along with his manifold connections, and his privilege of entering forbidden places—his omnipresence. His spying, intriguing tendencies are derived from Sir William Percy, who, in the capacity of government agent tracking down traitors, habitually gathered information by means which justified, in part, vindictive denunciation hurled against him, though Sir William, no more than M. Paul, was violating his sense of honor; he was serving his government, M. Paul his church. A friend of Sir William's remarked: "[He] seems to have eyes both before and behind"; and Lucy said of M. Paul: "It was very much his habit to wear his eyes before, behind, and on each side of him."

From Percy comes also M. Paul's habit of rising suddenly at Lucy's elbow and hissing into her ear some taunt or denunciation—Sir William was noted for his habit of dropping rankling remarks where they would do the most harm and leaving them to bear the desired fruits. "He had a way . . . of wandering about as if he could find no rest for the sole of his foot. No one could fix his place; he was at your elbow when you least dreamed of his presence. . . . He would drop a chilling word or two . . . and then wander away." Lucy remarks that, "No one ever knew his [M. Paul's] whim or his whereabouts," and Branwell compares Warner to quicksilver, because he was never long in one place. But Sir William did not hiss; nonchalance was a part of his technique. When he most wished to infuriate, he spoke his softest and coolest. "If he chanced to converse with anyone who spoke loud, he sank his own voice to a low insolent drawl. . . . The more warmly the other declaimed, the more provokingly inaudible grew Sir William's murmured answer." Perhaps it was M. Héger who changed his "chilling word" to a hiss.

Many small but significant touches indicate that Sir William Percy was before Charlotte's eyes as she painted Paul Emanuel. For instance, Charlotte once related that Elizabeth Hastings, coming unexpectedly upon Sir William Percy in the course of an evening's walk, heard her approach announced by "a sharp bark, not very furious" of a spaniel "standing guard over his master's gentlemanly looking hat and pair of gloves." Lucy Snowe writes that about Madame Beck's house was a small spaniel that "virtually owned" M. Paul as master. "A delicate, silky, loving and lovable little doggie she was, trotting at his side, looking with expressive, attached eyes into his face: and whenever he dropped his *bonnet grec* or his handkerchief, which he occasionally did in play, crouching beside it with the air of a miniature lion guarding a kingdom's flag."

Still another touch of Sir William in M. Paul is seen in his leaving Lucy to the agony of thinking herself deserted and forgotten while he was preparing her school as a somewhat childish surprise. His blindness is on a par with Sir William's selfishness in leaving Elizabeth Hastings to recover from the sorrow of her brother's disgrace, and to struggle with the problem of making her own living until it should suit his mood to look her up again, and Elizabeth's businesslike enterprise in setting up her school is the forerunner of Lucy's use of the equipment and capital entrusted to her. Elizabeth, Townshend tells us, set to work with the activity of an emmet. Summoning her address and ladylike manners to her aid, she called on the wealthy manufacturers of the city and the aristocracy of the seats around, showing them specimens of her accomplishments, and so pleasing them with her tact and quickness of wit, that "within a fortnight she had raised a class of pupils sufficient to supply her with the means of comfort and elegance."

Lucy herself relates realistically:

I commenced my school; I worked—I worked hard. . . . Pupils came— burgers at first—a higher class ere long. I ventured to take the house adjoining mine. . . . My *externat* became a *pensionnat;* that also prospered.

How much of M. Héger went into the making of Paul Emanuel only one who knew him intimately could say: his occupation, certainly, and his Catholicism; his appearance in part, perhaps, and some of his mannerisms. Coming under Charlotte's keen observation at a time when she was trying to give her Angrians a realistic aspect, he offered a perfect physical semblance for the spirit that was Warner Howard Warner.

Charlotte's admission that Dr. John Graham Bretton and his mother were drawn from her publisher, Mr. George Smith and his mother, whom she had visited in London, is but a part truth. In their relations to each other, mother and son were, no doubt, suggested by her kind friends; Mrs. Bretton may be a faithful portrait of Mrs. Smith, and Dr. John may bear a superficial resemblance to her son, but he is in actuality one phase of the many-sided Zamorna, following the original more faithfully in spirit and details than does Rochester in *Jane Eyre*.

Charlotte's early descriptions of young Arthur Wellesley, drawn when she was between thirteen and sixteen, show a youth of "tall, slender shape," with "auburn hair, curly and glossy, waving in a bright wealth of curls over a forehead of purest marble," a boy possessed of a "good-natured and amiable disposition," and an "elegant and cultivated mind given to pensive thoughts and meditation." Again she speaks of his "love of elegant literature and fine arts in general." Lucy Snowe (Charlotte as a mature artist) strips this picture of its conventional Byronism and calls it Graham Bretton at sixteen, "a handsome, faithless-looking youth," with "waved auburn hair," "supple symmetry," and "smile frequent, and destitute neither of fascination nor of subtlety."

Graham [Lucy says] was a boy not quite as other boys are. All his delight did not lie in action; he was capable of some intervals of contemplation; he could take a pleasure, too, in reading, nor was his selection of books wholly indiscriminating: there were glimmerings of characteristic preference, and even of instinctive taste in his choice.

Someone recalling Arthur Wellesley as a boy characterized him as "all laughing selfishness, even then," and Paulina Mary Home remembered that Graham at sixteen was "gay and careless, not much heeding those with whom he read or amused himself."

Again, Lord Charles concluded a description of a portrait of his brother at nineteen thus:

The figure seemed verily to rise into life. . . . It mingled the air of the deep student with something more awakening, a fiery dawn of the passions, such as did, I well remember, burn at that time in every glance of the original.

And Lucy Snowe, awakening from a delirium in the Bretton home, recognized on the wall of the room a portrait of the youthful Graham:

Any romantic little school-girl might almost have loved it in its frame. Those eyes looked as if when somewhat older they could flash lightning response to love.

And from this same Arthur Wellesley, uncontaminated by court life and the influence of Rogue, given wholesome home and school training, comes Dr. John, the youthful bourgeois physician—Zamorna, without a suggestion of the soldier, the tyrant, or the Oriental voluptuary, enjoying no power save that inherent in his charms, and no privileges save those accorded by love, a Zamorna frequently glimpsed in the Angrian stories on happy occasions when "hours of sociability softened the monarch's eyes."

Dr. John's tact with children is but a lightly sketched reminder of Zamorna's exquisite tenderness to all children—some of Charlotte's best scenes are those showing the Duke with his own youngsters. His benevolent kindness, never striking very deep into his emotions, never entailing any personal sacrifice, are a true carrying over of Zamorna's universal good will and unfailing kindness and helpfulness so long as the indulgence of this tendency of his nature does not interfere with a particular personal prejudice or desire. A comfortable sort of pleasure in the happiness and well-being of all about them is a part of the innate selfishness of both Zamorna and Dr. John. Graham with his sense of humor, his love of good-natured raillery and teasing, his easy adaptability which made him the "finest companion in the world," comes directly from Zamorna in relaxed and expansive moods. Dr. John Graham Bretton, the man of science, lover and connoisseur of art, critic of literature, and frequenter of the theatre and opera, is a humanized version of young Arthur Wellesley, Marquis of Douro, recipient of every honor and distinction the Angrian world of science could bestow, celebrated as patron of literary men and artists, and a mentor of the stage.

Innumerable verbal parallels offer their testimony to the identity of Dr. John and Zamorna, such as:

"Dr. John had a fine set of nerves."
[Zamorna] "Cast-iron could not be startled, no more was he."

[Dr. John] "Familiar shape, tall and grand. . . . He knew himself privileged."
[Zamorna] "Tall, grand figure; omnipotent and audacious self."

"Dr. John could think and think well, but he was rather a man of action than thought. . . . His natural attitude was not the meditative, nor his natural mood the sentimental."

"Zamorna was a man of no words at all on sentimental matters, though vigorous enough in his actions."

"Graham in a mirthful mood must not be humored too far. Just now there was a new sort of smile playing about his lips—very sweet, but it grieved me somehow—a new sort of light sparkling in his eyes; not hostile, but not reassuring."

[Zamorna] "Sweet as honey and bright with good humor, but in his glee there is so much of the devil that nobody that had their senses about them would trust him."

Dr. John was not perfect. . . . A god could not have the cruel vanity of Dr. John, nor . . . have resembled him in his occasional temporary oblivion of all but the present—in his passing passion for that present; shown . . . selfishly, by extracting from it whatever it could yield of nutriment to his masculine self-love; his delight was to feed that ravenous sentiment, without thought of the price of provender, or care for the cost of keeping it sleek and highly pampered."

[Zamorna] "He has too little of the moral great-heart in his nature. It is his creed that all things bright and fair live for him; by him they are to be gathered and worn as the flowers of his laurel crown."

An implication of faithlessness runs through the picture of Graham Bretton from the first stroke of the brush to the last. He is introduced as "a handsome, faithless-looking youth of sixteen." The child Polly saw something in his portrait that pained her keenly, and sent "a darkness . . . trembling through her sensitive eye." Lucy thought the young doctor's "eye glanced from face to face rather too vividly, too quickly, and too often." One of the discarded drafts of *Villette* goes even further in its implication of Graham's caprice in affection:

"Lucy," she [Paulina] said presently, "do you think Graham is inclined to be of a fickle nature?"

I replied that I was not sure whether he was fickle or not.

"I believe he is," she went on, "many ideas come into my mind about him, perhaps some of them unwarranted. I believe it would not be wise in any person to—to—what is called *love* him."

Small wonder that against such a carefully built-up background of distrust Charlotte's concluding declaration of Graham's constancy does not carry conviction: "Bright, too, was the destiny of his sweet wife. She kept her husband's love, she aided in his progress—of his happiness she was the corner-stone." Neither did Charlotte accept her own words, for too well Zamorna's creator remembered the fear gnawing always at Mary Percy's heart that when she should need the support of her husband's enfolding arms, they would not be there. It was not in the Angrian tradition that Zamorna should remain true in love. Graham Bretton's final faithfulness is but a bit of thin veneer suggested, perhaps, by Mr. George Smith.

The character of Graham Bretton, in spite of all the praise heaped upon it by Lucy Snowe, is not pleasing. She says he is good and kind and thoughtful and generous, but the reader knows he is inherently selfish and possessed of all the faults selfishness gives rise to; that he will be fickle, if not actually false in love; and that, having won a heart to a degree of adoration making it dependent upon him for its very life, he could doom it to death through forgetfulness and neglect. On the other hand Lucy is critical of her idol at times, she even abuses him in quite the old manner of Lord Charles abusing Zamorna, though it is plain that she, like her prototype, "is not in earnest" when she does so.

It is this recurring contradiction in the representation of Dr. John's character that makes Miss Sinclair say he never "comes off." She thinks it is because he is a "taken" character and has not passed through the life-giving medium of Charlotte's imagination. It is, rather, because he, with these same Byronic contradictions, had existed too long and too vividly in Charlotte's imagination to be amenable to the reforming suggestion of Mr. George Smith. He might be glossed over a bit, but he could not be made another person than his old self. And it must be admitted that Charlotte loved Zamorna's romantic vices too dearly to give them up. They were far more attractive to her than all the everyday virtues in Mr. Smith's calendar. It was Zamorna's sins that made him glorious. He hugged them to his bosom as a part of his precious ego— and the ladies, Charlotte among them, found him irresistible.

Nothing could be more characteristic of Zamorna than Dr. John's attitude toward Lucy Snowe: indifference until she was thrown upon his care; good-natured, careless kindness once she became attached to him; forgetfulness when a more lively interest presented itself; and general well-wishing when she came again under his notice.

There is no doubt that John Graham Bretton was, in Charlotte's mind, the real hero of *Villette*, for Zamorna could have no rival. He must have a wife young, beautiful, and wealthy, from the same group of fortunate, happy beings as himself. Lucy Snowe, a poor little moth of a governess, ventured too close to the great luminary and fell in agony to the earth, to be comforted in time by the lesser love of one on her own plane. But her heart always turned in adoration to Graham, even after she acknowledged to herself that she loved Paul Emanuel.

For this overlapping of Lucy's two loves, Charlotte has received severe criticism, and many explanations have been offered of the lapse. It is extremely doubtful that she was at all conscious of the situation or the problem involved in it. It was a matter of course in her mind that all women should love Zamorna. All of the wives of Angria kept secret shrines in their hearts for the worship of this divinity, and certainly no woman who came under his notice, as Lucy came under Dr. John's, could ever put him out of her heart. Lucy's situation is identical with that of Zenobia Ellrington, who confessed, years after her marriage, "there is a charm, a talisman, about him [Zamorna] which wins all hearts, rivets chains . . . which cannot be undone."

To make a proper wife for Graham, Charlotte blended Zamorna's two wives, Marian Hume and Mary Percy, into Paulina Mary Home. Marian's most marked characteristics were her simple purity and sweetness; her kinship to the fairies, indicated in her "fairy form," her "light, dancing step" and her occasional gaiety of manner and love of frolic; her resemblance to a lily-of-the-valley or a snowdrop, symbolized by her habit of dressing always in green and white: "Pure white or vernal green were the colours she constantly wore, without any jewels save one row of pearls around the neck."

The fairylike side of Paulina Mary is given full play in the scene on Christmas Eve in the kitchen at La Terrasse:

The little white Countess danced in a circle. . . . Paulina Mary still danced to and fro. . . .

"And is that a Scotch reel you are dancing, you Highland fairy?" asked her father. "Mrs. Bretton, there will be a green ring growing in the middle of your kitchen shortly. I would not answer for her being quite cannie; she is a strange little mortal."

And Graham Bretton, watching Paulina, "hardly knew how to blend together in his ideas the dancing fairy and delicate dame." Lucy Snowe, wandering alone in the park on a fete night, paused unrecognized to contemplate Paulina sitting between her father and lover, radiant in her betrothal happiness: "Within reach of my hand sat a figure like a fairy queen, whose array lilies and their leaves seem to have suggested; whatever was not spotless white, being forest-green."

An intermediate link between Marian Hume and Paulina Mary is Marian Fairburne of the transition fragments. To Marian Hume's delicacy of feature, exquisite complexion, deep blue eyes, and silky auburn curls, Marian Fairburne adds the diminutive form and financial opulence of Miss Victoria Delph, or Delphi, an heiress of Verdopolis, and passes them on to Paulina Mary. Notice how the appearance of being younger than she is runs as an identifying thread from Marian Hume to Marian Fairburne to Paulina Mary Home:

"She [Marian Hume] did not appear above fifteen years of age [she was seventeen]. She wore only a green silk frock and pearl necklace, and a myrtle branch twined among her luxurious auburn ringlets."

"At first sight you would have taken her [Marian Fairburne] for a little girl, she was so small and slightly formed, but when she looked up her face was not that of a child—it had the expression of seventeen years."

"She [Paulina Mary] is very light . . . like a child. . . . Is she a child, Lucy? Did you notice her age?"

"I am not a child—I am a person of seventeen," responded the patient, demurely and with dignity.

If Paulina Mary Home, descended from Marian Hume through Marian Fairburne, had followed the tradition consistently, she would have died of a broken heart through her love for Graham. Her capacity for suffering and Graham's carefully built up faithlessness in the early chapters of *Villette* prepare the way for such a tragedy. Why it was averted can only be guessed, but when little Polly of these early chapters reappears, near the middle of the book, as the rich and beautiful Countess de Bassompierre the danger is past. Perhaps it is because she has become identified in Charlotte's mind with Mary Percy, and Charlotte learned long since that she could not break the heart of that heroine.

Directly from Mary Percy, Paulina takes "the fineness of her beauty, the soft courtesy of her manner, her immature but real and inbred tact," which drew Graham Bretton as they had drawn Zamorna and held him against his natural tendency to stray. From Mary she takes also many of her more tangible features such as "the unmistakable poise of her head," "her delicate, rather fine profile," a touch of haughtiness, fastidious pride, a thin glazing of ice in her manner, a touch of petulance and wilfulness, and the assurance of high rank in life.

Mary Percy suited her fastidious husband, as no other woman ever suited him. He neglected and hurt her, and often forgot her superiority in lesser charms. "Still, she retained the power of awakening him at intervals to a new consideration of her price, and his Grace . . . would discover with surprise that he had a treasure always in his arms that he loved better, a great deal better, than the far-sought gems that he dived among the rocks so often to bring up." Just so Paulina and Graham suited each other perfectly. "All that was best in Graham sought Paulina; whatever in him was noble, awoke and grew in her presence. . . . Each liked the way the other talked, the voice, the diction, the expression pleased; each keenly relished the flavour of the other's wit; they met each other's meaning with a strange quickness, their thoughts often matched like carefully chosen pearls."

A distinct and significant reminiscence of Mary Percy in Paulina is her devotion to her father with its threat of tragedy in her life, for every reader of the Angrian stories remembers how cruelly Mary's heart was torn by her dual passion for a father and a husband often at mortal strife. And Mr. Home's acceptance of Graham as his son-in-law carries an echo of Percy's frequent curses upon Zamorna for the suffering his carelessness and neglect brought upon Mary: "Take her, John Bretton, and may God deal with you as you deal with her."

Mary Percy shows herself again in Paulina's anxiety that her father and Graham should be friends, and in her joy in the growing congeniality of the two beings upon whom her life depends. Lucy reports how she watched Paulina Mary, seated between her father and her lover, plait together wisps of hair from the head of each, bind the plait with a tress of her own hair, close it in a locket to be worn upon her heart. "Now," said she, "there is an amulet made which has virtue to keep you two always friends. You can never quarrel so long as I wear this."

In contrast to the complicated story of his daughter, Mr. Home's evolution is simple and direct. Among the original wooden soldiers of the Young Men's Play was one famous for his hard looks and proud manners who spoke with a Scotch accent. In course of time and the development of the play, this soldier, Bady, became Alexander Hume, Duke of Badry, described in Charlotte's first love story as "a Scotchman, who was physician to his Grace, and, though of gentlemanly manners and demeanor, yet harsh, stern, and somewhat querulous in countenance and disposition. . . . He was a widower and had but one child, a daughter." In *Villette* Mr. Home, Count de Bassompierre, a man of science, the father of Paulina Mary "was a stern-featured—perhaps I should say rather, a hard-featured man; his forehead was knotty, and his cheekbones were marked and prominent. The character of his face was quite Scotch. . . . His northern accent in speaking harmonized with his physiognomy. He was at once proud-looking and homely-looking." He, too, was a man of gentlemanly aspect and bearing, and in the one scene in which his disposition came out with any degree of distinction, when Graham asked him for his daughter's hand, he was quite stern, and showed himself "sorely crossed, annoyed—even bitter."

Miss Sinclair, summarizing the minor characters of *Villette*, remarks, "Experience may have partly accounted for Ginevra [Fanshawe]. It could hardly have accounted for the little de Hamal, and he is perfect, as far as he goes." Ginevra is not an Angrian, but de Hamal is one of the host of "fashionable ninnies" swarming around Jane Moore, who, Charles Townshend declared, "one and all wanted but a tail to make the prettiest counterfeit monkeys imaginable."

The most familiar scene in *Villette*, because so much played up by biographers as an account of Charlotte's own actual suffering in Madame Héger's school, is Lucy Snowe's agonizing dream, which climaxes the tragically realistic chapter headed, "The Long Vacation":

There was no way to keep well under the circumstances. At last a day and night of peculiarly agonizing depression were succeeded by physical illness, I took perforce to my bed. . . . I lay in a strange fever of the nerves and blood. Sleep went quite away. I used to rise in the night, look around for her, beseech her earnestly to return. . . . Sleep never came!

I err. She came once, but in anger. Impatient of my importunity she brought with her an avenging dream. By the clock of St. Jean Baptiste, that dream remained scarce fifteen minutes—a brief space, but sufficing to wring my whole frame with unknown anguish; to confer a nameless experience

that had the hue, the mien, the terror, the very tone of a visitation from eternity. Between twelve and one that night a cup was forced to my lips, black, strong, strange, drawn from no well, but filled up seething from a bottomless and boundless sea. . . . Having drunk and woke, I thought all was over; the end come and past by. . . . I rose on my knees in bed. Some fearful hours went over me; indescribably was I torn, racked, and oppressed in mind. Amidst the horrors of that dream I think the worst lay here. Methought the well-loved dead, who had loved *me* well in life, met me elsewhere alienated; galled was my inmost spirit with an unutterable sense of despair about the future. Motive there was none why I should try to recover or wish to live. . . . When I tried to pray I could only utter these words:—
"From my youth up Thy terrors have I suffered with a troubled mind."

Small wonder that readers give this chapter the credence of a personal confession, and yet Charlotte at fourteen, exulting in her power to create an atmosphere of horror, wrote:

I was racked by a dull torturing pain in my forehead which prevented me from sleeping. Sometimes my limbs were icy cold, sometimes burning hot. I could hear the violent throbbing of my temples; thrilling pain ran through my body from head to foot; a knot was in my throat and I felt dreadfully thirsty; my tongue was as dry as a dusty stick; and all my teeth were aching as if they were in want of the dentist's instrument and skill. . . . I rose and, tottering to the washstand, seized the ewer and drained its contents. Then I reeled back to bed and flung myself almost fainting upon it. After midnight I fell asleep and . . . dreamt many troubled, confused dreams, all of which have faded from my memory except . . . one. . . . Excruciatingly horrible is the remembrance of that frightful dream. . . . But to think of it is insupportable agony.

Other incidents of this, Charlotte's last novel, are reminiscent of earlier stories. Rachel's acting before the Belgian court, for instance, combines Charlotte's actual experience in a London theater with her purely imaginary picture of Mrs. Siddons's playing in the Theatre Royal of Verdopolis before the four monarchs of Ashantee, presented in "Arthuriana," 1833. The drama in the Bretton parlor when Graham compels little Polly to come to him for a much coveted colored picture is a reworking of a scene in Miss Percy's parlor from one of the transition fragments, when Arthur Ripley West tries, though unsuccessfully, to draw shy Marian Fairburne, Paulina Mary's direct prototype, to his side. Again, when Lucy Snowe would describe the effect of an opiate which

Madame Beck administers to her secretly, she uses the phraseology of Macara Lofty, an Angrian addict:

> The drug wrought. I know not whether Madame had over-charged or under-charged the dose; its result was not that she intended. Instead of stupor, came excitement. I became alive to new thought. . . . Imagination was roused from her rest, and she came forth impetuous and adventurous.

Lofty told his listener:

> The drug wrought quickly; in five minutes I, who had been the most miserable wretch under heaven, sat a rational, happy man, soothed to peace of mind, to rest of body, capable of creating sweet thoughts, of tasting bliss, of dropping those fetters of anguish which had restrained me and floating away with light frame and soaring into the fairest region imagination can disclose.

Lucy's description of the fateful storm at sea in which her lover is lost, the supreme culmination of Charlotte's creative imagery and lyrical expression, has a long background in Angrian literature. In "Stanzas on the Fate of Henry Percy," Charlotte at eighteen tried to weave in dramatic unity the separation of lovers by an evil person, a long voyage to a southern island, a storm encountered, and high tragedy haloed with mystery. A year earlier she introduced into "The Green Dwarf" a ballad picturing a young girl listening to the wind moaning wildly through the giant trees and thinking of her lover "asail on the mighty deep." The heroine's fears translate the moaning into the foreboding voice of a spirit and show her in imagination "her love's proud battleship" tossing wildly on the "storm-dark deep" until it lies before her "a wrecked and shattered hull," while "amid the rushing spray" she sees her Edward's "eagle plume." The singer of the ballad is aroused from her melancholy mood by the appearance of her lover himself.

Against Lucy's great prose song, "that sonorous dirge that rings high above all pathos, which is somehow a song of triumph, inspired by the whole power and splendour and magnificence of storm and death," there follows a paragraph which narrowly misses the effect of an anticlimax:

> Leave sunny imaginations hope. Let it be theirs to conceive the delight of joy born again fresh out of great terror, the rapture of rescue from peril, the wondrous reprieve from dread, the fruition of return. Let them picture union and a happy succeeding life.

This is as far as Charlotte dared indulge her old habit of resuscitating her hero.

Despite its faithful etching of buildings and streets, gardens and parks, theaters and holiday crowds, and its sustained conviction of actuality from beginning to end, *Villette* is the most Angrian of Charlotte's novels.

Wuthering Heights

There is little doubt that had we Emily Brontë's prose in proportionate completeness to Charlotte's Angrian literature, the "mystery of *Wuthering Heights*" would give way to a clear understanding of the process by which her Gondal-Titans became flesh and blood Yorkshire folk. But "Solala Vernon's Life," "Emperor Julius's Life," "Passages in the Life of an Individual," and "The Gondal Chronicles"—all "the good many books" that filled Emily's and Anne's leisure through adolescence and womanhood—have gone the crowded road of destruction, and with them information of the institutions, personalities, and events of the world in which *Wuthering Heights* was conceived. Only Emily's poems remain to explain the otherwise baffling psychology of her unique novel, but they suffice to show that *Wuthering Heights* was no sudden miracle of 1845–46 nor yet a reworking of Branwell's material, but, like *Jane Eyre* and *Villette*, it was the adaptation of a purely imaginary creation to the demands of realism.

Mr. Lockwood's nightmare, used to introduce the theme of *Wuthering Heights*, finds all its essential elements in a poem ("But dreams like this I cannot bear") dated October 14, 1837, depicting a sleeper in the grip of "an awful dream" induced by the scratching of a ghostly, snow-laden yew branch against an old vault's rail. Awakened, he is driven by "a frightened feeling, frenzy-born," out of the haunted room into the icy glory of a snow-covered world under moonlight.

In two distinct groups of poems Emily employs the situation of foster-brother and sister who become lovers. One of these groups, the Fernando story, has no particular significance, but the other, showing the adoption of the dark boy of sorrow by the golden-haired, blue-eyed child of gladness, is, to an interesting extent, the early Heathcliff-Catherine situation. The dark boy is killed as the assassin of King Julius, but the older Heathcliff is glimpsed in the unidentified Angrian wanderer of a poem beginning, "And now the house-dog stretched once more," whose presence chilled the friendly warmth of a shepherd's hearth where he sought shelter.

> Youthful he seemed, but worn as they
> Who spend too soon their youthful day.
>
> .   .   .   .   .
>
> But when upraised his eye would dart
> An icy shudder through the heart,
> Compassion changed to horror then,
> And fear to meet that gaze again.
>
> .   .   .   .   .
>
> . . . Lightning all unearthly shone
> Deep in that dark eye's circling zone,—
> Such withering lightning as we deem
> None but a spectre's look may beam;
> And glad they were when he turned away
> And wrapped him in his mantle grey,
> Leant down his head upon his arm,
> And veiled from view their basilisk charm.

Nelly Dean, the narrator in *Wuthering Heights,* once told Heathcliff his eyes held a couple of "black fiends so deeply buried, who never opened their windows boldly, but lurked glintingly under them, like devil spies." Later she remarked that his eyes were "deep set and singular," and still later that they were "full of black fire," burning at times with anguish, at times flashing fiercely. Heathcliff's wife spoke of his "basilisk eyes," and repeated Nelly Dean's figure: "The clouded windows of hell flashed a moment towards me; the fiend which usually looked out, however, was so dimmed and drowned that I did not fear to hazard another sound of derision." Near the end of his life, according to Nelly, Heathcliff's eyes and entire visage took on the aspect of an unearthly being.

Again Nelly Dean relates of Heathcliff, immediately following Catherine's death: "When I first looked into his face, I perceived that he had got intelligence of the catastrophe; and a foolish notion struck me that his heart was quelled and he prayed, because his lips moved and his gaze was bent on the ground." When she spoke to him, however, she was met with curses instead of prayers. Her experience is identical with that of an unknown person in one of Emily's poems:

> . . . That stormy breast
> At length, I said, has deigned to rest;
> At length above that spirit flows
> The waveless ocean of repose.
>
> Let me draw near: 'twill soothe to view
> His dark eyes dimmed with holy dew;
> Remorse even now may wake within,
> And half unchain his soul from sin.

Drawing near to the suffering man, the speaker was repulsed even as Nelly Dean, and exclaimed,

> Oh! crime can make the heart grow old
> Sooner than years of wearing woe,
> Can turn the warmest bosom cold
> As winter wind or polar snow.

Heathcliff, near the end of his life, recounting to Nelly Dean the efforts of his spirit to break through the flesh to Catherine, said, "The most ordinary faces of men and women—my own features—mock me with a resemblance." Just so "A.G.A." in the poem beginning "Where were ye all?" saw in chance faces about her resemblances to the one stamped indelibly upon her heart.

More than once Catherine declared that both Linton's and Heathcliff's love had brought her nothing but pain, echoing Angelica's complaint that she had known many kinds of love and "*all* made the loved one rue." Catherine in her frenzy wished that Linton and Heathcliff might suffer as they had made her suffer, and over and over Heathcliff retaliated, cursing her for separating herself from him by her marriage to Linton, just as Gondal men and women cursed their false lovers:

> Oh! could I know thy soul with equal grief was torn,
> This fate might be endured, this anguish might be borne.

and

> Well, thou hast paid me back my love!
> But, if there be a God above,
> Whose arm is strong, Whose word is true,
> This hell shall wring thy spirit too!

On first meeting Catherine as Mrs. Linton, Heathcliff says, "I've fought through a bitter fight since I last heard your voice," and that night, Catherine, referring to the long separation, confided to Nelly, "Oh, I've endured very, very bitter misery, Nelly." In their last tragic meeting Catherine accuses, "Why shouldn't you suffer? I do," and Heathcliff retorts, "You teach me how cruel you have been. . . . *I* have not broken your heart—you have broken it; and in breaking it you have broken mine"; and Catherine answers, "If I've done wrong, I am dying for it." The defense of each might be summed up in the Gondalan plea:

> If I have sinned; long, long ago
> That sin was purified by woe.

When Nelly carried word of Catherine's death to Heathcliff, waiting under the trees, he exclaimed to Catherine's spirit, "Oh, you said you cared nothing for my sufferings, and I pray one prayer—I repeat it until my tongue stiffens—Catherine Earnshaw, may you not rest as long as I am living! You said I killed you—haunt me then! . . . Be with me always—take any form—drive me mad! Only *do* not leave me in this abyss, where I cannot find you! Oh, God! it is unutterable! I *cannot* live without my life! I *cannot* live without my soul!" Long before a Gondalian had prayed the spirits of a dead lover:

> If grief for grief can touch thee,
> If answering woe for woe,
> If any ruth can melt thee,
> Come to me now!

and

> Oh, come again! What chains withhold
> The steps that used so fleet to be?
> Come, leave thy dwelling dank and cold
> Once more to visit me!

Just as Catherine and Heathcliff "pay each other back torture for torture, and pang for hopeless pang," yet cling together in love that is stronger than death, so Lord Alfred, thinking of one who had driven him to self-destruction, exclaims:

> Oh, could that lost heart give back, back again to thine,
> One tenth part of the pain that clouds my dark decline!

yet dies confessing,

> *Life* bows to my control, but *Love* I cannot kill.

Catherine, ill unto death, declared, "I am tired of being enclosed here. I am wearying to escape into that glorious world, and to be always there; not seeing it dimly through tears and yearning for it through the walls of an aching heart, but really with it, and in it." Heathcliff's life went out, not of bodily illness, but of the constant beating of his spirit against the limitation of material existence. He declared: "I have a single wish, and my whole being and faculties are yearning to attain it. They have yearned toward it so long, and so unwaveringly, that I am convinced that it *will* be reached—and soon—because it has devoured my existence: I am swallowed up in the anticipation of its fulfillment. . . . I'm too happy, and yet I'm not happy enough. My soul's bliss kills my body, but does not satisfy itself. . . . I have nearly attained *my* heaven." In "The Prisoner," written about the time Emily began *Wuthering Heights,* and published in *Poems* of 1846, a girl captive likewise exults in impending freedom of her soul from its body:

> Then dawns the Invisible; the Unseen its truth reveals;
> My outward sense is gone, my inward essence feels:
> Its wings are almost free—its home, its harbour found,
> Measuring the gulf, it stoops—and dares the final bound.

Heathcliff, cursing Catherine in his agony at her going, begs, "You said I killed you—haunt me then! The murdered *do* haunt their murderers, I believe. I know that ghosts *have* wandered on earth." Nelly, having concluded the story of Heathcliff's death and burial, adds:

But the country folks, if you ask them, would swear on the Bible that he *walks;* there are those who speak to having met him near the church, and on the moor, and even within this house. . . . That old man by the kitchen fire affirms he has seen two on 'em, looking out of his chamber window, on every rainy night since his death:—and an odd thing happened to me about a month ago. I was going to the Grange one evening—a dark evening threatening thunder—and just at the turn of the Heights, I encountered a little boy with a sheep and two lambs before him; he was crying terribly; and I supposed the lambs were skittish, and would not be guided.

"What is the matter, my little man?" I asked.

"There's Heathcliff and a woman, yonder, under the t'nab," he blubbered, "un' I darnut pass 'em."

Ghosts were undoubted realities in Gondal, and it was probably from his Gondalan incarnation that Heathcliff carried over his conviction "that ghosts *have* wandered on earth." There was King Julius's ghost from beyond the gulf "o'er which mortality has never, never been," and, even more clearly drawn, was the ghost of Lord Alfred haunting Aspin Castle, though it should have wandered

> Three thousand miles beyond the wave,
> Where his exilèd ashes lie,
> Under the cope of England's sky.

The shepherds of the neighborhood and the narrator had often seen it at close range—

> It always walks with head declined,—
> The long curls move not in the wind;
> Its face is fair, divinely fair;
>   But brooding on that angel brow
> Rests such a shade of deep despair,
>   As naught divine could ever know.
>
> How oft in twilight, lingering lone,
>   I've stood to watch that phantom rise,
> And seen, in mist and moonlit stone
>   Its gleaming hair and solemn eyes!

Nature, wooing Emily Brontë from her absorption in Gondal to old-time intimacy ("Shall earth no more inspire thee,") urged:

> Few hearts to mortals given,
>   On earth so wildly pine;
> Yet few would ask a heaven
>   More like this earth than thine,

anticipating Cathy's dream that she was so homesick in heaven that the angels in disgust cast her out upon her own moors, where she awoke sobbing for gratitude.

Catherine, in her death delirium, begging for the cold northwest wind across her bed, "Do let me feel it—it comes straight down the moor—

do let me have one breath," speaks in the voice of the Gondalan suicide,

> . . . 'Tis Gondal's wind that blows;
> I shall not tread again the deep glens where it rose.
> I feel it on my face: "Where, wild blast, dost thou roam,
> What do we, wanderer, here, so far away from home?"

In a poem headed, "A.S. to G.S. December 19, 1841," Emily pictures a girl trying to console her brother for the death of their mother:

> And from that world of heavenly light
> Will she not always bend
> To guide us in our lifetime's night,
> And guard us to the end?

Ellen Dean reports that on the night that Mr. Earnshaw, senior, died, she found the children, Cathy and Heathcliff, in a room upstairs, comforting each other with better thoughts than she could have hit upon: "No parson in the world could have pictured heaven so beautifully as they did, in their innocent talk."

Mr. Lockwood, returning to Gimmerton Valley after long absence, concludes his description thus: "Had I seen it nearer August, I'm sure it would have tempted me to waste a month among its solitudes. In winter, nothing more dreary, in summer nothing more divine, than those glens shut in by hills, and those bluff, bold swells of heath." "The Outcast Mother" used the same contrast in describing the death-glen of her child:

> I've seen this dell in July's shine
> As lovely as an angel's dream.
>
> .   .   .   .
>
> Wakes up the storm more madly wild,
> The mountain-drifts are tossed on high.

Rosina's "weeks of wild delirium" connected with the birth of a baby girl about the time of Julius's assassination suggests Catherine's brain fever which brought on the premature birth of her daughter.

Nelly Dean, recounting the birth of Catherine Linton II, then eighteen years of age, living in friendless misery at Wuthering Heights, said: "An unwelcome infant it was, poor thing. . . . Its beginning was as friendless as its end is likely to be." Ten years before Emily had made the lonely boy of the Gondal poems declare himself to be as friendless after eighteen years, as lone as on his natal day.

With even a partial reconstruction of Gondal, such as can be made from Emily's poems, disappears the last vestige of probability attaching to the theory that *Wuthering Heights* was written or inspired by Branwell Brontë, for what is there in the novel beyond the imaginative experiences of a woman who for half her life had ruled kingdoms, languished in prisons, led armies, wandered with outlaws, murdered ruthlessly, and ministered tenderly? Branwell had no part in Gondal; why should his hand be needed to explain *Wuthering Heights?*

APPENDICES

Appendix I

RECONSTRUCTING GONDAL

K NOWING that Emily Brontë's voluminous *juvenilia* had been destroyed, I began my study of the Parsonage family without hope of adding anything to the scant knowledge of her genius and its development. Her birthday notes of July 30, 1841, and July 31, 1845, apparently the sole remaining traces of an extensive Gondal literature, were tantalizing reminders of what might have been learned. But, in her own words, repining was "hopeless and vain," and I omitted Emily from my plan of Brontë study.

Her first challenge to my attention came through a catalogue card lent me by Mr. Henry H. Bonnell, describing a then unpublished journal fragment in his collection of Brontë manuscripts, signed by both Emily and Anne and dated November 24, 1834, when Emily was sixteen. Amid household commonplaces came a sentence that excited my imagination: *"The Gondals are discovering the interior of Geraldine."* The Gondals, I knew from the birthday notes, were the people of Emily's imaginary world, but who or what was Geraldine. The sentence suggested nothing more sensible than a group of small children exploring the sawdust interior of a doll.

I was still puzzling over this picture when Mr. Bonnell died, and his rich collection was transferred, according to his wishes, to the Brontë Museum and Library at Haworth, England. There, two years later, in the course of my work, I turned up the "Geraldine" sheet, the mysterious sentence fairly jumping at me from the small page of minute hand printing. I read: "The Gondals are discovering the interior of—" not *Geraldine,* but—*"Gaaldine."* That made a different story. I had never heard the name Gaaldine, but it had a familiar Brontësque sound that was reassuring.

Very soon after this discovery I left Haworth for a time, and during my absence I was tormented by that sentence beating itself into my brain: "The Gondals are discovering the interior of Gaaldine." It ran into my dreams at night until I prayed the spirit of Emily Brontë for relief. It was Anne, however, who took pity and answered.

Back at Haworth, I came across a little volume in the Bonnell collection entitled *A Grammar of General Geography,* by the Rev. J. Goldsmith, 1823. Near the end I found "A Vocabulary of Proper Names" to be committed to memory, into which Anne had penciled alphabetically the Gondalan place names quoted on page 103. Here at last was an outline map of Emily's secret world: "Gondal, a large island in the North Pacific" with Regina as its capital; "Gaaldine, a large island newly discovered in the South Pacific," comprising five independent kingdoms and one province governed by a Gondalan Viceroy. I saw her Gondalan vikings, strong, bold, and adventurous, steering their fast-sailing ships to the exploration and conquest of the newly discovered island continent in the tropical seas; and I guessed at once that the name in Anne's birthday notes of 1845, transcribed *Gaul* by Shorter —"The Unique Society, about half a year ago, were wrecked on a desert island as they were returning from Gaul"—was originally written Gaaldine. Reference to the manuscript confirmed this guess.

Most of the names in this fanciful list added by Anne to the Rev. J. Goldsmith's useful "Vocabulary" were already familiar to me from Emily's poems—Almedore, Ula, Regina, Zalona, and Zedora—and they now recalled an article of several years before by Madeleine Hope Dodds (*Modern Language Review,* January, 1923), attempting to fit a group of Emily's poems into a Gondal story plot. In sleepless excitement, I read and re-read Mr. Hatfield's *Complete Poems of Emily Brontë* until I fixed in my mind not only the words of the poems, with their every tangible characteristic of style, but their most subtle shadings of atmosphere and emotion. Making my connection through the place name Ula, or Ulah—"Ula, a kingdom of Gaaldine governed by four sovereigns" —I learned from a poem beginning " 'Twas yesterday at early dawn" that Gaaldine was a land of tropical prairies bright with flowers and clear flowing rivers, in contrast to Gondal's dreary mists and moorlands, "and sleet and frozen gloom." Then picking up another thread by the personal name of Julius—"Emily is engaged in writing the Emperor Julius's life"—I traced it through ten or more poems, unfolding the bare outlines of a story plot, having this sovereign as hero.

In addition I was able to bring together in groups a goodly number of poems relating to other characters. For instance, I isolated four poems having to do with the fortunes of a youth named Fernando. Fernando, leaving Gaaldine for Gondal, bade farewell to his sweetheart, who was also his adopted sister, in vows of eternal love, but in the far-away country, on Lake Elderna's shore, he fell under the spell of an evil woman for whom he joyfully cast away "virtue and faith and heaven." She, after leading him into crime and shame, threw him into prison and left him to madness. Back at home the girl whom he had betrayed refused to share the world's scorn of him, declaring that a God of pity who had seen his suffering in life would never punish him after death.

I singled out also half a dozen poems held together by the name of Elbë, though neither their collective significance nor their relation to each other was clear to me, and I felt that these same Elbë poems were connected, though I could not tell how, with a somewhat larger, but less distinct group gathering around a woman identified by the signature A. G. Almeda or simply the initials A.G.A., whose story I could not work out to any degree of satisfaction. She was first the sweetheart of this man, then the wife of that, with never an indication of the transition from one state to the other. In one poem she reigned a queen. In the next she pined in prison. In still another she was an outcast or fugitive tending her darling child in a cave. Yet another poem pictured this "child of love" freezing to death in a mountain snowstorm.

A number of single dramatic poems excited me greatly by their suggestion of high adventure and stark human tragedy. One of particular interest pictured a youth standing in the moonlight before his sweetheart's door, breathing a silent farewell, knowing that the morrow's morn will brand him as coward and traitor because he holds his inner faith more precious than honor's name.

I had gleaned, I knew, but the barest outline of the Gondal story, for only about twenty-five of the poems had moved into the pattern. So many more, however, displayed unmistakably the Gondalan spirit that I began to suspect that the whole group was written as an epic of Emily's imaginary world.

What help would the original manuscripts give me? The text I had so meticulously impressed upon my memory was faulty indeed, as I well knew. Emily herself, and Charlotte following her example, deleted from the poems they printed all names and other traces of Gondal. Later editors, unable in many instances, to decipher Emily's crabbed and blurred microscopic hand printing, by misreadings and omissions obscured, lost, and even changed her meaning. Mr. Hatfield told me that he edited the volume I was using from transcripts furnished by Clement Shorter, and was now examining all manuscripts for himself, hoping to bring out a perfect text with every poem correctly dated.

Fortunately Emily's manuscripts have remained pretty well together. Her two notebooks of transcribed poems belonged, at that time, to Sir Alfred Law of Honresfeld and Alexander Murray Smith of London, while a group of twelve odd leaves were in the Bonnell collection at Haworth. A number of poems on loose pieces of paper were known to have been at one time in the possession of Harry B. Smith, an American book dealer. The Bonnell and Honr feld poems were accessible, but all efforts to secure a sight of the London manuscript failed, and the whereabouts of the group in America was unknown to me. Strangely enough, soon after my return the group in this country was offered me for purchase. In one of them I found the answer to a pivotal question raised by a poem in the Bonnell collection, recounting Julius's joint coronation with Gerald Exina as King of Gondal:

> King Julius lifts his impious eye
> From the dark marble to the sky;
> Blasts with that oath his perjured soul.

I had long pondered wherein lay Julius's coronation perjury. In my hands was the manuscript of a poem that I knew under the printed title "Harold," though the name, I saw, was not Harold, but Gerald. Thus I learned that Julius, breaking his oath, threw Gerald into prison and made himself sole ruler of Gondal.

This group of manuscripts was bought by Mr. W. T. H. Howe of

other than is implied in the place name, Alcona, a province in Gondal. The identity of Rosina with A.G.A., apparent from her physical features and personality, is demonstrable through the three other poems beginning: "O Mother, I am not regretting," "Alcona, in its changing mood," and "Thy sun is near meridian height."

Through the heading "M. Douglas to E. R. Gleneden" attached to the manuscript beginning "The moon is full this winter night," and the personal name Gleneden, replaced by a general term in the printed text, I recognized the tantalizing youth before his sweetheart's door as one of the conspirators in the death of Julius, awaiting the hour set for the assassination.

Thus the reconstruction of the Gondal epic has gone on through ten years, with occasional discoveries that compensate for barren months. Half of Emily's approximately two hundred extant poems and fragments now fit together in definite story pattern. Of the remainder, eight are subjective poems acknowledging the dominant place of Gondal in her life, many are short lyrics reflecting the Gondal theme and atmosphere, but lacking definite marks of identification, while a large proportion are mere fragments of a few lines each. Whatever the nature of the unidentified residue, it is evident that the majority of Emily's poems belong to an epic of Gondal's Queen, Augusta Geraldine Almeda.

Emily's and Anne's scant prose fragments contain references to three periods of Gondal history: (1) the discovery, exploration, and conquest of Gaaldine—"Gaaldine, a newly discovered island in the South Pacific," and "The Gondals are discovering the interior of Gaaldine"; (2) the first wars—"I [Emily] am at present writing a work on the First Wars"; (3) the Republican Revolution—"The Royalists are at present hard driven by the victorious Republicans," and "The Republicans are uppermost, but the Royalists are not quite overcome." None of Emily's poems have to do with the first period. A half dozen, perhaps, belong to the last period. All those centering around A.G.A. seem to fall into the period designated as "the First Wars." Five poems in the British Museum volume include in their headings dates belonging to a distinct Gondal chronology, by which it would appear, every event of the epic was definitely calendared in Emily's mind:

"From a Dungeon Wall in the Southern College—J.B. Sept. 1825."

"From a D[ungeon] W[all] in the N[orth] C[ollege]. A.G.A. Sept. 1826."

"Written on returning to the P[alace] of I[nstruction] on the 10th of January, 1827."

"To A.S. 1830."

"Rodric Lesley. 1830."

A suggestive outline for reading Emily Brontë's poems as an epic of Gondal is offered in C. W. Hatfield's new volume called *The Complete Poems of Emily Jane Brontë Edited from the Manuscripts*.

Appendix II

ANNE BRONTË'S GONDAL POEMS

VALUABLE as Anne Brontë's prose fragments are in reconstructing Gondal, her verse adds nothing to the understanding of Emily's epic, though her poems—those that pertain to Gondal—are concerned for the most part with Emily's favorite theme: the separation of loved ones through imprisonment. Anne's captives, however, bear different names from Emily's, while her meek and patient lover-prisoners are unimpressive beside her sister's kings, patriots, innocent maidens, and cutthroats, who sicken in body and break in mind under the torture of confinement. It appears that the younger Brontë girls were not so close in their literary work as has been supposed, not nearly so close as were Charlotte and Branwell.

The few points of critical interest in Anne Brontë's Gondal poems are noted in the following list:

1. Verses by Lady Geralda
    "Why, when I hear the stormy breath"

December, 1836

A girl leaves her hopeless home, seeking comfort for her weary heart in activity.

2. Alexander and Zenobia
    "Fair was the evening and brightly the sun"

July, 1837

This poem is distinctly reminiscent of the Angrian story of Alexander Percy and Zenobia Ellrington, though Anne's Alexander is "a boy of just fourteen," and Zenobia, "a slender girl." Their connection with the Gondal cycle is indicated in the lines:

> At break of day I must return
> To distant Gondal's shore,

and

> Zenobia, do you remember
> A little lonely spring
> Among Exina's woody hills?

3. A Voice from the Dungeon
"I'm buried now; I've done with life"

Marina Sabia.
October, 1837

A woman in prison dreams of seeing her child and his father.

4. The Captive's Dream
"Methought I saw him, but I knew him not"

Alexandrina Zenobia.
January 24, 1838

A girl in prison dreams that she sees her lover but cannot speak to tell him where she is that he may set her free.

5. The North Wind
"That wind is from the north; I know it well"

Alexandrina Zenobia.
January 26, 1838

A girl captive addresses the north wind, which tells her that her native mountains still are free. This is a companion poem to Emily's "To A Wreath of Snow by A.G.A." December, 1838.

6. The Parting (I and II)
"The chestnut stood by the gate"

Alexandrina Zenobia, 1837
Anne Brontë, July 9-10, 1838

The Lord of Alzerno, bidding affectionate farewell to his young wife Eliza, rides away never to return. Eliza's grief is accentuated by uncer-

tainty of his fate. The narrator assures her that only death could keep her
husband from her, confessing aside, however:

> But more than this I would not tell,
> Though all the while I knew so well
> The time and nature of his death;
> For when he drew his parting breath,
> His head was pillowed on my knee.

This stanza is a companion piece to Emily's vignette describing the death
of Lord of Elbë:

> "None but one beheld him dying,
> Parting with the parting day;
> Winds of evening sadly sighing,
> Bore his soul from earth away."

7. Verses to A Child
   "Oh, raise those eyes to me again"
   Alexandrina Zenobia.
   August 21, 1838

A mother tells her daughter Flora of her father's treachery.

8. Self-congratulation
   "Ellen, you were thoughtless once"
   Olivia Vernon.
   January 1, 1840

A woman boasts that she has learned to meet a certain man without betraying emotion.

9. An Orphan's Lament
   "She's gone; and twice the summer's sun
   Has gilt Regina's towers
   And melted wild Angora's snows
   And warmed Epina's [Exina's?] bowers."
   A[lexandrina] Z[enobia].
   January 1, 1841

This is a companion poem to Emily's "A.S. to G.S." December 19, 1841.

10. The Appeal

"Oh, I am very weary"

August 28, 1841

This is a companion piece to a poem of the same title by Emily:

"I cannot be more lonely,
    More drear I cannot be!
My worn heart throbs so wildly,
    'Twill break for thee."

11. The Captive Dove

"Poor restless dove, I pity thee"

October 31, 1843

This, whether a Gondal poem or not, is a companion to Emily's "And like myself lone, wholly lone," February 27, 1841.

12. The Student's Serenade

"I have slept upon my couch"

Alexander Hybernia.
February, 1844

This poem is a companion piece to Emily's "All day I've toiled, but not with pain."

13. The Dungeon

"Though not a breath can enter here"

Lines inscribed on the wall of a dungeon in the Southern P[alace] of I[nstruction] by A[lexander] H[ybernia]. April, 1826
December 16, 1844

This poem is an interesting companion piece to Emily's "From a Dungeon Wall in the Southern College—J.B. Sept. 1825." November 11, 1844.

14 & 15. Song

"We know where deepest lies the snow"

September 3, 1845

Song
"Come to the banquet; triumph in your songs"
September 4, 1845

These are songs of the triumphant Republicans celebrating the overthrow of the Royalists.

16. Parting Address from Z.L. to A.E.
"Oh, weep not, love! each tear that springs"
Zerona.
October 1, 1845

A girl vows fidelity to her lover despite the cruel opposition of her parents. This, with other Zerona poems that follow, is apparently Anne's equivalent of Emily's "Julian M. to A. G. Rochelle." October 9, 1845.

17. Mirth and Mourning
"Oh! cast away your sorrow"
Zerona.
July 15, 1846

A girl grieves for her lover who is in prison for her sake.

18. "Weep not too much, my Darling"
A— E—
July 20, 1846

A.E. in prison hopes that Zerona is happy in her freedom.

19. The Power of Love
"Love, indeed thy strength is mighty"
A.E.
August 13, 1846

A.E. urges his sweetheart to keep up hope for his sake.

20. The Prison
"A prisoner in a dungeon deep"
(n.d.)

This, next to the poem that follows (No. 21), is the strongest of Anne's Gondal pictures.

21. I Dreamt Last night
"I dreamt last night, and in that dream"

E.Z.
September 12, 1846

This is the best of Anne's Gondal poems, in that it tells a story and presents a graphic picture. In its theme: the horrors of civil war, it is a close companion to Emily's last poem, dated two days later. In point of its characters, it recalls Emily's "D.G.C. to J[ulius] A[ngora]. October 2, 1844." One stanza seems to echo the assassination of Julius.

"Back, foolish tears! the man I slew
    Was not the boy I cherished so;
And that young arm that clasped the friend
    Was not the same that stabbed the foe;
By time and adverse thoughts estranged,
    And wrongs and vengeance, both were changed."

Appendix III

A LIST OF GONDAL PERSONAL NAMES
AND INITIALS

I. Those used by Emily in prose fragments and poems:
Augusta Geraldine Almeda, commonly designated as A.G.A., but
variously called Augusta, Geraldine, A. G. Almeda, and Rosina of
Alcona; Amedeus; Henry Angora; Juliet Angusteena; Blanche; Julius
Brenzaida, Prince of Angora, King of Almedore and Emperor of
Gondal, designated in turn by each of his titles and their abbreviations;
Claudia; Douglas and M. Douglas (probably one person); Edmund;
Ella and Julian Egremont; Rosabella Esmalden; Arthur and Gerald
Exina; Cordelia Fitzaphnold; Flora; Francesca; Arthur Gleneden; R.
Gleneden (man); E. R. Gleneden (woman); Iërne; Lord Lesley;
Marcius; Rodric Lesley; Julian M.; Roland Macalgin; Mary; Catherine
Navarre; Mary R.; Regina; A. G. Rochelle; Alexander S., Lord of Elbë;
Angelica S.; Alfred S., Lord of Aspin Castle; Marcellus Stewart; Ronald
Stewart; Fair Surrey; Lord Eldred W.; A.A.; H.A.; M.A.; M.A.A.;
D.G.C.; R.C.; E.G.; H.G.; I.G.; M.G.; I.M.; R.M.; M.R.; A.S.

II. Those used by Anne in prose fragments and poems:
Alexander; Isabelle Abrantez; Cornelia Alzerno; Julian An[gora];
Lucia Angora; Catherine T. G. Angusteena; Una Campbell; Halbert
Clifford; Alexander D.; Helen Douglas; Harriet Eagle; Arthur and
Gerald Exina; Rosalind Fizherbert; Florian; Flora; Gerald; Lady Ger-
alda; Alexandrina Zenobia Hybernia; Edward Hybernia; Eliza Hyber-
nia; Zerona L.; Archibald Mac Ray; Isadora Montara; Marina Sabia;
Adolphus St. Albert; Isabella Senland; Xirilla Senland; Eustace So-
phona; Henry Sophonia; Albert Vernon; Olivia Vernon; A.E.; and E.Z.

Appendix IV

A PARTIAL LIST OF MANUSCRIPTS, PRINTED BOOKS, AND PERIODICALS USED IN THIS STUDY

Manuscripts

All MSS. are in minute hand-printing unless described otherwise. The length of prose pieces is given in words; verse in lines.

By Charlotte Brontë

"There was once a little girl and her name was Ane." c. 1824. Six colored illustrations. 16 pp., 4 blank: 125 words. 2½" × 1½".
  Bonnell Collection, Brontë Museum and Library, Haworth, Eng.
Two Romantic Tales. 11 pp.
  1. The Twelve Adventurers. April 15, 1829. 4,500 words.
  2. An Adventure in Ireland. April 28, 1829. 1,000 words.
    Library of Sir Alfred Law, Honresfeld, Littleborough, Eng. (now dispersed.)
List of Painters Whose Work I Wish to See. 1829.
  Bonnell Collection.
The History of the Year. March 12, 1829. 550 words.
  Bonnell Collection.
Fragment: "The Origin of the O'Deay's is as Follows." On reverse of the above sheet. 57 words.
The Enfant. July 13, 1829. 800 words.
  Bonnell Collection.
"Sir,—It is Well Known That The Genii." July 14, 1829. 1 p.: 220 words. 3¼" × 2½".
  Bonnell Collection.
The Keep of the Bridge. July 23, 1829. Two pencil sketches. 3 pp.: 38 lines. 3½" × 2¼".
  Library of W. T. H. Howe.

Blackwood's Young Men's Magazine. August 1829. Ed. by the Genius, C.B. 20 pp. 2" × 1½".
The Amy Lowell Collection, Harvard University Library.

Fragment: "One Cold Night in the Month of December." August 8, 1829. 300 words.
Bonnell Collection.

Fragment: "On the Third Day I Came to a Wide Plain." August 8, 1829. 340 words.
Bonnell Collection.

The Search After Happiness. July 28–August 17, 1829. 16 pp.: 4,000 words plus 28 lines. 2" × 1½".
Ashley Library, British Museum.

Blackwood's Young Men's Magazine. October 1829. 16 pp. 2" × 1½".
Amy Lowell Collection.

Anecdotes of the Duke of Wellington. July 8–October 2, 1829. 2 pp.: 440 words. 2⅛" × 1⅞".
Bonnell Collection.

Sunset. October 8, 1829. 24 lines.
Bonnell Collection.

Sunrise. October 9, 1829. 32 lines.
Bonnell Collection.

Blackwood's Young Men's Magazine. November, 1829. 16 pp. 2" × 1½".
Lowell Collection.

Blackwood's Young Men's Magazine. December (1), 1829. 1⅞" × 1⅜".
Brontë Museum and Library, Haworth, Eng.

Blackwood's Young Men's Magazine. December (2), 1829. 18 pp. 2½" × 1½".
Ashley Library.

Characters of the Great Men of the Present Time. By Capt. Tree. December 17, 1829. 16 pp.: 2,500 words. 2" × 1⅜".
Law Collection.

Written upon the Occasion of the Dinner Given to the Literati of the Glass Town. January 9, 1830. 68 lines.
Bonnell Collection.

Two Poems:
  1. A Wretch in Prison. By Murry. February 1, 1830. 32 lines.
  2. "Of College I Am Tired." Signed C[harles] W[ellesley]. February 1, 1830. 18 lines.
Bonnell Collection.

The Adventures of Mon. Edouard de Crack. By Lord Charles Wellesley. February 22, 1830. 21 pp.: 3,000 words. 2½" × 2".
Lowell Collection.

Miscellaneous Poems. By Charlotte Brontë. May 31, 1830. 12 pp.: 289 lines plus 1,000 words.
Bonnell Collection.

Prose Fragment and Poem:
"Overcome with that delightful sensation."
"Lo, stretched beneath the clustering palm." c. June, 1830. 250 words plus 64 lines.
Bonnell Collection.

An Interesting Passage in the Lives of Some Eminent Men of the Present Time. By Lord Charles Wellesley. June 18, 1830. 16 pp.: 4,300 words. 2″ × 1⅜″.
Lowell Collection.

"The Following Strange Occurrence." June 22, 1830. 1 p̈. 3¾″ × 1¾″.
Bonnell Collection.

Miss Hume's Dream. By the Islander Lord Wellesley. June 26, 1830. 2 pp.: 64 lines.
Bonnell Collection.

The Evening Walk: a Poem by the Marquis of Douero, in Pindaric metre. June 28, 1830. 276 lines.

Leisure Hours. ("I wrote this in the space of one hour—C.B. Charles Wellesley"). June 29, 1830. 2 pp.: 700 words. 7⅞″ × 3¾″.
Bonnell Collection.

The Poetaster. A Drama in Two Volumes. By Lord Charles Wellesley.
Vol. I. July 8, 1830. 18 pp.: 2,275 words; 1½″ × 1¼″.
Lowell Collection.
Vol. II. July 12, 1830. 14 pp.: 2,200 words. 1½″ × 1¼″.
Bonnell Collection.

Young Men's Magazine. Second Series. August, 1830. 20 pp.: 3,500 words plus 40 lines. 2⅛″ × 1½″.
Bonnell Collection.

Catalogue of My Books with the Periods of Their Completion up to August 3rd, 1830. 2 pp. 4″ × 2½″.
Bonnell Collection.

Translation into English Verse of the First Book of Voltaire's *Henriade*. August 11, 1830. 12 pp.: 457 lines. 4″ × 2″.

Young Men's Magazine. Second Series. October, 1830. 20 pp.: 2,900 words plus 88 lines. 2⅛″ × 1 9⁄16″.
Bonnell Collection.

Albion and Marina: a Tale by Lord Charles Wellesley. October 12, 1830. 16 pp.: 4,000 words plus 53 lines. 2¾″ × 1½″.
Palmer Collection, Wellesley College Library.

Young Man Naughty's Adventure. October 14, 1830. 36 lines.

Matin and Vesper. Two Poems by Charlotte Brontë. November 11–12, 1830. 2 pp.: 104 lines. $2\frac{11}{16}'' \times 2\frac{3}{16}''$.
Ashley Library.

The Violet: a Poem with Several Smaller Pieces. By the Marquis of Douro. November 14, 1830. 16 pp. $3\frac{3}{4}'' \times 2\frac{1}{4}''$.
Howe Collection.

Young Men's Magazine. Second Series. December (1), 1830. 20 pp. $2'' \times 1\frac{3}{8}''$.
Law Collection.

Young Men's Magazine. Second Series. December (2), 1830. 20 pp.: 3,550 words plus 77 lines. $2\frac{1}{4}'' \times 1\frac{1}{2}''$.
Bonnell Collection.

Visits in Verreopolis. Volume I. By Lord Charles Wellesley. December 7–11, 1830.

Visits in Weropolis. Volume II. By the Honorable Charles Albert Florian Wellesley, aged 10 years. December 18, 1830. 32 pp.: 6,000 words. $3'' \times 2''$.
Law Collection.

"And Music All on Earth Unknown," followed by prose fragment signed Lord Charles Albert Florian Wellesley. July 11, 1831. 4 pp.: 100 words plus 92 lines. $3\frac{1}{2}'' \times 2\frac{1}{2}''$.
Bonnell Collection.

"The Trumpet Hath Sounded." December 11, 1831. $2\frac{1}{2}$ pp.: 84 lines. $3\frac{3}{4}'' \times 2\frac{3}{8}''$.

"Oh! There is a Land Which the Sun Loves to Brighten." December 25, 1831. 56 lines.
Bonnell Collection.

The Bridal. July 14–August 20, 1832. 18 pp.: 4,000 words plus 84 lines. $3\frac{3}{4}'' \times 2\frac{1}{2}''$.
Bonnell Collection.

The African Queen's Lament. February 12, 1833. 56 lines plus 350 words (longhand) plus 69 words.
Bonnell Collection.

"Fair Forms of Glistering Marble Stand Around." March 26, 1833. 48 lines.
Bonnell Collection.

The Foundling. A Tale of Our Own Times. By Captain Tree. May 31–June 27, 1833. 18 pp.: 34,000 words. $7\frac{5}{16}'' \times 4\frac{9}{16}''$.
Ashley Library.

The Green Dwarf: a Tale of the Perfect Tense. By Lord Charles Albert Florian Wellesley. September 2, 1833. 25 pp.: 34,000 words.

Stark Collection, University of Texas Library.

Arthuriana, or Odds and Ends. By Lord Charles A. F. Wellesley. September 27–November 20, 1833. 18,600 words plus 278 lines.
J. Pierpont Morgan Library.

The Last Will and Testament of Florence Marion Wellesley, Marchioness of Douro, Duchess of Zamorna, and Princess of the Blood of the Twelves. 4 pp.: 1,000 words. $4\frac{1}{2}'' \times 3^{11}\!/_{16}''$.
Bonnell Collection.

A Leaf from an Unopened Volume. Edited by Lord Charles Albert Florian Wellesley. Preface by Sergeant Tree. January 17, 1834. 20,000 words.
Library of A. Edward Newton.

High Life in Verdopolis. In Six Chapters. By Lord Charles Albert Florian Wellesley. February 20–March 20, 1834. 22 pp.: 38,000 words.
British Museum.

Corner Dishes: Being a Small Collection of Mixed and Unsubstantial Trifles in Prose and Verse. By Lord Charles Albert Florian Wellesley. May 28–June 16, 1834. 19,100 words plus 282 lines.
Henry E. Huntington Library.

A National Ode for the Angrians. By Arthur Augustus Adrian Wellesley. July 17, 1834. 66 lines.
Bonnell Collection.

The Spell: an Extravaganza in Eight Chapters. By Lord Charles Albert Florian Wellesley. June 21–July 21, 1834. 26 pp.: 42,000 words.
British Museum.

My Angria and the Angrians. By Lord Charles Albert Florian Wellesley. October 14, 1834. $17\frac{1}{2}$ pp.: 22,000 words.
Law Collection.

The Scrap-Book: a Mingling of Many Things. Compiled by Lord C. A. F. Wellesley. March 17, 1835. 31 pp.: 53,000 words.
British Museum Library.

To the Horse Eagle That I Rode at the Battle of Zamorna. 20 lines.
Howe Library.

Diary Fragments, 1835–1839:
1. "Well, here I am at Roe Head." 3 pp.: 1,400 words.
2. "Now, as I have a little bit of time." Friday Afternoon, February 4, 1836. 416 words.
3. "All this day I have been in a dream." October 14, 1836. 1,700 words.
4. "About a week since I got a letter from Branwell." 400 words.
5. "Mr. Sanderson did not speak again." 1,339 words.
6. "My compliments to the weather." 5,400 words.
7. "I have now written a great many books." $\frac{1}{4}$ p.: 510 words.
Bonnell Collection.

We Wove a Web in Childhood. December 19, 1835. 6 pp.: 185 lines plus 350 words.
Huntington Library.
Passing Events. By Charles Townshend. April 21, 1836. 20,000 words.
Morgan Library.
Poem (Zamorna's Exile). July 19, 1836. 12 pp.: 575 lines. $7\frac{1}{4}'' \times 4\frac{1}{2}''$.
Bonnell Collection.
Poem (Zamorna's Return). January 9, 1837. 436 lines. $7\frac{1}{2}'' \times 4\frac{3}{4}''$.
Bonnell Collection.
Story (Zamorna's Return). c. 1837. 35 pp. $7\frac{1}{4}'' \times 4\frac{1}{2}''$.
Law Collection.
"Dream of the West! The moor was wild." 36 lines.
Bonnell Collection.
"He could not sleep!—the couch of war." 28 lines.
Bonnell Collection.
"It is not at an hour like this." 24 lines.
Bonnell Collection.
Fragment: "Two gentlemen in earnest conversation were walking in St. Mary's Grove." $\frac{3}{4}$ p.
Bonnell Collection.
The Teacher's Monologue. May 5-12, 1837. 90 lines (last 16 lines in longhand).
Bonnell Collection.
"If thou be in a lonely place." May 14, 1837. 48 lines.
Bonnell Collection.
"Is this my tomb, this humble stone?" June 4, 1837. 80 lines.
Bonnell Collection.
"There is, reader, a sort of pleasure." June 29, 1837. 36 pp.: 15,000 words.
Wrenn Library, University of Texas.
Group of Angrian Stories and Poems. July 21, 1837. 42 pp.: 15,000 words.
Law Collection.
Marian. July 21, 1837. 51 lines.
Bonnell Collection.
"The last scene in my last book concluded within the walls of Alnwick House." January 17, 1838. 35 pp.: 18,000 words plus 14 lines. $7\frac{1}{4}'' \times 4\frac{1}{2}''$.
Law Collection.
"There's no use in weeping." January 29, 1838. 36 lines.
Bonnell Collection.
Story. By Charles Townshend. June 28, 1838. 34 pp.: 20,400 words plus 44 lines.
Bonnell Collection.

'Tis the siesta's languid hour, June 7, 1838. 48 lines.
Bonnell Collection.

Review at Gazemba. July 7, 1838. 78 lines.
Bonnell Collection.

A Volume of Stories by Charles Townshend and Sir William Percy. July 21, 1838. 42 pp.: 28,000 words.
Law Collection.

Fragment: "But it is not in society that the real character is revealed." c. 1839. 800 words.
Bonnell Collection.

Caroline Vernon. March 26, 1839. A novel in 3 books containing 17 chapters. Signed "Charles Townshend." 67 pp.
Harry Elkins Widener Collection, Harvard University Library.

Henry Hastings. By Charles Townshend. February 22–March 20, 1839. 49 pp.
Widener Collection.

Fragment: "Miss Percy and Miss Thornton being both settled in Yorkshire." 2,672 words.
Bonnell Collection.

Fragment: Mr. Ashworth.
Widener Collection.

Note on inside cover of Russell's General Atlas of Modern Geography. 1843. 71 words.
Bonnell Collection.

Copybook (longhand) containing revisions of eleven earlier poems.
"He saw my heart's woe, discerned my souls anguish." c. 1846. 1 p.: 32 lines.
Bonnell Collection.

Discarded drafts of *The Professor* (longhand).
"I had the pleasure of knowing Mr. Crimsworth well." 400 words.
Bonnell Collection.

[The Moores] (longhand). 34 pp.
A. S. W. Rosenbach.

Poem: "Look, wife, the clouds are full of snow." 57 lines.
Bonnell Collection.

Preface to Second Edition of *Jane Eyre* (longhand).
A. S. W. Rosenbach.

Prose fragment: "I never had much time for writing." Jan. 23, 1850. 2 pp.: 600 words.

Fragment: "There was once a large house called Gateshead."
Bonnell Collection.

Three rejected fragments of *Villette* (longhand). 1,000 words plus 1,300 words plus 650 words.
Bonnell Collection.
Three fragments (longhand): Willie Ellin. 1853.
One in Bonnell Collection, two in the Howe Library. All were printed by C. W. Hatfield in Brontë Society Publications. 1936.

By Branwell Brontë

The Battle of Wch-not-on. March 12, 1827. Water-color illustrations. 8 pp. $2\frac{1}{2}'' \times 2\frac{1}{4}''$.
Brontë Museum and Library.
History of the Rebellion in My Army. 1828 (longhand and large printing). 6 pp. $4\frac{1}{2}'' \times 4\frac{1}{4}''$.
Brontë Museum and Library.
Magazine. January, 1829. Pencil illustrations. 9 pp. $2\frac{1}{4}'' \times 1\frac{1}{4}''$.
Lowell Collection.
Branwell's Blackwood's Magazine. June, 1829. 18 pp. $2'' \times 1\frac{1}{2}''$.
Lowell Collection.
Branwell's Blackwood's Magazine. July, 1829. 22 pp. $2'' \times 1\frac{1}{2}''$.
Lowell Collection.
A Collection of Poems by Young Soult the Rhymer. Illustrated with Notes and Commentaries by Monsieur Chateaubriand. In two volumes. September 30, 1829. $2\frac{3}{4}'' \times 2\frac{1}{8}''$.
Brontë Museum and Library.
Laussane: a Dramatic Poem by Young Soult the Rhymer. December 1–23, 1829. 14 pp. $3\frac{3}{4}'' \times 2\frac{1}{4}''$.
Bonnell Collection.
The Liar Detected. By Captain Bud. 1830. 12 pp.: 2,200 words. $2\frac{1}{2}'' \times 2''$.
Bonnell Collection.
The Revenge: a Tragedy in Three Acts by Young Soult. In two volumes. November 23, 1830. 14 pp. $4\frac{1}{8}'' \times 3\frac{5}{8}''$.
Brontë Museum and Library.
The History of the Young Men, from Their First Settlement to the Present Time. By John Bud. December 15, 1830–May 7, 1831. Folding map and plate. 18 pp.: 15,000 words. $7\frac{3}{4}'' \times 6\frac{1}{2}''$. Introduction is in longhand.
Ashley Library.
Poems (in longhand):
  1. The Fate of Regina (incomplete). May, 1832.
  2. Ode on the Celebration of the Great African Games. June 26, 1832. 177 lines.
  3. The Pass of Thermopylae. March 3, 1833. 56 lines.

4. An Hour's Musing. By Alexander Percy. November 16, 1834.
Brontë Museum and Library.

The Pirate: a Tale by the Author of Letters from an Englishman. February 8, 1833. 15 pp.: 5,250 words.
Bonnell Collection.

The Monthly Intelligencer No. 1. March 27–April 26, 1833. 4 pp. 9" × 7½".
Brontë Museum and Library. (This seems to be the only number issued.)

The Politics in Verdopolis: a Tale by Captain John Flower, M.P. November 15, 1833. 18 pp.: 16,900 words. 7½" × 4½".
Bonnell Collection.

Northangerland's Address to the Angrians. 1834. 2 pp.
Brotherton Collection, Leeds University. (Transcript received from C. W. Hatfield.)

Fragments describing the "Massacre of Dongola" and the Battle of Loango, January, 1834. 10 pp.
Brotherton Collection and Bonnell Collection (Transcripts received from C. W. Hatfield.)

The Wool is Rising, or the Angrian Adventurer. A Narrative of the Proceedings of the Foundation of the Kingdom of Angria by the Right Hon. John Baron Flower and Viscount Richton. June 26, 1834. 24 pp.: 30,000 words. 7⅜" × 4⁹⁄₁₆".
Ashley Library.

Fragments. June–September, 1834. 12 pp.
1. "Sound the loud trumpet o'er Africa's bright sea." 41 lines.
2. Anthem of the Coronation. 33 lines.
3. Prose account of the coronation of Zamorna as Emperor of Angria.
4. List and descriptions of the provinces of Angria.
Brontë Museum and Library.

Fragments. September–October, 1834. 9 pp.
1. MS opening with "The Angrian Welcome."
2. Poem by Henry Hasting: "History stood by her pillar of fame."

Fragments: An account of the opening of the First Angrian Parliament. By Lord Richton. September–October, 1834. 9 pp.
(Transcript received from C. W. Hatfield.)

A New Year Story. January 7, 1836–August 31, 1836. Pen and ink sketches. 38 pp.: 32,000 words. 7⅜" × 4¾".
Ashley Library.

Fragment pertaining to the Angrian War. November–December, 1836. 8 pp.: 6,200 words.
Bonnell Collection.

Poems and fragments. 1836. 458 lines.
Bonnell Collection.

Fragments. 1837. 32 pp.: 25,000 words.
> Ashley Library, Bonnell Collection, and Brotherton Collection.

The Life of Warner Howard Warner. By the Right Hon. John Earl of Richton. February 1, 1838. 4 pp.: 7,200 words.
> Bonnell Collection.

The Wanderer. A Tale in Verse. Bradford. July 31, 1838. 12 pp.: 509 lines.
> Ashley Library.

And the Weary Are at Rest. c. 1845.
> (Transcript received from C. W. Hatfield.)

By Anne Brontë

"A prisoner in a dungeon deep." c. 1844. 2 pp.: 58 lines. $4\frac{1}{8}'' \times 3\frac{1}{2}''$.
> Bonnell Collection.

"When sinks my heart in hopeless gloom." (Signed "Alexander Hybernia.") February, 1844.
> Howe Library.

Five poems. December 13, 1840–June 1, 1845. 12 pp.: 140 lines. $4\frac{1}{2}'' \times 3\frac{5}{8}''$.
> Bonnell Collection.

"Gloomily the clouds are sailing." October 6, 1846. 44 lines.
> Bonnell Collection.

"Love, indeed thy strength is mighty." A.E. August 13, 1846. 60 lines.
> Bonnell Collection.

"I dreamt last night." E.Z. September 14, 1846. 150 lines.
> Bonnell Collection.

The Three Guides. August 11, 1847. 216 lines.
> Bonnell Collection.

"Severed and gone so many years." April, 1847. 68 lines.
> Bonnell Collection.

"A dreadful darkness closes in." January 28, 1849. 68 lines.
> Bonnell Collection.

List of Gondal names.
> Stark Collection.

Notes in Goldsmith's *A Grammar of General Geography*, 1823.
> Bonnell Collection.

By Emily Brontë

Thirty-one poems and fragments. 1836–1838. On separate bits of paper of varying sizes.
> Howe Library.

Two poems.
> Stark Collection.

Sixty-two poems and fragments. 1836–1844.
  Bonnell Collection.
Volume headed "Gondal Poems," containing 44 poems, March 6, 1837–May 14, 1847. 68 pp. 6″ × 4″.
  British Museum.
Volume of Poems. November 11, 1837–December 2, 1846.
  Law Collection.

By Emily and Anne Brontë

Journal fragment. November 24, 1834. 2 pp.: 350 words. 4″ × 2½″.
  Bonnell Collection.
Birthday notes. July 30, 1841. 850 words.
Birthday notes. July 31, 1845. 1,276 words.
  Law Collection.

Printed Books

Brontë, Anne: The Complete Poems of Anne Brontë. Ed. by Clement Shorter; with a Bibliographical Introduction by C. W. Hatfield. London, Hodder and Stoughton, 1923.

Brontë, Charlotte: The Adventures of Ernest Alembert: a Fairy Tale. Privately printed by T. J. Wise, 1896.

—— The Complete Poems of Charlotte Brontë. Ed. by Clement Shorter; with Bibliography and Notes by C. W. Hatfield. London, Hodder and Stoughton, 1923.

—— Four Letters from Charlotte Brontë to M. Constantin Héger. Ed. by Marion H. Spielman. *The Times*, June 29, 1913.

—— Jane Eyre, to which is added The Moores, an unpublished fragment by Charlotte Brontë; with Introduction by W. Robertson Nicoll. New York, Dodd, Mead and Company, 1902.

—— Tales of the Islanders. June 31, 1829–July 30, 1830. *Nash's Magazine*, December, 1911.

—— The Twelve Adventurers and Other Stories. London, Hodder and Stoughton, 1925.

—— Emma: *The Cornhill Magazine*, April, 1860, pp. 487–98.

Brontë, Emily Jane: The Complete Poems of Emily Jane Brontë. Ed. by Clement Shorter. Arranged and collected, with Bibliography and Notes, by C. W. Hatfield. London, Hodder and Stoughton, 1923.

—— Gondal Poems by Emily Jane Brontë. Now first published from the MS in the British Museum. Ed. by Helen Brown and Joan Mott. Oxford, Shakespeare Head Press, 1938.

Brontë, Charlotte, Emily, and Anne: Poems by Currer, Ellis, and Acton Bell. London: Aylott and Jones, 1846.
—— Wuthering Heights and Agney Grey. By Ellis and Acton Bell. With a Selection from Their Literary Remains, and a Preface, by Currer Bell. London, Smith, Elder, and Co., 1850.
—— Poems by Charlotte, Emily, and Anne Brontë. New York, Dodd, Mead and Company, 1902.
—— Brontë Poems. Ed. by Arthur C. Benson. London: Smith, Elder, and Co., 1915.
Brontë, Charlotte, Branwell, Emily, and Anne: Definitive Edition of the Brontës. Ed. by Alex Symington and Thomas J. Wise. Oxford, Shakespeare Head Press, 1934–36.
Brontë Society Publications.
Gaskell, E. G.: The Life of Charlotte Brontë. London, Smith, Elder, and Co., 1857.
Goldsmith, J.: A Grammar of General Geography for the Use of Schools and Young Persons. 1823.
Haldane, Elizabeth S.: Mrs. Gaskell and Her Friends. London, Hodder and Stoughton, 1930.
Leyland, Francis A.: The Brontë Family, with Special Reference to Patrick Branwell Brontë. London, Hurst and Blackett, 1886.
Oliphant, Mrs. Margaret: Annals of a Publishing House. William Blackwood and His Sons, Their Magazine and Friends. Edinburgh, W. Blackwood and Sons, 1897–98.
Sinclair, May: The Three Brontës. London, Hutchinson and Company, 1912.
Shorter, Clement: Charlotte Brontë and Her Circle. New York, Dodd, Mead and Company, 1896.
Shorter, Clement: The Brontës Life and Letters. London, Hodder and Stoughton, 1908.

Periodicals

Currer Bell. *The Palladium*, September, 1850, pp. 161–75.
Dodds, Madeleine Hope: (1) Gondaliand (2) A Second Visit to Gondaliand. *Modern Language Review*, January, 1923, and January, 1926.
Nussey, Ellen: Reminiscences of Charlotte Brontë by "A Schoolfellow." *Scribner's Monthly*, May, 1871.
Review of *Jane Eyre. Quarterly Review*, December, 1848, pp. 162–76.
Review of *Jane Eyre, Wuthering Heights,* and *The Tenant of Wild-fell Hall. North American Review*, October, 1848, pp. 355–60.

INDEX